LONDON
MUSEUMS AND
COLLECTIONS

Edited by G.M.S. Scimone and M.F. Levey

London Tourist Board
Award Winner

CPC ◉ GUIDEBOOKS

Canal Publishing Company
London

© Canal Publishing Company 1989

First edition 1986

Canal Publishing Company
gratefully acknowledge the help received from

Glaxo

with this revised and expanded second edition.

British Library Cataloguing in Publication Data
London museums and collections. –
    2nd. ed. – (CPC Guidebooks, ISSN 0269-6584)
    1. London. Museums. Visitors' guides
    I. Scimone, Giuseppe   II. Levey, Michael
    069'.9421
    ISBN 0-907237-25-8

Photography and Picture Research: Charles Love, Fiona Smith.

Advertisement and Distribution: Peter Betts, Barbara Satchell.

Design and Production: Mikiko Hara, Hooker Serowka, Stuart Sepple.

Typesetting: Stratatype.

Cartography: FWT Studios Ltd.

Printing: Bournehall Graphic Ltd.

LRT U/G Map Reg. User No. 89/798

CPC⊚GUIDEBOOKS is an imprint of
Canal Publishing Co Ltd, 23 Golden Sq, London W1R 3PA
Tel 439 8639. Tx 295929. Fax 437 0696.

CONTENTS

The Entries

ACKNOWLEDGEMENTS

Canal Publishing wishes to thank the many museums, archives, organizations,
photographers and individuals who have given their help and made available
copyright material for reproduction. Special thanks are due to the Bank of
England, BTA, British Library Board, British Museum, Corporation of London,
Department of Environment (Crown Copyright), English Heritage, Alan Irvine
Esq, National Gallery, National Monuments Record (Crown Copyright), National
Portrait Gallery, Public Record Office, Board of Trustees of the Royal Armouries,
Science Museum (Crown Copyright), Tate Gallery, Victoria and Albert Museum
(Crown Copyright), Wallace Collection (Crown Copyright), Dean and Chapter
of Westminster.

FOREWORD

By

Dr Dennis Farr, MA DLitt FRSA FMA
Director, Courtauld Institute Galleries

In its museums and collections, public and private, big and small, world famous and known mainly to locals and specialists, London has a rich heritage, unequalled in extent and variety in any other capital city.

The great institutions – the British Museum, the National Gallery, the Tate Gallery, the Victoria and Albert Museum – are perhaps unlikely to be missed, but it is often the smaller ones, like the idiosyncratic Sir John Soane's Museum in Lincoln's Inn Fields, the Dickens House in Doughty Street, the Geffrye Museum in the East End, which give a specially rewarding insight into the nation's cultural and social history. Local museums like the Barnet Museum and Vestry House in Walthamstow are often particularly valuable for the young, giving historical events a background of everyday life.

This edition, like its predecessor, here up-dated and expanded, is aimed not only at visitors but also at Londoners who wish to learn more about their own heritage. It also provides information about specialist collections, research facilities and services of use to scholars.

The range of its many knowledgeable contributors lends variety to its entries, each of which is the fruit of fresh and personal observation and research. Its place among London books of reference is surely established.

London, October 1989

5

PREFACE

By Austen Kark CBE, MA (Oxon)
Chairman
Canal Publishing Company

Museums are more than just storehouses of art and artifacts or, for that matter, mere monuments to older generations' acquisitiveness. They are repositories of human skills, achievements and enthusiasms. They affirm a continuous link with our past. They introduce us to antiquity and make it plausible. They trace the rise and fall, the confluence and the flowing apart, of civilizations. They store knowledge as well as things of beauty and virtue. They tell us as much about ourselves and our neighbours as about our common ancestors. They tell us about Art and Nature and Science. They help us to understand history and perceive genius.

Of course, they should be exciting; they should be fun; and, in an ideal world, they should be free, as London's publicly maintained collections traditionally were. Economic pressures, particularly in the public sector, have made it increasingly difficult to maintain the policy of free entry and readers should make maximum use of those that between them still provide a most marvellous range of free cultural attractions.

If it is one object of this book to make the many and varied museums and collections of London as easily accessible to the visitor as to the Londoner, to the student as to the research scholar, another has been to reveal the rewards and excitements each contains. Some are specialist museums designed for specialists and a few of these need to be approached in advance before they will allow anyone to study or examine their collections. But these are rare, reminders that it is also the function of museums to provide for scholarship and research. The overwhelming majority are intended to be used by the general public as well as by specialists and are designed accordingly. Some, the Natural History and the Science Museums are excellent examples, make themselves especially attractive to children with things, even for the very young, to do and find out, and try out, and learn.

This new edition, up-dating, correcting, amending, and adding new entries to the list of **London Museums and Collections**, and weeding out those that no longer qualify, is part of a series of long-term projects which CPC Guidebooks is undertaking. They are designed to run alongside and supplement our well-established annual multi-lingual guides to London (and the rest of Britain) published in English, French, German, Italian, Spanish and Japanese.

In this book we have attempted to describe and examine in appropriate detail the wide and rich assortment of museums and collections in London, ranging from the world famous, such as the British Museum, the V&A, the National Gallery, the Tate, to the esoteric and eccentric (such as collections of early surgical instruments; artillery and ammunition; or amulets and charms to ward off the evil eye) in which, as the pages of this book demonstrate, London is peculiarly rich. If London's museums do not show you something, somewhere, to surprise, fascinate and delight you and make you resolve to know more and come back again, then you are hard to please. But we hope and believe that you will return to London's museums and collections, and to this book as an introduction to their riches.

Finally and personally I should like to thank Sir Paul Girolami, Chairman of Glaxo plc, for his support, Dr. Dennis Farr for contributing the Foreword, Michael Levey and his colleagues for writing or editing some 212 entries, the many directors and heads of museum departments who took considerable trouble to help make the book accurate and comprehensive, and the designers, printers and production team who, under the energetic and dedicated co-ordinating direction of Dr. G.M.S. Scimone, the Editor-in-Chief of the series, managed to produce this edition so quickly and efficiently.

HOW TO USE THE BOOK

The book presents an extensive survey of museums, collections and permanent exhibition-places within the Greater London area. The museums are arranged in strict alphabetical order, either by their official name or by the title by which they are generally known, regardless of size, status, subject matter or location. Please bear in mind that admission to certain museums and collections is restricted and *prior application* is imperative. Telephone numbers have been included so that visitors can check beforehand. Where available a number with recorded information is given in brackets after the main number of the museum. At some places where admission is free a donation is appreciated.

In *the essentials* details are necessarily brief. They are correct at the time of going to press. Of course changes may occur according to circumstances.

Some museums and collections close on Public Holidays. As a general rule almost all close on Good Friday, Christmas Eve and Christmas Day, and the first Monday in May.

'Shopping' indicates that there is an opportunity to buy something to commemorate the visit. 'Publications' means that the institution publishes its own catalogue, or other descriptive matter. 'Photography' is almost always limited to the hand-held variety for non-commercial purposes, and flash is seldom permitted. It is always wise to ask first. 'Research' means essentially academic research and an appropriate letter or other introduction is usually necessary. 'Staff opinion' indicates the availability of experts to offer guidance (not valuation) on items brought to their attention. Anyone planning to bring an organized party or a disabled person, especially in a wheelchair, is urged to ring first.

With a number of contributors, variations in spelling, terminology and general approach are inevitable, and the editors have thought it best to resist the temptation to over-edit for the sake of consistency. All were allowed complete freedom to express their own personal opinions; with these CPC does not, of course, necessarily agree.

ABBREVIATIONS AND CONTRACTIONS

As a rule the use of abbreviations and contractions in the text has been avoided. Those which follow are the exceptions:

AD	Anno Domini	d	died
att	attributed to	ext	extension (telephone)
BC	before Christ	mss	manuscripts
BR	British Rail	qv	see
c	circa	RAF	Royal Air Force
C	Century	Tel	telephone
cf	compare with	V & A	Victoria and Albert Museum

■ ALL HALLOWS BY THE TOWER UNDERCROFT MUSEUM

Byward Street EC3R 5BJ.   Tel 481 2928
Admission *charge*

The significance of the church derives from its long history of about 1,300 years and its proximity to Tower Hill, place of execution of prominent persons who somehow displeased Authority. Their remains were buried in the church.

In the Undercroft are a Roman pavement, a model of Roman London, a Saxon arch and cross with inscription, an altar constructed from stones of a Crusader castle in Palestine and a collection of historical silver-gilt plate which is still used on festive and special occasions. Also to be seen are church registers which record the baptism of William Penn, founder of Pennsylvania, and the marriage of John Quincey Adams, sixth president of the US, as well as the burial of Archbishop William Laud.

Although the church was lucky to avoid being destroyed by fire during the Great Fire of London in 1666 (Samuel Pepys wrote the account of the Great Fire from the tower of the church), it was unable to avoid this fate during the Blitz of 1940. Remnants of the original oak doors were recovered and can be seen today.

---

the essentials

Underground Tower Hill (Circle, District Lines). **Open** Mon-Fri 0900-1800, Sat-Sun 1000-1800. **For the disabled** access to Church only, not to Undercroft. **Refreshments** restaurant (Mon-Fri) 1200-1400. **Shopping. Publications. Visitors' services** guided tours for groups by appointment.

■ ARTS COUNCIL OF GREAT BRITAIN COLLECTION

105 Piccadilly W1V 0AU.   Tel 629 9495
Admission *prior application*

The Arts Council Collection of post-war British Art includes about 6,000 items: over 2,000 sculptures, paintings, drawings and works in mixed media; 1,500 artists' prints, by foreign as well as British

All Hallows by the Tower.

Arts Council Collection: Nicholas Pope,
Three Wood Block, 1978.

artists and 1,800 photographs. Purchasing was begun during World War II when CEMA (the Council for the Encouragement of Music and the Arts) bought paintings and drawings to form touring exhibitions with funds obtained from the Pilgrim Trust. These works were inherited by the Arts Council when it was founded in 1946 and the Council continued the practice of buying works of art for touring exhibitions. A few works dating from the earlier part of the century were acquired but, by 1955, purchasing was almost exclusively concentrated on acquiring (funds permitting) the best available recent work by living British artists.

This is a loan collection administered by the Arts Council to provide material for the Council's own touring exhibitions and is the largest and most accessible source of post-war British long-term loans to museums, galleries, universities and other public buildings throughout the country. Acquisitions, excepting artists' prints, are listed in two fully illustrated catalogues, Arts Council Collection Volume I 1942-78 and Volume II 1979-83, available from the Arts Council Publications. All enquiries regarding the collection, and about exhibitions at the Council's own **Hayward** [Belvedere Road SE1 8XZ] and **Serpentine** galleries [Kensington Gardens W2 3AX] should be sent to the above address. (IJ)

─────────────────────── *the essentials* ───────────────────────
Underground Green Park (Jubilee, Piccadilly, Victoria Lines). **Open** Mon-Fri 0930-1700. **Cloakroom. Toilets. Publications. Research** library.

■ ASHMOLE ARCHIVE
King's College, Strand WC2R 2LS.   Tel 836 5454 ext 2343
Admission *prior application*

Although this unique collection of *photographs of Greek and Roman sculptures* is used mainly by the teaching staff of the Department of Classics within King's College, University of London, it is at the same time made available to any serious student, collector, or person in the art world engaged in research on the subject.

It contains more than 10,000 photographic prints and many rare negatives assembled by Professor Bernard Ashmole during his long and distinguished career as scholar of classical sculpture.

Ashmole Archive: Roman bronze portrait bust of the Greek comic poet Menander, now in the S. Paul Getty Museum, Malibu, California, USA. This small copy (C1) is the only one to be inscribed with Menander's name and thus assures the identification. Discovered in the art market by Professor Bernard Ashmole, and first published by him in 1975.

─────────────────────── *the essentials* ───────────────────────
Underground Temple (Circle, District Lines). **Open** Mon-Fri 0930-1700. **Toilets** within King's College. **Public telephones** within King's College. **Refreshments** restaurant, snacks within King's College. **Educational facilities. Staff opinion.**

Bank of England Museum: Sir John Soane's Bank Stock Office (1792) (restored).

■ BANK OF ENGLAND MUSEUM

Bank of England, Bartholomew Lane EC3R 8AH.   Tel 601 5545 (601 5792)
Admission *free*

The Museum illustrates the history of the Bank of England and includes a unique collection of bank notes, together with gold bars from Roman times to the present day and many of the Bank's original documents, including the Royal Charter. An inter-active video allows the visitor to follow a path around the modern Bank and discover the secrets held behind each door, while a dealing desk gives the visitor an insight into the activities of the financial markets as they happen. The museum is set around the Bank Stock Office, designed by Sir John Soane and regarded as the finest neoclassical interior in Europe.

the essentials

Underground Bank (Central, Northern Lines). **Open** Oct 1-Thur before Easter Mon-Fri 1000-1800; Good Friday – 30 Sept Mon-Sat and Public Holidays 1000-1800, Sundays 1400-1800. **Cloakroom. Toilets. For the disabled** access difficult, but Braille, cassettes, toilets available. **Shopping** publications, gifts. **Educational facilities** visits, films, talks by prior arrangement. **Visitors' services** guided tours. **Research** archives and historical collections open by prior arrangement.

■ BANKSIDE GALLERY

48 Hopton Street SE1 9JH.   Tel 928 7521
Admission *charge*

The gallery, situated on the south of the River Thames not very far from Blackfriars Bridge, is a national centre for the appreciation of watercolours, prints and drawings. From 1980 it has been the home of the Royal Society of Painters in Watercolours (founded in 1804) and the Royal Society of Painter-Etchers and Engravers (1880). The two societies, commonly known by the initials RWS and RE, have had amongst their members such prominent watercolour painters as Cox, Cotman, De Wint, Burne-Jones, Holman Hunt, Sargent, Rackham and Russell Flint and well-known printmakers like Tissot, Legros, Sickert, Griggs, Drury, Brockhurst, Gross and Hayter.

Both societies maintain permanent collections. The **RWS Diploma Collection** consists of about *500 watercolours* by past and present members and has been assembled over the years by gifts and bequests together with the Diploma works given on their election by the artists in return for which they receive the Society's Diploma, signed by the Sovereign. This applies also to the **RE Diploma Collection** which comprises over *300 etchings and engravings*. Both collections, not until recently shown to the general public, are accessible to researchers and serious students.

Each society holds a Spring and Autumn show. Important loan exhibitions of historical and contemporary work are presented from time to time, as well as exhibitions open to non-member artists. These are the most important open exhibitions for watercolourists and printmakers held annually in the London area.

the essentials

Underground Blackfriars (Circle, District Lines). **Open** Tue-Sat 1000-1700, Sun 1400-1800. **Cloakroom. Toilets. For the disabled** access, toilets. **Shopping. Publications. Photography. Educational facilities** by prior arrangement. **Visitors' services** guided tours, films, lectures by arrangement during exhibitions. **Research** library.

■ BANQUETING HOUSE

Whitehall SW1A 2ER. Tel 930 4179
Admission *charge*

Focal point of the Court and scene of the fall of Charles I, who was beheaded in 1649 on the scaffold erected just outside this historic building, the Banqueting House's major appeal nowadays is the ***nine large paintings*** by Peter Paul Rubens. The works of the Flemish artist cover the entire ceilings of the Banqueting Hall, the main apartment of this magnificent building designed by Inigo Jones, the greatest British architect. With Raphael's Cartoons at the Victoria and Albert Museum and the Triumphs of Caesar at Hampton Court Palace, these paintings are amongst the finest in the possession of the Crown. They were commissioned by Charles I to commemorate his father James I and put in place in 1653. Rubens received payment of £3,000 for them and a knighthood.

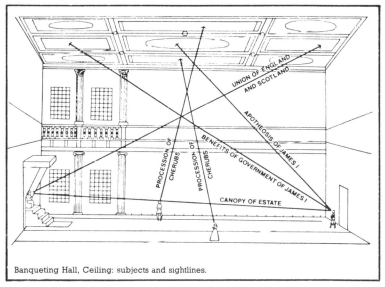

Banqueting Hall, Ceiling: subjects and sightlines.

The best vantage point to admire the paintings is the north entrance doorway of the hall, which at the time of the Stuarts was also the entrance used by distinguished visitors seeking audience with the Sovereign, who was usually seated on a throne at the south end of the room. The central oval, *The Apotheosis of James I*, depicts the King rising to heaven. Flanking this great oval are a procession of cherubs in a kind of Bacchic triumph. The painting *The Benefits of the Government* of James I — placed almost above the throne — shows the Monarch surrounded by Wisdom (attired as Minerva) confronting War (Mars trampling on the King's enemies), while Mercury points to the nether regions as their destination. With a sweeping gesture the King indicates Peace and Plenty while a cherub holds aloft the royal crown. In the oval, to the left, is the figure of Abundance holding the cornucopia bestriding the bound figure of Avarice. In the right oval, Reason holds a bridle above the cramped figure of Intemperate Discord.

The northern pictures, best seen from just in front of the throne, describe, in the central square, the *Union of England and Scotland*.

Here James I in full regalia leans forward from his throne towards a naked child symbolising the new-born Union of the northern and southern kingdoms. The child is supported by two figures and above his head Britannia holds the joined crowns of England and Scotland. In the ovals on the sides are, on the left, *Heroic Virtue* in the guise of Hercules crushing Envy, and the right *Heroic Wisdom* in the form of Minerva striking Ignorance with a spear.

Banqueting Hall: the Rubens paintings.

the essentials

Underground Charing Cross (Bakerloo, Jubilee, Northern Lines). **Open** Tue-Sat 1000-1700, Sun 1400-1700. **Cloakroom. Toilets. Public Telephones. Shopping** sales desk. **Publications.**

■ BARNET MUSEUM

Wood Street EN5 4BE.   Tel 449 0321
Admission *free*

The Museum stands in the centre of the busy suburb of Barnet. The shell of the building dates from the early C19 but it was gutted and most handsomely refitted by the London Borough of Barnet, starting in 1979. It is now occupied and run by the local history society. As you enter, on the **ground floor** you will see a fine fireplace whose presence was unsuspected when the renovators moved in, but the room's centre is given over to Barnet's own 'red letter day', the great Battle of Barnet of April 1471, when Edward IV, newly back from Flanders, defeated and killed Warwick the 'Kingmaker'. A *plan of the battle* is superimposed on the grid of modern-day Barnet.

Go **downstairs** to inspect the excellent *display of ladies' period dresses and bonnets*, and then **upstairs** to see some outsize enlarged photographs of Old Barnet, the ***Watson Collection*** of locally-made scientific instruments, and a fully-furnished late-Victorian sitting-room.

A real miscellany of bygones, all beautifully kept and displayed in a warm and welcoming setting. The **garden** at the back leads you straight into an equally pleasant park.

--------- *the essentials* ---------

Underground High Barnet (Northern Line). **Open** Tue-Thur 1430-1630, Sat 1000-1200, Sun by appointment only. **Toilets. Parking. For the disabled** access to ground floor. **Shopping** sales desk. **Publications. Photography. Educational facilities. Research** map library on application.

■ HMS BELFAST

Symons Wharf, Vine Lane SE1 2JH.   Tel 407 6434
Admission *charge*

In 1971 the Royal Navy's last big-gun ship, the cruiser HMS Belfast was towed into the Thames to be moored opposite the Tower of London and became a floating museum.

HMS Belfast was built in the city whose name it bears and was commissioned just one month before the outbreak of World War II. In October 1939 she captured the German liner Cap Norte which was bound for Germany and shortly after, in November 1939, she was severely damaged by a magnetic mine, and remained under repair until October 1942. She then began her service guarding the Russian convoys, and it was at Christmas 1943 when, as the flagship of the 10th Cruiser Squadron, she helped to sink the single greatest danger to the Russian lifeline, the German battle cruiser Scharnhorst. HMS Belfast served throughout the rest of the war, leading the cruiser bombardment which supported the Allied landings on D-Day, saw action in the Korean War, and eventually ended her active career in 1963.

A warship of this class was like a floating city with 800 men living, working and fighting on board; there is a lot to see from 'A' *Turret* housing part of the ship's main armament of 6-inch guns, to the ship's laundry and the cavernous machinery spaces. The ship has been left as nearly as possible in her original condition, and her *Operations Room* is set up as it would have been at Christmas 1943 when she was in action against the Scharnhorst.

The *Admiral's Cabin* is arranged as it was when occupied by Vice-Admiral Burnett who had HMS Belfast as his flagship during the engagement with the Scharnhorst. Visitors can also see how

The cruiser HMS Belfast.

the ordinary sailors lived, ate and slept, with their mess cutlery and uniforms neatly arranged for inspection. There is a tableau showing how the ship's surgeon worked in the *Sick Bay*, operating on an injured seaman; one of the ship's eight bakers is seen preparing bread in the *Bakery*, while next door the *Ship's Company Galley* — the kitchen — gets ready for a meal. There are special displays on board. The Royal Ulster Rifles were affiliated to the ship and there is an exhibition 'Who shall separate us?' dedicated to the regiment. There is also a Battleship Exhibition, a D-Day Exhibition, Conflict at Sea, a Rum Display, and a special display showing the Royal Navy's role today. The *Cruiser Museum* studies the class of warship Belfast belonged to, which played so great a part in the C20 annals of the Royal Navy. (ST)

—————————————— *the essentials* ——————————————

Underground Tower Hill (Circle, District Lines). **Open** daily. Summer 1100-1750, Winter 1100-1600. **Toilets. Public telephones. For the disabled** by prior arrangement. **Refreshments. Shipping. Publications. Photography. Educational facilities. Visitors' services** films, slides, talks by prior arrangement, linguistic aid (French) (Mon-Fri) by prior arrangement.

■ BETHNAL GREEN MUSEUM OF CHILDHOOD

Cambridge Heath Road, E2 9PA. Tel 980 2415
Admission *free*

The museum is a branch of the Victoria and Albert Museum (qv) and its guide defines the difference between the two: "The V & A is concerned with the beautiful things man has made for his own use. Its Bethnal Green branch is concerned with what man has made for his children" - toys, clothes and furniture, books. The building is an archetype Victorian Museum - in fact, it is the original building of the South Kensington Museum, now the V & A, which was moved piece-by-piece and re-erected here in 1872. It displayed artefacts relating to this then specially depressed part of London's East End. When Sir Roy Strong became the V & A's director in 1974 he decided the museum would become the Museum of Childhood, remaining a branch of the V & A, and the transformation process is now almost complete.

In March 1986 the new *toy galleries* were completed, and these are a joy for adults and children alike. Starting with the simplest of playthings such as marbles, every toy imaginable is here: fantastical automata, so popular with the Victorians, Dinky toys, teddy bears, clockwork train sets, optical toys, lead soldiers, miniature furniture and a whole toy circus - covering about four centuries to the present day.

The *collection of dolls' houses,* from the intriguing Nuremburg house of 1673 to modern ones, is unique and must not be missed, nor the re-creations of rooms with all the implements and furniture in perfect miniature. There is a special display of *puppets and marionettes* following the history of these fascinating toys, and another of *pedal cars and scooters. Dolls* throughout the ages receive special attention too. The model of Queen Victoria in her Coronation Robes made in the 1840s shortly after her accession is particularly interesting.

In the process of being arranged on the top floor are the displays recounting the history of child life, with clothes, children's furniture and learning toys. The huge *Renier collection of children's books* – numbering 70,000 volumes so far and still growing – is available to researchers by appointment.

Temporary exhibitions are held at the museum, and each Christmas there is a special seasonal exhibition. There is also a lively Education Department with special activities organised during each school holiday. (ST)

––––––––––––––––––––––––––––– *the essentials* –––––––––––––––––––––––––––––
Underground Bethnal Green (Central Line). **Open** Mon-Thur, Sat 1000-1800, Sun 1430-1800. **Cloakroom** luggage lockers. **Toilets. Parking. For the disabled** by prior arrangement. **Shopping. Educational facilities. Staff opinions.**

Bethnal Green Museum: Puppet and toy theatre gallery.

■ BEXLEY MUSEUM

Hall Place, Bourne Road, Bexley DA5 1PQ. Tel (0322) 526574
Admission *free*

The museum is part of the Bexley Museum Service, created in 1972 as an integral part of the Local Studies Section of the London Borough of Bexley. It is divided into permanent and temporary display areas. The **permanent display** consists of exhibits showing some of the geology, archaeology and natural history of the areas. The **temporary displays** (usually three a year) are concerned with social and industrial local history. Past topics have included the agricultural history of Bexley, the life of the Borough during the War, the use and effect of the Thames in the Borough and an exhibition on photography and local photographers.

The building which houses the museum is a Tudor mansion of stone (some very likely taken from a destroyed medieval monastery) and bricks, which was enlarged in the C17.

─────────────── *the essentials* ───────────────

BR Bexley Station (from Charing Cross Station). **Open** Summer Mon-Sat 1000-1700, Sun 1400-1700; Winter Mon-Sat 1000-dusk. **Toilets. Parking. For the disabled** access to ground floor of the house. **Refreshments** snacks. **Shopping** sales desk. **Photography. Educational facilities. Visitors' services**, lectures, guided tours by prior arrangement. **Research** library.

■ BRITISH ARCHITECTURAL LIBRARY DRAWINGS COLLECTION

21 Portman Square W1H 9HF. Tel 580 5533
Admission *prior application*

Since its foundation in 1934, the Royal Institute of British Architects (RIBA) has amassed a rich and diverse collection of architectural drawings. It has its home in a handsome Adam building in Portman Square. Originating in 1838 with Sir John Drummond-Stewart's gift of French and Italian designs, it has since been augmented by gifts from members and others and the total now stands at 350,000. In 1894 the outstanding **Burlington-Devonshire collection** of drawings by the great Andrea Palladio was acquired, followed in 1926 by the **Smythson collection** of late Elizabethan designs. The earliest drawing (1520) is of a chantry in Winchester Cathedral.

The variety is wide-ranging, from the early simple plans and elevations, through the C19 elaborate large-scale watercolour perspectives to drawings by Frank Lloyd Wright, Le Corbusier, Mies van der Rohe and others. There are also a number of models. Accessible by appointment, the collection's value for scholars, students and those concerned with planning, conservation and design for films and television is enormous.

The RIBA **Heinz Gallery** (entrance in Gloucester Place) for special exhibitions was developed with a generous gift from Mr and Mrs Henry J Heinz II. It presents an average of six special exhibitions a year on the work of either contemporary architects or their distinguished predecessors.

─────────────── *the essentials* ───────────────

Underground Bond Street (Central, Jubilee Lines), Marble Arch (Central Line). **Open** ☐ Drawings Collection: Mon-Fri 1000-1300. ☐ Heinz Gallery: Mon-Fri 1100-1700, Sat 1000-1300 (during exhibitions). Both Collection and Gallery are closed during August.

■ BRITISH COUNCIL COLLECTION

11 Portland Place W1N 4EJ.　Tel 930 8466
Admission *prior application*

Founded in 1934, the British Council exists to promote cultural, educational and technical co-operation between Britain and other countries. Within that broad framework the Visual Arts Department of the Council is concerned with the presentation overseas of British art both of the past and of the present day, to demonstrate its qualities and vitality. This is carried out largely through the provision of exhibitions, normally in response to invitations from museums and other institutions, and also through the circulation of works from the Collection to other countries over as wide an area as possible.

This Collection is a major public representation of C20 British art consisting of over 5,000 items: paintings, sculpture, drawings, graphics, photographs and mixed media works. It is particularly rich in important works by Henry Moore, Barbara Hepworth and Graham Sutherland and there are many other well-known British artists whose works are included, such as Matthew Smith, Ben Nicholson, Lucian Freud, Alan Davie, Eduardo Paolozzi, Bridget Riley, Anthony Caro, Richard Smith and David Hockney. Most of the works are post-1944. The Collection proper started the following

British Council Collection: David Hockney, Man in a Museum, 1962.

19

year, although the first purchases were made before World War II from a donation of £1,000 made by Lord Wakefield.

Funds available for purchase have fluctuated since then, but the annual purchase grant has recently been between £30,000-£40,000.

A high proportion of acquisitions is made specially in order to make up the modestly-scaled Circulating Exhibitions, which can tour indefinitely throughout the world. The Council may also buy works to supplement and strengthen major loan exhibitions, which are assembled through the generosity of public and private owners.

Many works are displayed within Council offices and centres abroad and larger works are sometimes placed on long loan to foreign museums. Short-term loans are also made whenever possible to exhibitions organised by museums and institutions both in Britain and overseas. All enquiries regarding the Collection should be sent to the Visual Arts Department at the above address.

the essentials

Underground Oxford Circus (Bakerloo, Central, Victoria Lines). **Open** Mon-Fri 1000-1700. **Cloakroom. Toilets. For the disabled** access, toilets. **Publications. Research facilities** by application.

■ BRITISH DENTAL ASSOCIATION MUSEUM

64 Wimpole Street W1M 8AL. Tel 935 0875
Admission *prior application*

The museum is perhaps one of the best on dentistry in Europe and possibly in the world. Its origin goes back to 1934 when the Board of the British Dental Association accepted a proposal to create and name it after J Smith Turner (a father figure of the dental profession in England).

The various items on permanent display (only 10% of the rich collections assembled through the years) are cleverly arranged to achieve the aim of illustrating the drastic changes that have taken place within the dentistry profession especially during the last hundred years. Beside many dentures using so-called 'Waterloo teeth', there is the ivory plate specially made for Edmund Burke who delivered his nine-day speech for the impeachment of Warren Hastings in 1794. Not less important are the collection of *historic surgical instruments* from as far back as the C16, including some very early extractors, keys and artefacts connected with the making of dental porcelain and the tremendous advance following the discovery of vulcanization.

But perhaps most interesting of all are the reconstructions of two *dental surgeries*, complete with original furniture and instruments of the C19 period, when dentistry evolved from being a kind of sub-branch of mechanical engineering towards an activity where medical science has much more to contribute.

the essentials

Underground Bond Street (Central, Jubilee Lines). **Open** Mon-Fri 1000-1600. **Cloakroom. Toilets. Photography** by prior arrangement. **Research** library by prior arrangement.

■ BRITISH LIBRARY

Great Russell Street WC1B 3DG. Tel 636 1544
Admission *free* (Exhibition Galleries); *reader's pass* * or *prior application* (rest)

The British Library easily fits the description of being one of the richest, if not the richest, public collections of books and related materials in the world. It resulted from the merger, following an 1972 Act of Parliament, which brought together several major organisations to form the United Kingdom's national library.

The British Library in Figures 1989	
· Shelving	376 miles
· Books and (bound) periodicals (volumes)	18 million
· Western & Oriental manuscripts (volumes)	165,000
· Cartographic items	1.6 million
· Music scores	1.6 million
· Newspapers (volumes)	over 0.5 million
· Patent specifications	29 million
· Serials (current titles)	over 170,000
· Philatelic items	6 million
· Recorded sound (discs)	0.7 million
(tapes)	47,000 hours

Currently dispersed over more than ten locations in London and a complex in Boston Spa (West Yorkshire LS23 7BQ) the library's best-known collections are those housed in the British Museum (qv) building. Here are the exhibition Galleries, a must for every visitor to London; the unique Map, Music and Official Publications libraries; part of the vast Philatelic Collection (the bulk being lodged in Store Street WC1E 7DG); the renowned Department of Manuscripts; the famous Round Reading Room devised by Panizzi and, of course, the cavernous North Library.

☐ The **Exhibition Galleries** present a remarkable display both in terms of the very high qualilty of the contents and the way they are arranged. They are four in number (the Middle Room, the Manuscript Saloon, the King's Library and the Map Gallery) and occupy most of the ground floor and mezzanine of the British Museum's East Wing, where the Crawford Room is also located (see the British Museum Floor Plans).

● The **Middle Room** formerly housed copies of the plays submitted to the Lord Chamberlain for approval. Some of the Library's Western illuminated manuscrips are now displayed there. On entering, the first case contains the *Lindisfarne Gospels* which were written and illuminated about 698 in the Northumbrian island monastery of Lindisfarne. This manuscript demonstrates the outstanding achievement of Northumbrian artists in the earliest period of English Christianity. Other notable exhibits are the C8 *Vespasian Psalter* from Canterbury – a collection of psalms written in Latin bearing the

---

* A *reader's pass* is in general issued to those of 21 years and over studying at above first-degree level. Application must be made in person at the Reader Admission Office.

British Library (King's Library): a page from the Gutenberg Bible, printed in Mainz c1455, by Johann Gutenberg, Johann Frist and Peter Schoeffer.

earliest known historiated initial; the *Benedictional of St Ethelwold,* a collection of blessings written for the saint's personal use when he became Bishop of Winchester in 963; the *Bedford Hours,* produced in the early C15 for the Duke of Bedford, an outstanding example of the standard book for popular devotion in Western Europe during the late Middle Ages and Renaissance. It contains nearly 300 leaves, every one of which is illuminated; the *Luttrell Psalter,* in Latin, made before 1340 for Sir Geoffrey Luttrell, a Lincolnshire landowner. Its marginal decoration is one of the richest surviving sources for illustrations of everyday life in the Middle Ages. The Continental selection includes secular manuscripts, as well as Byzantine manuscripts and manuscripts from the Carolingian Empire including the *Harley Golden Gospels,* a copy of the four Gospels, written entirely in gold and lavishly illuminated, made about 800 probably at the court of Emperor Charlemagne at Aachen.

● The **Manuscript Saloon** is primarily devoted to manuscripts of historical and literary interest. Royal autographs are prominent among the historical letters and documents and almost every major literary figure is represented in the section given to English literature. There are also displays of Bibles, heraldry, maps and music. Famous items on display include *Magna Carta* and the *Articles of the Barons,* the demands placed before King John at Runnymede in June 1215. Accepted by him and sealed with his seal (shown next to the document), they formed the basis of Magna Carta, regarded by all who have adopted English laws as their chief constitutional defence against arbitrary or unjust rules. The Codex Sinaiticus and the Codex Alexandrinus are two of the three earliest and most important manuscripts of the Bible. The *Codex Sinaiticus*

British Library (Middle Room): The Nativity from the Benedictional of St Ethelwold. It is the outstanding example of the so-called 'Winchester school' of illumination which flourished in England in the century preceding the Norman conquest.

was written in Greek about the middle of the C4 and the *Codex Alexandrinus* during the first half of the C5. Both manuscripts are on vellum. *Sumer is icumen in* is one of the most familiar medieval musical compositions and the earliest to have both sacred and secular words provided for the same tune. The manuscript was probably written at Reading in the mid-C13. A special 'Manuscript of the Month' case is used to show items of particular interest and topicality.

● The **King's Library** was built in 1823-26 to house the library of King George III, whose books may still be seen in the glass wall-cases around the gallery. This was the first part of the present British Museum building to be erected. The showcases at the south end of this gallery display *Oriental treasures* including fine examples of the art of the book in Asia, Africa and Europe. They show splendidly illuminated manuscripts and scrolls in Arabic, Persian, Turkish, Hebrew, Ethiopic, Coptic, Syriac and Armenian, and superbly illuminated items from the Indian sub-continent, China, Japan, and other Central and South East Asian and Far Eastern countries. These consist not only of manuscripts on paper, vellum and palm leaves, but include unique and rare early printed books of great significance and value. The history of writing and writing material is also extensively documented. The centre of the gallery is used for temporary exhibitions. Near to Roubiliac's 1758 *statue of Shakespeare* is a case of documents relating to the bard, including a mortgage bearing his signature, and a copy of the *Shakespeare First Folio, 1623*, the first collected edition of Shakespeare's plays, which was printed from sources that represent the plays as performed in the theatre. The engraved portrait is the only printed contemporary likeness of the author.

The displays in the north of the gallery show the impact made by the printed book on many aspects of society. Notable specimens of early printing include the *Diamond Sutra,* dated 868, the earliest complete and dated extant block - printed book in the world, and the *Gutenberg Bible* (completed c 1455), the first book printed in movable type. The introduction of printed books into England is represented by the work of William Caxton and Wynkyn de Worde as well as by books printed on the Continent and imported into England through the booktrade. The importance of the printed book in spreading and refining knowledge of all kinds is amply illustrated. Displays show the role of the printed word in bringing information to a wider audience than previously possible. Discoveries of new lands (eg *Columbus's letter on his finding America),* progress in language studies (dictionaries), and in understanding the human body (anatomies), the scholar's use of books as steps towards further progress (commentaries, criticism, citations) and the use of books as the vehicle for opinion (eg King Henry VIII on the authority of the church and on wives, Thomas Cranmer on heresy) are just some of the themes for the visitor to follow. The transition from Latin to the vernacular is also exemplified with specific language displays illustrating different aspects of new readership. There are C16 German books on subjects of topical interest (emancipation of the peasants, legal rights) as well as those encouraging the illiterate to read; English books printed for women; Slavonic language books reflecting greater national awareness; and

C16 Italian books 'for every pocket' as well as the examples of the use of the Italian language in famous books such as the *Dante edition illustrated by Botticelli*. The north end of the gallery also displays music and approximately 6,000 album leaves taken from the library's philatelic collection. They include rarities such as the *1840 Great Britain Penny Black* and the *1847 Post Office issues of Mauritius.*

British Library (Map Library): terrestrial globe by John Senex (d1740).

● The **Map Gallery** displays examples from the Map Library. The display is normally changed once a year to commemorate anniversaries and to illustrate special themes in the history of cartography.

● The **Crawford Room** accommodates special exhibitions which require a compact venue.

□ The **Map Library** is one of the world's most important cartographic collections; its treasures include four *C13 manuscripts* by Matthew Paris in what are the first scientific maps of Britain since the time of Ptolemy (C2). George III's own library contributed (1828) some 50,000 maps, plans and charts of North America, and acquisitions over the years have brought the total to over 2 million

SECVNDA
MVSCVLO.
RVMTA
BVLA.

British Library (North Library): Andrea Vesalius, De humani corporis fabrica, Basle, 1543. The first complete illustrated account of human anatomy based on dissection.

items. The Map Library is the British Library's centre of geographical studies, with an information service, reading-room, facilities and an open-access reference library.

☐ The **Music Library** aims to be the complete archive of British published music and its collections include all periods and types, world-wide, of music publications. More than 11 million pieces cover the history, from C16 to today, of printed music. Its foundations were laid in the C18 with the Hanoverian Royal Music Library, particularly rich in Handel autographs. The vast Hirsch Library, acquired in 1946, enriched the Library's holdings of the Viennese classics. The valuable collection of autograph musical and literary manuscripts formed by the Austrian writer Stefan Zweig was given to the Library in 1986: this bequest is commemorated by a series of concerts, lectures and exhibitions each Spring. These magnificent music collections can be studied with a reader's pass.

☐ The **Official Publications Library** is the reading room for holdings of British and Foreign Official Publications. A reader's pass is necessary.

☐ The **Department of Manuscripts** is the national repository of the written word and is one of the original departments of the British Museum. It contains manuscripts of all kind and all ages in Western languages, ranging from single documents to books containing as many as 500 or more leaves. Reflecting the history of Western civilisation in general and in the UK in particular, the collection includes Greek and Latin papyri, ancient Biblical codices, illuminated manuscripts of incalculable value, other medieval manuscripts both secular and religious, great archives and post-medieval historical papers, famous literary autographs and vast collections of music, maps, plans, topographical drawings, charters and seals. The reading room is accessible by a supplementary pass.

☐ The **Philatelic Collection**, numbering some 6 million items, originated in 1891 with the huge Tapling Collection bequest. The present-day main reference basis is the Universal Postal Union Collection, which receives reference sets of every new postage stamp issued from virtually every postal administration in the world. The *Fletcher Collection* illustrates postal history from the mid C17 to the 1960s. All can be studied by prior application.

☐ The **Round Reading Room** and the **North Library.** Until 1857 various areas provided reading rooms, but in that year was opened the spectacular domed masterpiece of Sir Anthony Panizzi, Keeper of Printed Books, and the architect Sydney Smirke. For it they used the courtyard which lay at the centre of the building. The project cost the (in those days) very large sum of £150,000, and was completed at very great speed, thanks to the use of cast iron. The vast dome is only two feet less in diameter than the Pantheon in Rome. Great care was devoted to the decorations and fittings, and the Round Reading Room is still one of the great triumphs of Victorian architecture, and the best-known writer's-workshop in the world. Visitors are shown into the Room on the hour, 1100-1600. Rare books are made available for study in the North Library, a separate

British Library: Panizzi's Round Reading Room.

galleried reading room built after World War I. Access to both reading rooms is by reader's pass only.

Other London-based collections include those of the India Office Library and Records (qv), the National Sound Archive (qv), the Newspaper Library (qv), the Oriental Collections (qv) and the Science Reference and Information Service (qv). The professional library and information communities of the UK are served by the **British Library Information Service** [7 Ridgmount Street WC1E 7AE, Tel 323 7688].

The building of a new headquarters in Euston Road, next to St Pancras Station, lies at the heart of the British Library's plans for the future. It will provide an opportunity for preserving, managing, exploiting and presenting the national collections more effectively for the benefit of future users. The building will be opened to readers and the general public from 1993.

---

the essentials

Underground Holborn (Central, Piccadilly Lines), Tottenham Court Road (Central, Northern Lines). **Open** Mon-Sat 1000-1700. Sun 1430-1800. **Cloakroom. Toilets. Public telephones. For the disabled** access, toilets. **Refreshments** snacks. **Shopping. Photography. Educational facilities. Visitors' services** talks on special subjects, Acousta Guides. **Research** by prior arrangement. **Staff opinion** but not valuations.

■ BRITISH MUSEUM

Great Russell Street WC1B 3DG. Tel 636 1555 (580 1788)

Admission *free*   (in the text, numbers in **bold** refer to the Plan)

The British Museum is one of the world's greatest museums. Since 1759 people have been making their way along Great Russell Street to gaze at what has been called a 'noble and magnificent cabinet', 'the world's greatest storehouse of priceless treasures', a 'labyrinthine lumber room', 'an interesting monster' and 'history's great treasure trove'. It is one of the wonders of the world and should on no account be missed. Here under the Museum's seven acres of roof are the finest collection of Assyrian reliefs outside the Middle East, the Rosetta Stone, the Anglo-Saxon treasure from Sutton Hoo, the oldest Christian silver yet found in the Roman Empire, 3,000 clocks and watches, half-a-million coins, two-and-a-half-million prints, the best collection of Islamic pottery outside the Islamic world, Indian sculptures, Chinese porcelain, Egyptian mummies.

Its title is misleading for it is not really a 'British' museum. Founded by Act of Parliament in 1753 to house the multifarious collections of the physician, naturalist and collector, Sir Hans Sloane (1660-1753), the Cottonian library and Harleian manuscripts, it is a universal collection reflecting the rich variety of man's works. Once it was even more universal - the natural history collection was transferred to the British Museum (Natural History) (qv) in the 1880s and the library is now part of the British Library (qv) although much remains on the same site.

The British Museum contains some of the finest pieces of art in the world but it has never been an art museum. Alongside the masterpieces is a vast collection of flints, scraps of pot, cuneiform tablets, etc for as well as catering for the 'curious' visitor (mentioned thus in the 1753 Act) who comes to look at the galleries, it is a research institution publishing profound works of scholarship and catering also for the 'studious' from all over the world. The problem therefore for the casual visitor is putting limited time to best use. If time is short then look at a selection of the world's greatest treasures listed below. If you have more leisure or prefer not to go with the crowd then it is well worth lingering in some of the more obscure of the Museum's 2½ miles of galleries. The collections number several million items and the Museum reckons, with a few exceptions, to display all its first-rank material (or at least a representative selection).

The building is itself as fine an exhibit as any. The Museum acquired a C17 mansion on this site in 1754. This has now disappeared under the largest neoclassical building in the British Isles, the greater part designed by Sir Robert Smirke (1781-1867). Work started on the oldest section, the King's Library, in 1823 and, as the visitor will probably discover, appears to have been going on ever since as the Museum regularly outgrows its space (gallery closures are listed in the Front Hall). To reach the great entrance, turn off Great Russell Street through the massive gates erected in 1852 and up the steps below a crowded pediment by Richard Westmacott showing 'The Progress of Civilisation' (note the intriguing way the sculptor managed to fit in an elephant, lion and crocodile, not to mention Astronomy, into minimal space).

Probably the best introduction to the Museum is to turn left from the main Entrance Hall past the bookshop and into the 'Assyrian Transept' **26**. There may be a special exhibition in Room **27** but, if you want to start with GREECE continue straight ahead through the 1300 BC columns from the 'Treasury of Atreus' at Mycenae and past the enigmatic marble figures of the Bronze Age Cyclades **1**. There are some interesting pieces in Rooms **1-3** but these are not the best-represented periods in the Museum. The mysterious Aegina Treasure with the strange gold figure of the 'Master of the Animals' **2** is worth pausing at. Dating from c1700-1500 BC it

● **Upper floors** rooms 35–73, 90–94

● **Ground floor** rooms 1–34

● **Basement** rooms 77–89 *Basement level is reached from the west stairs and rooms 12, 16 and 17*

Floor plans

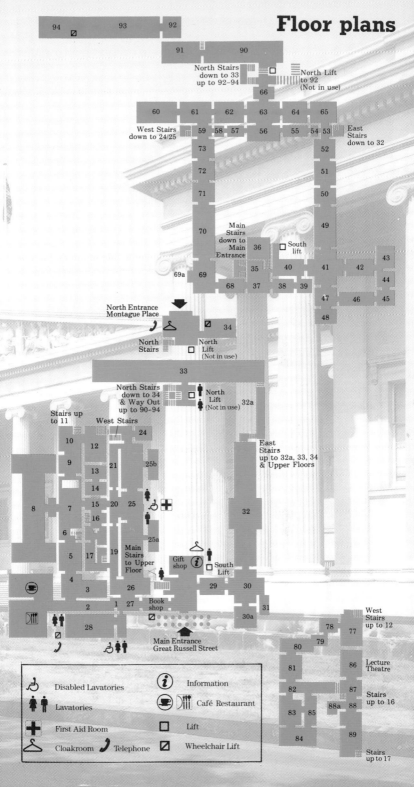

British Museum: the Townley Collection, C1 and C2 Roman sculpture (Room 84).

British Museum (Egyptian Antiquities): detail of sheet 5 of the papyrus
of Hunefer, 19th Dynasty c1310 BC (Room 62).

probably belonged to Minoan Cretans and was found in a tomb on the island of Aegina. In Room **3** is a display on Archaic Greece 1000-500 BC. The staircase leads down to a study display of Greek vases **3a.** Room **5** contains sculptures and small objects including some fine vases. Of particular note is the *Harpy tomb* from Xanthos, named from the rather sinister human-headed birdlike creatures, spirits of the storm and the wind, carrying the souls of the departed members of the Lycian family for whom the tomb was erected c480-470 BC. The mezzanine upstairs **6** contains battling Greeks and Amazons, Lapiths and Centaurs from the C5 BC Temple of Apollo at Bassae, the earliest known sculptured frieze decorating the inside of a Greek temple.

Walk through the doorway and silhouetted against an Aegean blue background is the *Nereid Monument* from Xanthos **7**, one of the finest tombs of the Chieftains of Lycia, c400 BC, which takes its name from the figures in clinging drapery between the columns, once thought to be Nereids but now identified as Aurae or breezes. To the left **8** is one of the half dozen or so things everyone should see, the mid-C5 BC *Sculptures of the Parthenon*, part of the collection rescued by Lord Elgin at the beginning of the C19. The marble has been transformed into a jostling procession - horses with flaring nostrils, lowing cattle and human attendants circle the room towards a dignified gathering of the great gods. At each end of the gallery are surviving figures from the pediments of the temple, that to the north portraying the Birth of Athena and that to the south her contest with Poseidon for the land of Attica. Also acquired by Elgin were a *Caryatid* and a *column* from the east porch of the *Erechtheion* **9.** The imposing structure in Room **10** is yet another tomb from Xanthos, built by the unknown Payava in the C4 BC. A permanent exhibition of Athenian red-figured vases is displayed in the mezzanine **11.** Next door **12** are more sights not to be missed - remains of two of the Seven Wonders of the ancient world - the C4 BC *Mausoleum at Halicarnassus* including a superb horse, the survivor of four which towered 150 feet above the ground at the summit of the Mausoleum. Beyond the sculptures known as 'Maussollos' and 'Artemisia' is a column base from the C4 BC *Temple of Diana* (Artemis) at Ephesus which stood when St Paul preached.

If you have time, detour into the basement Wolfson Galleries **78-85.** A fascinating collection of Greek and Roman architectural remains **77** illustrates in handy form what particular bits looked like - Doric, Ionic, Corinthian orders, architraves, capitals, cornices, etc. The Inscription Room **78** contains a selection of Greek and Latin civic, religious and funerary texts including a grand temple dedication by Alexander the Great. Some inscriptions are carved with great skill but there are one or two intriguingly poor efforts whose length the craftsman seems to have miscalculated. In Rooms **79-81** are early Greek sculptures - more tombs from Lycia, C6 seated figures from the Sanctuary of Apollo at Didyma, sculptured tombs from Classical Athens. There are the hindquarters of a horse, the remains of a Persian rider and other fragments from the Mausoleum, little figures from the temple of Athena Polias at Priene and more pieces from the Temple of Diana.

Across the corridor in the ROMAN Room **83** is a collection of sculpture and sarcophagi (some virtually mass-produced) and the largest foot in the Museum (from Alexandria C2). At the far end the *Townley collection of Roman sculpture* **84** is displayed in a crowded basement to reflect its origins - a C18 gentleman's collection once kept in his private house. The sculptures, largely from C18 excavations in Italy include the well-known 'Discobolus' (the discus thrower), the Townley Venus and 'Clytie' (Townley's favourite) - perhaps Antonia, daughter of Mark Antony and mother of the Emperor Claudius.

At the end of the detour (or after Room 12) don't miss another of the Museum's great treasures, the *Portland Vase* **14** which will in due course move to **70**. Dating from the reign of Augustus or Tiberius (27 BC-AD 37), it is one of the finest pieces of glass to have survived from the ancient world. Made of two layers, cobalt blue and white, it portrays the wooing of the sea-goddess Thetis by the mortal hero Peleus. From Room **15** you now enter EGYPT. Those who prefer to start here should on arrival turn right on leaving the postcard shop, passing the fearsome gateway guardians from the North-West Palace of the Assyrian King Ashurnasirpal (883-859 BC) from the city of Nimrud **26**. Just beyond this (left) is the famous *Rosetta stone*, carved c196 BC **25**. An unassuming slab of basalt, it was discovered in 1799 when all knowledge of the ancient Egyptian heiroglyphic script had been lost. Its triple inscription (a similar text repeated in heiroglyphs, demotic – the cursive form, and Greek) enabled scholars to reconstruct the ancient Egyptian language. Before you lies the finest collection of *Egyptian sculpture* outside Egypt, dominated by the remains of two colossi – the head and arm of a king, perhaps *Amenophis III* c1390 BC from Thebes and the upper half of a statue of *Ramesses II* c1270 BC which has been in the Museum since 1818. There are also smaller objects – wall paintings, inscriptions, jewellery, bronzes and massive sarcophagi including that made for Nectanebo II, last native ruler of Egypt, c345 BC. Don't miss a detour into Room **17** which is lined by the relief sculptures of the *Lion Hunt of Ashurbanipal* (668-627 BC) from the North Palace of the ASSYRIAN city of Nineveh. These reliefs of dying lions and lionesses pierced with arrows shot by the king from his resplendent chariot are some of the finest animal sculptures of antiquity. The *Black Obelisk of Shalmaneser III* 825 BC, in the middle of Room **19**, shows the delivery of tribute including that from Jehu, King of Israel c841 BC.

In nearby galleries **16-20, 21** are more reliefs from the palaces of the Assyrian kings, showing the king as invincible under divine protection and plentiful corpses resulting from the bloody campaigns of his much-feared armies. If time permits, Room **89** downstairs is worth a visit for the famous Battle of the River Ulai, an early form of strip-cartoon from the South-West Palace at Nineveh showing Ashurbanipal's defeat of the Elamite King Teumman in 653 BC. At the far end of the Egyptian Sculpture Gallery, at the foot of the West Stairs, is the Ancient Palestine Room **24** which features a reconstruction of a burial from Bronze Age Jericho c2100-1900 BC, with added grave robbers C18-17 BC.

Upstairs in Rooms **60** and **61** is the Museum's fine collection of *Egyptian mummies, coffins, human and animal remains.* The oldest inhabitant is 'Ginger', a 5000-year-old body preserved in hot sand

British Museum: 1. The Royal Gold Cup, Paris c1380, with scenes from the life of St Agnes (Room 42); 2. The Rosetta Stone, c196 BC (Room 25); 3. The Portland Vase, C1 BC or AD (Room 14); 4. Horse of Selene from the east pediment of the Parthenon, mid-C5 BC (Room 8); 5. Human-headed lion from Ashurnasirpal II's palace at Nimrud, c865 BC (Room 26).

before the development of mummification techniques, which are well illustrated in the popular but gruesome collection next door. Beyond **62** are *papyri* including sections from the world's longest, the Great Harris c1150 BC, the Rhind mathematical papyrus c1575 BC, the Harris Tomb robbery papyrus c1175 BC and many fine Books of the Dead. There are *tomb paintings*, including a lively Banquet Scene c1400 BC from the tomb of Nebamun, Thebes, the guests sitting with perfumed wax dripping down their wigs. In **63** is a selection of the things Egyptians took with them to the tomb which they had used in everyday life - food, clothing, furniture, tools, cosmetic jars and little models to work for them after death.

A rather traditional display of small sculptures **64** leads into a new display, *Egypt in Africa*, opening 1991 **65**. Parallel is a range of galleries starting with ancient South Arabia **59**. Next come intricately carved ivories, many found at the bottom of a well in the Assyrian city of Nimrud, having survived its sack by Medes and Babylonians in 612 BC **58**, worth visiting particularly for the strange 'Woman at the Window' pieces and the superb lioness and negro. The next gallery **57** covers ancient SYRIA. On one of the walls ancient portraits from Palmyra C1-2 stare down impassively at the passerby. A new display on MESOPOTAMIA **56**, opening 1991, will include the dazzling 4500-year-old jewellery and other items (remains of a sledge, harp, lyre, 'standard' – whose purpose no one has yet worked out) from the *Royal Cemetery at Ur* (thought to be the Biblical Ur of the Chaldees). Some of the earliest writing in the world comes next **55**; among the exhibits is the famous C7 BC tablet from Nineveh (case 5) which recounts a tale of a flood similar to that in the Bible. Room **54** has ancient pottery from WESTERN ASIA with, in the centre, the 9000-year-old Jericho skull. From Ur you turn right into a display of objects from Anatolia and Iran **51, 52**. At the end of the gallery is the fabulous *Oxus Treasure*, a perplexing mixture of objects, possibly the offerings to a temple dating from c600-300 BC, found on the banks of the River Oxus in the last century. At present there is a small display of COINS AND MEDALS off Room **69** and selections in appropriate galleries. Room **49** and **50** will be used for special exhibitions until 1990 and there may be a charge.

Room **41**, reached by lift or stairs from the Front Hall, traces the rise of MEDIEVAL EUROPE from its roots in the Late Antique world of the C3 and C4 to c1100. Don't miss the *Esquiline Treasure* which dates from the second half of the C4 and includes a massive silver casket, perhaps part of a wedding present to Secundus and Projecta. The C4 *Lycurgus cup* is also stunning, cut from a single piece of glass it changes colour from wine red to pea green according to the light. The *Sutton Hoo Treasure* is a must. This was found in Suffolk in 1939, buried c625 in the remains of a 27m boat accompanying a dead ruler, perhaps Raedwald, High King of Anglo-Saxon England. There are silver bowls, a great silver salver from Byzantium, the remains of a fearsome helmet, shield and sword, a cauldron, drinking horns and lyre. The brilliant jewellery includes a great gold buckle decorated with writhing beasts and shoulder clasps set with brittle blood-red garnets.

The next room, chronologically, is **42**. Only a few items can be mentioned in such a rich assemblage but don't miss the *Lewis chessmen*, the finest set from the ancient world, made of walrus ivory carved in the C12 and found, no one knows why, in the remote

British Museum: gilt bronze figure of the Bodhisattva Tara from Sri Lanka, C10 (Room 34); inner coffin of the Lady of the House Takhebkhenem, c450 BC, from Thebes (Room 60).

Outer Hebrides. There is the oldest surviving major English musical instrument of the Middle Ages, a gittern with intricately carved foliage, beasts and hunters c1290-1330, which once belonged to Queen Elizabeth I or her doomed favourite the Earl of Leicester. One of the finest objects in the Museum is the *Royal Gold Cup*. Made in Paris c1380, it passed from French to English sovereigns before ending up in a Spanish convent and returning to England in 1892.

The sounds next door come from the Museum's *collection of clocks* **44**. These are set to strike at various times but the most imposing is undoubtedly the great *Carillon Clock* made in 1589 by Isaac Habrecht of Strasbourg which puts on a lively performance culminating in a squawk from the bird at the top. The 'Congreve' rolling ball timepiece c1810 is irresistible, even if its action is limited to the perpetual rolling of a steel ball which tips the movement every 30 seconds. Room **45** is modelled on a Renaissance 'schatzkammer' or treasure house and holds the glittering *Waddesdon Bequest* given by Baron Ferdinand de Rothschild in 1898. The centrepiece is the *Holy Thorn Reliquary*, made of gold and enamelled in Paris c1400-10. Surrounding it are Limoges enamels, Italian maiolica, silver gilt dishes, intricate boxwood carvings, Venetian glass, jewellery - not everything suits all tastes but the general effect is magnificent. The Corridor **46** leading from it now houses collections dating from the Renaissance to the C18 and is due to be remodelled, opening in 1992. A very fine collection of C18 Huguenot silver and other European objets d'art to the left is paralleled by British miscellanea which include Oliver Cromwell's death mask, Dr Dee's magic mirror, Prime Minister Palmerston's garter, Mary Queen of Scot's signet ring, the Marlborough gold ice pails and royal seal dies. In the next room **47** surrounded by pottery, porcelain and glass, is a collection of jewellery put together by Mrs Anne Hull Grundy, not containing great pieces, but very enjoyable to look at and of immense value to students of jewellery. Room **48** has the beginnings of the Museum's modern collection – objects made after 1845 are modern by Museum standards.

The next range of galleries takes you back 2000-5000 years to the beginnings of PREHISTORIC EUROPE. Rooms **38** and **39** have some of the finest pieces of Celtic art in existence - six gold torcs (neck rings) from Ipswich, the Desborough mirror, the Witham and Battersea shields, two helmets - the only surviving examples from Iron Age Britain (one horned like those the Vikings were supposed to wear but didn't) and the magnificent 400 BC bronze wine flagons from Basse Yutz, France. Next door **40** are three great treasure troves from ROMAN BRITAIN - the C4 silver from *Mildenhall*, Suffolk, including a solid silver dish weighing 8,256 gm, one of the finest sets of tableware to be found anywhere in the Roman Empire, the *Water Newton hoard*, hidden in the C4 although some items were made earlier - the earliest group of Christian silver yet found - and the strange C4 gold and silver pagan hoard found in 1979 at *Thetford*, Norfolk, some of it dedicated to the elusive pagan god Faunus. Other items which illustrate aspects of life in Roman Britain include writing tablets from the pre-Hadrianic frontier outpost of Vindolanda, the bronze head of the Emperor Claudius and Christian wall paintings from a villa at Lullingstone, Kent.

In the Central Saloon **35** is the earliest representation of Christ yet found in Britain – the C4 mosaic from Hinton St Mary, Dorset. This area also contains small temporary exhibitions and the remains of the 2,000-year-old Lindow Man. The mezzanine above **36** displays prehistoric objects – including 3-million-year-old tools from Olduvai Gorge, Tanzania; an intricately carved mammoth tusk portraying swimming reindeer, 10,500 BC, from Montastruc, Bruniquel, France; a piece of reindeer skull perhaps used for hunting or ritual 7,500 BC from Yorkshire. Adjacent **68** are bronzes from Greece, Etruria, Sardinia and Rome and terracottas from Rome and Greece including delightful and realistic little figures from Boetia (Tanagra) 330-200 BC. Beyond this **69** is a display of Greek and Roman life which will interest children – gladiators, chariot, racing, medicine, games, soldiers are some of the topics covered. Galleries **70-71** are being remodelled to hold displays on *Rome City and Empire* opening in 1991. In **72** is a new display of *Cypriot antiquities* and in **73** the *Greeks in Southern Italy*. The main stairs from the Central Saloon **35** return you to the Front Hall, passing on the way a display of C15 and C16 brass plaques from the African Kingdom of BENIN – a foretaste of the display at the Museum of Mankind (qv). The two lions flanking the stairs are from the Mausoleum of Halicarnassus.

This (fairly) rapid tour has not included the Museum's rich ORIEN-

Gallery of Japanese Antiquites

The British Museum houses the most comprehensive collection of Japanese art and antiquities in Europe. It covers every period from the late Jomon (about 3000BC) until the present day, and every type of material with the exception of costume and contemporary crafts, which are collected by the Victoria and Albert Museum. The earliest highlights are a splendid large group of pottery and metalwork recovered from the moated tombs of the Great Tomb Period (Kofun).

The collections of Buddhist material are particularly wide, beginning with moulded clay plaques of the C8. They include many early paintings on paper and silk, including the splendid C13 *hanging scroll of Fuku Kenzaku Kannon*. The finest sculptures are a magnificent pair of wooden figures of Monju and Fugen, carved in the early C17. Later sculpture is represented by the nearly 2000 carved miniature netsuke, thought to be the finest in Europe. Of the arts of the samurai, the swords are outstanding. From the collection of over 200, the earliest are from the C13. The sword-fittings of later periods (C16-19) are large and comprehensive. The lacquered wares represent every century from the C13 to the present.

The British Museum's most splendid holdings, however, lie in the paintings, prints and woodblock ehon of the premodern (Kinsei) period In particular, the *paintings of the Marujama-Shijo* and *Ukiyoe Schools* are outstanding while the Ukiyoe prints and books (about 8000 in number) form one of the greatest collections in the world. The collection of C20 prints (about 2000) is also the only comprehensive one in Europe. (LS)

Porcelain jar with enamelled decoration in Kakiemon style, early C18.

TAL COLLECTIONS. Because of the way the building is constructed, with the inaccessible British Library Reading Room in the middle, it is not possible to reach these galleries directly via the ground floor. Either go up the West or East stairs, crossing via Room 66 or, if your first interest is Oriental, use the North Entrance situated in Montague Place. On the ground floor **34** is a new gallery featuring an extensive display of the museum's rich *Islamic collections* and including the Godman collection – the finest assemblage of Islamic pottery outside the Islamic world. Above **33** are superb collections from the Orient – India, China, Tibet, Sri Lanka, Korea and elsewhere including examples from the finest collection of Chinese porcelain in Europe, the best holdings of Indian sculpture outside India and Pakistan and a particularly outstanding collection of ancient Chinese bronzes. Rooms **90** and **91** house temporary exhibitions of PRINTS AND DRAWINGS and oriental material. Above, opening spring 1990, is a new Japanese gallery which features a changing display of major treasures, a teahouse together with loan exhibitions from Japan. (MLC)

---
the essentials

Underground Holborn (Central, Piccadilly Lines), Russell Square (Piccadilly Line), Tottenham Court Road (Central, Northern Lines). **Open** Mon-Sat 1000-1700, Sun 1430-1800. **Cloakroom. Toilets. Public telephones. For the disabled** access, toilets. **Refreshments** licensed restaurant (self service) and snacks. **Shopping** bookshops. **Publications** general guide in several languages, others on specific collections. **Photography. Educational facilities. Visitors' services** guided tours on special subjects, films, lectures. **Research** by prior arrangement. **Staff opinions** given but not valuations.

39

■ BRITISH OPTICAL ASSOCIATION FOUNDATION MUSEUM

British College of Optometrists, 10 Knaresborough Place SW5 0TG.
Tel 373 7765
Admission *prior application*

The Museum preserves and displays the works of spectacle and instrument makers from early times and is adjacent to a well-stocked library. The exhibits include early Chinese spectacles, and very colourful spectacle cases, many with coloured tassels, which were worn by men. Most of the spectacles are glazed with quartz lenses (pebbles) as distinct from the usual glass or plastic.

The museum collection of original early UK spectacles and cases begins with examples of the bow spectacle of the C16 and C17, with the frames often made from bone, ivory, brass, horn or leather. They were made before sides on spectacles were invented, and kept on the nose by pressure often from a spring bar. Many of the spectacles' cases are made from wood, some being carved inside the cases the same shape as the spectacles. Specimens of the first spectacles with side pieces can be seen; they are often called wig or temple spectacles and are of the C18 and C19. This illustrates the great technical advance that has been made. The museum also has an outstanding collection of hand-held optical aids, such as quizzing glasses, lorgnettes and spy glasses. (HO)

———————————————————— *the essentials* ————————————————————

Underground Earl's Court (Circle, District, Piccadilly Lines). **Open** Mon-Fri 0930-1300, 1400-1700. **Toilets. Photography** by arrangement. **Research** library.

■ BROMLEY MUSEUM

The Priory, Church Hill, Orpington BR6 0HH.   Tel (0689) 31551
Admission *free*

The nucleus of the museum came from the extensive archaeological and ethnological collections of the first Baron Avebury (1834-1913), now on display in the Great Hall of the Priory. This was

Bromley Museum: a Saxon burial excavated in Orpington.

originally a typical early C12/C13 manor house, much altered in recent times, but still incorporating C15 and C16 features in the windows, ceiling and fireplaces and the half-timbered south-wing. Avebury, a friend of Charles Darwin, wrote the earliest book on pre-history in 1865. He amassed a vast collection of antiquities during his world-wide travels, and bequeathed some to the British Museum and the remainder to the Orpington Historical Society, which in turn permanently loaned it to the Bromley Museum.

The theme is the development of Man from Pre-history to Today, in a changing environment. Exhibits range from relics of the Old, Middle and New Stone Ages to the Bronze and Iron Ages. The Romans and Saxons are also well represented with *pottery, building material, coins, jewellery* and various pieces of metal found from local excavations. Objects from the C16 to the early part of the C20 relate to early education, items used in the home, clothing and a *Queen Anne fire engine*, together with old watercolours, photographs, prints and manuscripts from the area. Most are on permanent display but some exhibits are regularly changed, and several exhibitions by outside Groups are put on display in the Gallery throughout the year.

―――――――――――――――――――――― *the essentials* ――――――――――――――――――――――

BR Orpington (from Charing Cross Station). **Open** Mon, Wed 0900-1800, Tue, Fri 0900-2000, Sat 0900-1700. **Toilets. Parking. For the disabled** access, toilets nearby in the Park. **Publications. Photography** by application. **Educational facilities. Visitors' services** guided tours, lectures by arrangement. **Research** library.

■ BRUCE CASTLE MUSEUM

Lordship Lane N17 8NU.   Tel 808 8772
Admission *free*

Bruce Castle is one of Haringey's oldest buildings, but it is hardly a castle, though the tower gives it a certain air. Its name comes from the Bruce family but although there was a moated manor house on the site in medieval times, when the land was owned by the Bruces, they never lived there. It was for long the seat of the Lords of the Manor of Tottenham, and the house now dates substantially from the C18 with survivals from before, and many additions and alterations after that date.

The exhibitions, which are changed periodically, include many items from the Haringey local history collections with fine enlargements of old photographs of local scenes. A display of early domestic equipment includes a primitive hand-operated *washing machine*. A huge *grandfather clock* might better be called a 'goalkeeper' — it came from the famous Tottenham Hotspur Football Club. There is also a well-researched and documented feature on postal history using items from the deposited ***Morten Collection of British Postal History***.

Ascend the massive mid-C18 staircase to the **Museum of the Middlesex Regiment** ('The Diehards') — with some gorgeous *uniforms, medals* and other reminders of bravery for King, Queen and Country. Note the *Chinese machine-gun* captured in Korea; surely so primitive as to have threatened operator and enemy alike. From World War II there is a *German field telephone switchboard*. The list of subscribers to this select exchange are a blood-chilling roll-call — Goering, Himmler, Keitel, Bormann and Der Führer himself.

---
the essentials

Underground Wood Green (Piccadilly Line) then **Bus** 243. **Open** Mon-Fri 1300-1700, Sat 1000-1200, 1300-1700, Sun 1300-1700. **Parking. For the disabled** limited access. **Refreshments** vending machine. **Shopping** sales desk. **Photography. Visitors' services** guided tours, lectures by arrangement.

■ BRUNEL'S ENGINE HOUSE

Tunnel Road SE16 4JJ.   Tel 318 2489
Admission *charge*

The museum is housed in the boiler house used by Marc Isambard Brunel (1769-1849) and his son Isambard Kingdom Brunel (1806-1859) when they were supervising the construction of the world's oldest under-river tunnel. The tunnel links Rotherhithe on the south side of the Thames with Wapping on the north bank. It took 18 years to complete and was opened as a pedestrian route in March 1843 at a cost of £468,249. In 1865 it was sold to the East London Railway and it is still used by the Metropolitan Line. The tunnel should not be confused with the Rotherhithe Tunnel which was built much later (1908) mainly for the use of road traffic.

The museum contains a *steam engine* similar to that used by Brunel for draining water from the works, and a small exhibition on the tunnel. From time to time exhibitions are held on other local topics. The museum acts as a focal point for an area full of historic survivals. Almost opposite the museum is the Mayflower pub — once used by the Thames Tunnel Directors — which derives its name from the fact that the captain of the Pilgrim Fathers' ship hailed from Rotherhithe and is buried there.

---
the essentials

Underground Rotherhithe (East London Line). **Open** first Sun of each month only 1100-1500. **Shopping** sales desk. **Photography. Publications. Photography.**

■ BURGH HOUSE

New End Square NW3 1LT.   Tel 431 0144
Admission *free*

What has been called 'London's finest Queen Anne house' dates from 1703, when fashionable London was flocking to the Long Room in Well Walk nearby to 'take the waters'. The Spa's physician, Dr William Gibbons, lived at Burgh House, hence the initials 'WG' in the wrought-iron gates. The house saw a succession of occupants, including the Reverend Allatson Burgh, who gave his name to it and who was so unpopular as vicar of St Lawrence Jewry in the City that his parishioners petitioned Queen Victoria to have him removed.

The house today belongs to Camden Council but is leased to an enterprising Trust which maintains it as a centre for local meetings and cultural activities and the small **Hampstead Museum**. There is space for a succession of art exhibitions and rooms upstairs (by way of a fine staircase) with displays and items of Old Hampstead, including giant fresh-water mussels found in the Leg o'Mutton Pond when it was drained in 1906 to facilitate the digging of the Hampstead Tube. But the great pride of Burgh House is its delightful

Music Room, panelled in natural pine from the former Spa Long Room, with handsome fluted pilasters framing the door at one end and the shallow bow window at the other. The Hampstead Music Club's recitals in this room must indeed be a pleasure.

In the basement is the *Buttery*, an excellent cafeteria which also offers light lunches, and you can take your refreshment at tables on the terrace at the front of the house.

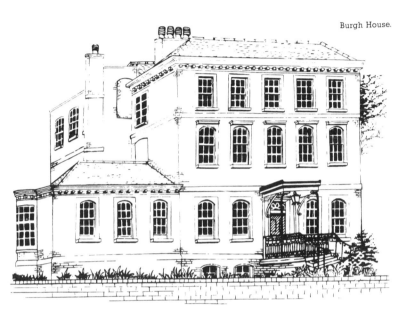

Burgh House.

———————— *the essentials* ————————
Underground Hampstead (Northern Line). **Open** Wed-Sun 1200-1700. **Toilets. Public telephones. For the disabled** access not easy, toilets. **Refreshments** restaurant, snacks. **Shopping** sales desk. **Photography. Visitors' services** guided tours by arrangement, projector and screen for slides.

■ CABINET WAR ROOMS

Clive Steps, King Charles Street SW1A 2AQ.   Tel 930 6961
Admission *charge*

The clock stands at 5 o'clock and the room is set as it was on October 15, 1940. At 5pm on that day one of over 100 meetings of Winston Churchill's War Cabinet was about to start in this room, where many of the most crucial decisions of World War II were made between Churchill's appointment as Prime Minister in May 1940 and the end of the war five years later. It is the main room in the suite which formed the Cabinet War Rooms, the underground protected accommodation used by Winston Churchill, the War Cabinet and the Chiefs of Staff of Britain's armed forces in World War II.

This is the ***Cabinet Room***, Room 69, and the first that visitors come to. It had originally been intended as an air raid shelter for about 80 people when the underground complex was constructed in 1938 in anticipation of war. Gradually, more rooms were taken over as it became necessary to accommodate the whole of the Cabinet Secretariat and military chiefs of staff and their secretariats. The first War Cabinet meeting was held, under Neville Chamberlain, Churchill's predecessor, in October 1939.

Leaving Room 69, the visitor walks along the corridor which connects all the rooms, passing the weather board which gave the conditions on the surface (traditionally it would read "windy" during air raids) and the **Transatlantic Telephone Room** from which, after August 1943, Churchill could talk to President Roosevelt without fear of enemy interception. Other rooms provided the accommodation for the typists and telephonists; rooms used by Churchill's top military and civilian advisors as both offices and sleeping accommodation and the rooms from where Britain's defence would have been so co-ordinated if the invasion, uppermost in minds that evening, had taken place.

Room 65 was the **Map Room**, manned day and night throughout the war, where all the latest information was collected, analysed and plotted on maps for the King, the Prime Minister, the War Cabinet and the Joint Chiefs of Staff to see the war's progress at a glance. The long table was where the Map Room officers sat in three daily shifts, their coloured telephones connecting them with operations centres on the surface. Here, the date has moved on to 1945 for the maps in use at the end of war that August have been kept just as they were left.

But perhaps the most fascinating is Room 65A, which was originally intended to be the Cabinet's main meeting room. It never was, for after briefly serving as accommodation for the Joint Planning Staff, it was **Churchill's combined office and bedroom**. It was from this room that he made some of his most famous BBC broadcasts — the invasion warning, the speech to the defeated French people in 1940, and the broadcast after the United States entered the conflict in December 1941. (ST)

─────────────────── *the essentials* ───────────────────

Underground Westminster (Circle, District Lines). **Open** Tue-Sun 1000-1750. **Cloakroom. Toilets. For the disabled** access, toilets. **Shopping. Publications** catalogues in several languages. **Photography. Educational facilities. Visitors' services**. Acousiguide

■ CARLYLE'S HOUSE

24 Cheyne Row SW3 5HL.   Tel 352 7087
Admission *charge*

The home from 1834 of the Scottish philosopher and historian Thomas Carlyle (1795-1881). It was here that he wrote 'The French Revolution'; 'The Life and Letters of Oliver Cromwell' and 'Frederick the Great'. The house contains many letters and paintings relating to Carlyle and his wife, including a small collection of valentines, Carlyle's hat and pipe, and the dog Nero's lead.

An unusual item of furniture is the kitchen dresser incorporating the maid's bed. The front parlour is of particular interest, since the painting by Robert Tait, *A Chelsea Interior c1857*, now hanging to the left of the fireplace, shows Mr and Mrs Carlyle in that room, and demonstrates the painstaking nature of the restoration. The house is in the care of the National Trust. (IO)

———————————— *the essentials* ————————————
Underground Sloane Square (Circle, District Lines). **Open** Apr-Oct Wed-Sun 1100-1700. **Toilets**.

	1	
2		3

Cabinet War Rooms: 1. The Map Room; 2. Churchill's Bedroom. 3. Carlyle's House.

■ CHARLES KING COLLECTION OF HISTORICAL ANAESTHETIC APPARATUS

Association of Anaesthetists of GB and Ireland, 9 Bedford Square WC1B 3RA. Tel 631 1650
Admission *prior application*

This private museum of historical anaesthetic apparatus, known as the Charles King Collection, after the instrument maker who collated the initial apparatus, displays the evolution of the speciality of anaesthesia with particular reference to equipment. The content is changed on a yearly basis usually in June/July, and illustrates specific topics. The museum resources include an unequalled collection of anaesthetic apparatus, from the earliest days to the present time, extensive library facilities and a photographic and video collection relating to anaesthesia, together with specific memorabilia and archival material. Visitors are welcome on Fridays by prior appointment only. (DW).

─────────────── *the essentials* ───────────────

Underground Goodge Street (Northern Line). **Open** Fri only 1030-1500. **Toilets. Shopping** slide sets. **Photography** by prior arrangement. **Visitors' services** Curator on site. **Research** by prior arrangement.

■ CHARTERED INSURANCE INSTITUTE MUSEUM

20 Aldermanbury EC2V 7HY.   Tel 606 3835
Admission *prior application*

The museum contains some of the finest examples of artefacts relating to the early history of insurance companies and is run by the Chartered Insurance Institute, a professional body with over 57,000 members. The rise of the insurance company is closely connected with fire and early attempts to control this hazard reflected in a number of hand-operated appliances, sundry helmets, fire buckets and instruments used by firemen shown in the museum. The display also includes many original firemarks (plates).

Before the Great Fire of 1666, responsibility for dealing with fire rested with the parish. As their intervention proved inadequate, insurance companies formed their own uniformed body of firefighters and for nearly two centuries these provided virtually the only protection. In the early days of fire insurance many premises had no formal address, so the fire mark was vital evidence that a policy relating to the damaged building had been taken out. Additionally it was used to prevent fraudulent claims. It was also important as a guide to the insurance company's fire fighting party. The earliest firemarks carried numbers corresponding to those of the policies, but this practice was discontinued after the 1800s. Numbered marks were usually made of lead, after which copper became the preferred material, followed by iron and tin from 1820-25. Interestingly, each variant in the collection is different from others in design, material or original colouring.

Many items, including firemarks and appliances, were given by Sir Ernest Bainy in 1934. The collection of firemarks was further expanded with the Alexander Bashall Dawson bequest in 1953.

─────────────── *the essentials* ───────────────

Underground Moorgate (Circle, Metropolitan, Northern Lines). **Open** Mon-Fri 0915-1700. **Shopping** sales desk. **Photography.**

Chartered Insurance Institute Museum. 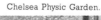 Chelsea Physic Garden.

■ CHELSEA PHYSIC GARDEN

66 Royal Hospital Road SW3 4HS. Tel 352 5646
Admission *charge*

Founded by the Society of Apothecaries in 1673 to supply medicinal herbs, it has been a centre for the study of horticulture for over 300 years. During the C18 the garden had an unrivalled reputation for the collection and introduction of new species from the New World and from the East. Until quite recently it was closed to the public but a change in ownership enabled this very secret place to become a must for garden enthusiasts.

Seeds from the 4-acre square patch in the heart of London have helped to transform the economies of far-distant regions and countries, most notably the cotton seeds sent to Georgia which started the cotton plantations. Exotic *Mediterranean plants* thrive outdoors as the garden is kept warm by its sheltered position and heat from surrounding buildings in winter, and there is an exceptionally diverse range of plants and trees to be seen.

The influence of Philip Miller, curator between 1722 and 1770, is much in evidence today. The intention is to recreate parts of the garden as it existed in his time, to contain plants that were important to pharmacology, horticulture and industry in the C18. A continuing role for the garden is envisaged in teaching and research so that the tradition of scholarly contributions to horticultural literature, which were Miller's aims, is maintained.

---
the essentials

Underground Sloane Square (Circle, District Lines). **Open** mid Apr-mid Oct Wed, Sun 1400-1700 or by appointment. **Cloakroom. Toilets. Public telephones. For the disabled** access, toilets. **Refreshments** snacks (Sun only). **Shopping** sales desk. **Publications. Photography. Visitors' services** guided tours by prior arrangement. **Research** library for scholars by prior arrangement.

■ CHISWICK HOUSE

Burlington Lane W4 2RS. Tel 995 0508
Admission *charge*

Chiswick House

Built in about 1725 by the third Earl of Burlington, this fine example of English Palladian architecture is worth visiting for its splendid park as well as for its architecture. The interior of the house was designed by William Kent (1684-1748), and is complicated yet fascinating with its small-scale symmetrical rooms, which have been carefully restored to their original appearance. It should be noted that this was not a residence but a setting for the entertainment of friends and the cultivated 'conversazioni' beloved of the C18.

There is a comprehensive display of the plans and drawings for the house, and also interesting information showing how the restoration was carried out. The house is most notable for its rich and elaborate *decorations* and extraordinary collection of *classical busts*. The garden is laid out in a formal manner, containing a large number of statues and pieces of assorted architecture. The two taken together give a clear and unusual picture of how one man chose to create a complete environment for himself. (IO)

---
the essentials

Underground Turnham Green (District Line). **Open** mid Mar-mid Oct Mon-Sat 0930-1830, Sun 1400-1830, mid Oct-mid Mar Wed-Sun 0930-1600. **Toilets. Parking. Refreshments** snacks. **Shopping** sales desk. **Publications. Photography. Visitors' services** guided tours. **Research. Staff opinion.**

■ CHURCH FARM HOUSE MUSEUM

Greyhound Hill NW4 4JR.   Tel 203 0130
Admission *free*

In an area one does not immediately associate with antiquity, Hendon's oldest house is satisfyingly ancient, dating from the mid-C17, and its use as a local history museum should ensure its further survival as a type of building fast vanishing from London; a farmhouse

Church Farm House Museum: the Kitchen (c1815).

with alterations down the years which tell the continuing story of its occupants and uses.

Church Farm House stands in a harmonious ensemble alongside pub and church. As you enter, the room to your left contains a walnut grand piano, a good long-case ('grandfather') clock and some archaeological finds. To the right you pass through a pleasant panelled room with some old furniture to the *Kitchen*, dominated by the fireplace crammed with gadgets for roasting, grilling, turning, basting, boiling . . . Around is a display of *kitchenalia*. Note the *salamander* for instant browning of meat, the tongue and meat press, the *sugarcutters* and the ingenious flycatcher. All are identified and explained on a well-planned information sheet.

The centre passage continues through the heart of the central chimneystack to the stairs. Above are rooms for decorative arts and local and social history exhibitions, and above again are the *attics* (ask to see them) with open internal box gutters and tiled roof supported by heavy timbers. Note the thin layer of thatch as insulation between the timbers, and the hand-made tiles fixed with oak pegs.

From the shady garden at the back you can walk out into the open meadows, with fine trees and views, of Sunny Hill Park. During licensed hours the Greyhound next door amply compensates for the lack of a tea bar.

──────────────── *the essentials* ────────────────

Underground Hendon Central (Northern Line). **Open** Mon-Sat 1000-1300, 1400-1730 (closed Tue pm); Sun 1400-1730. **Toilets. Shopping** sales desk. **Publications. Photography. Visitors' services** guided tours by prior arrangement. **Staff opinion.**

■ CITY LIVERY COMPANIES COLLECTIONS

☐ Mercers ☐ Grocers ☐ Drapers ☐ Fishmongers ☐ Goldsmiths ☐ Skinners ☐ Merchant Taylors ☐ Haberdashers ☐ Salters ☐ Ironmongers ☐ Vintners ☐ Clothworkers ☐ Armourers and Brasiers ☐ Apothecaries ☐ Pewterers ☐ Saddlers

Admission *prior application*

Among the most valuable collections of secular treasures in the City of London are those belonging to the Livery Guilds or Companies.

From medieval times the Guilds have played an important role in the life and government of the City, especially as the chief civic officers the Lord Mayor and Sheriffs are elected by the Liverymen each year. They have also had the duty of ensuring that Londoners maintained a high standard in regard to craftsmanship and in the quality of the goods and produce sold.

Of the 96 Companies in existence today just over a third possess Halls where plate and other treasures are housed and sometimes displayed. The fact that there is a great abundance of plate is due largely to benefactions on the part of members, though sometimes such donations have been made in lieu of the responsibility of holding office as Master or Warden. To view these collections it is generally necessary to obtain permission of the Company's governing body, known as 'the Court', by writing first to the Clerk. However, on certain days during the summer a number of Halls are open to the public, and a list of containing dates and times is available from the Corporation of London (Tel 606 3030 ext 2456/7).

In the case of Companies which have no Hall, it may be more difficult to inspect a particular collection, though scholars will usually be granted access if they write to the Clerk stating the purpose of their research. Incidentally, the most enjoyable way of seeing a Hall and its treasures is to have the privilege of being invited as a guest to a Livery Company dinner! As regards the Company records and archives, it should be noted that most, although not all, of these have now been entrusted to the care of the Department of Manuscripts, Guildhall Library, Aldermanbury EC2V 7HP.

Some of the finest treasures are those of the Twelve Great Livery Companies, which are treated here in order of precedence, bearing in mind that the Skinners and the Merchant Taylors have seniority in alternative years, the result of a dispute settled in the C15 by Mayor Billesden.

☐ **Mercers** [Ironmonger Lane EC2V 8HE]. Although the Hall and Chapel (the only Company to possess its own) were destroyed in World War II, they have been rebuilt in a manner befitting the premier Livery Company. Its most treasured holding is the *Leigh Cup*, given by a former Master and mentioned in an inventory of 1569. A beautiful early C16 full-length figure of *Christ*, now in the annexe, was discovered during the rebuilding in 1954. The Company's records are kept at the Hall under the care of an archivist who frequently puts a selection on display for the benefit of members.

☐ **Grocers** [Princes Street EC2R 8AQ]. Sadly, the C19 Hall, which escaped bombing, was accidentally destroyed by fire in 1965 when many treasures, including the Company's charters, were lost. The new Hall was opened by the Queen Mother in 1970. It contains *tapestries* designed by John Piper and made near Aubusson. There are also beautiful collections of *glass* and *china*.

☐ **Drapers** [Throgmorton Avenue EC2N 2DQ]. One of the few Halls to have a garden — it once belonged to Thomas Cromwell. During the Great Fire the plate was saved by being buried in a well in the garden. There is a *Tudor cup* presented by William Lambard in 1578, and a set of four *Gobelin tapestries* of 1774 showing Jason and the Golden Fleece.

☐ **Fishmongers** [London Bridge EC4R 9EL]. Of all the Companies this Hall has the most imposing site. It contains treasures old and new. Among the former is the *dagger with which William Walworth*, fishmonger and Mayor, *slew Wat Tyler* in 1381, and a *funeral pall* of pre-Reformation date embroidered with scenes from the life of St Peter. A recent acquisition is the first *portrait of the Queen* by Annigoni, specially commissioned by the Company.

☐ **Goldsmiths** [Foster Lane EC2V 6BN]. As one would expect of this Company, there is a splendid collection of plate, one of the most interesting pieces being a *C16 cup and cover* of silver gilt and rock crystal with the armorial bearings in coloured enamel of Alderman Sir Martin Bowes. This is believed to have been used by Elizabeth I at her Coronation Banquet in 1558. The famous *gilt dish and ewer* by Paul de Lamerie (1741) has a place of honour on special occasions. There is also some excellent modern silver. Exhibitions of silver and other works are held from time to time in the Hall, built in the classic style in 1835 to the design of Philip Hardwick.

☐ **Skinners** [8 Dowgate Hill EC4R 2SP]. The Dining Hall is adorned with panels painted by Sir Frank Brangwyn R A, depicting scenes connected with the history of the Company and the fur-trade. There is good C17 *panelling* in the Court Room.

1	
2	**3**

1. Fishmongers' Hall: embroidered C15 pall (detail).
2. Goldsmiths' Hall: C16 silver gilt and rock crystal cup and cover.
3. Apothecaries' Hall.

1. Saddlers' Hall: Ballot Box (1614).
2. Vinters' Hall: the Courtroom (1959).

☐ **Merchant Taylors** [30 Threadneedle Street EC2R 8BA]. Prior to the Reformation many Companies had their own *funeral palls* or hearse-cloths for use when a Liveryman died. The Merchant Taylors still possess two magnificent examples dating from 1490 and 1520. The large Dining Hall contains a fine *organ* from a former City church.

☐ **Haberdashers** [Staining Lane EC2V 7DD]. In common with several other Companies, this has the custom of crowning the Master and Wardens after their election, and there are velvet garlands with silver badges for the purpose. *Paintings* include works of Sir Joshua Reynolds, and of the modern artist R A Cundall depicting the newly-rebuilt Haberdashers Hall, with St Paul's in the background, surrounded by the ruins caused during the severe bombing of the area in World War II.

☐ **Salters** [Fore Street EC2Y 5DE]. The Hall, opened in 1976, was designed by Sir Basil Spence and is in a truly modern style. The Dining Hall is ash panelled. Two huge *blocks of crystallized salt* donated to the Company are a reminder of its past association.

☐ **Ironmongers** [Shaftesbury Place EC2Y 8AA]. Although of Tudor appearance, the Hall dates only from 1925. It had a miraculous escape in World War II. There is a C16 silver-mounted *coconut cup*. Like all the Livery Companies, Ironmongers are involved in charitable works. The Company's original almshouses now form the attractive Geffrye Museum (qv).

☐ **Vintners** [Upper Thames Street EC4V 3BE]. Among the Company's great treasures is a *tapestry* of 1466 showing its patron saint, Martin of Tours, dividing his cloak with a beggar. He also appears on an early C16 pall. There is a C17 *silver-gilt vessel* in the form of a milkmaid, containing two cups from which newly-admitted members were expected to drink without spilling the contents! On an outside wall is a C19 figure of a Vintry Ward schoolboy made of Coade stone.

☐ **Clothworkers** [Dunster Court, Mincing Lane EC3R 7AH]. The Hall was rebuilt after its destruction in World War II. Samuel Pepys, the diarist, was Master in 1677, and the *cup, rose-water dish* and *ewer* presented by him are among the Company's most cherished possessions.

Of the treasures belonging to the 'minor' Companies, some of which have fascinating objects relating to their particular craft or trade, the following must be regarded as simply representative:

☐ **Armourers and Brasiers** [81 Coleman Street EC2R 5BJ]. A magnificent set of *weapons* and *armour* which includes the suit worn by the champion of Elizabeth I, Sir Henry Lee, adorn the Hall. The Company was fortunate in that its Royalist members buried the plate in their gardens during the Commonwealth, so enabling it to be saved. The oldest piece is a silver-mounted earthenware *jug* in the form of an owl.

☐ **Apothecaries** [Blackfriars Lane EC4V 6EJ]. Its Hall, which is the oldest and least-altered of the Company Halls, contains a valuable collection of apothecaries' *jars*, and of *pill-slabs* which used to be hung up by dispensers as evidence of their qualification. There are paintings of James I and Charles I and also of past Masters.

☐ **Pewterers** [Oat Lane EC2V 7DE]. On permanent display at the Hall is a fine collection of *pewterware*. This includes an Elizabethan *flagon* — the earliest known example in existence — and a rare Charles II *tankard*.

☐ **Saddlers** [Gutter Lane EC2V 6BR]. The annual election of a new Master is an important event in the life of every Livery Company. A *ballot-box* is required, of which the most interesting example is that belonging to this Company. Painted and inlaid, it was made in 1619 for the East India Company whose arms it bears. Its design is such that it is impossible to discern how anyone dropping a ball in to one of the three boxes has voted — thus upholding those standards of integrity and fair dealing for which the City of London and its Livery Companies have long been renowned.

As for the Clockmakers' Company Collection (qv) this is displayed in the library building within the precinct of Guildhall, in the heart of the City of London. (GH).

■ CLOCKMAKERS' COMPANY COLLECTION
Guildhall Library, Aldermanbury EC2P 2EJ.   Tel 606 3030
Admission *free*

The oldest surviving clocks date from the C14, and their makers were members of the Blacksmiths' Company. In 1631 the Clockmakers' Company was formed. Many City companies have

| 1 | 2 | Clockmakers' Company Collection: |
| | 3 | 1. Long-case clock by Edward East, c1675. 2. Table clock by Henry Archer, c1625. 3. Marine watch by John Harrison, 1770, with key and oiler. |

little or no connection with their original craft, but the Clockmakers are not only still actively concerned with the making of clocks and watches, but own the valuable and important collection which has been at the Guildhall for more than a century.

The gallery is at the entrance to the Guildhall Library, on the west side of the Guildhall itself. The earliest exhibits predate the Company, but the emphasis is naturally on those made during the Company's life, and, for reasons of space, on watches, of which there is a dazzling display. Note the *star-shaped watch* of 1625. This was made by David Ramsey, watch-maker to King James VI of Scotland and first Master of the Company. The watch was owned at one time by King Farouk of Egypt but was recovered at that unhappy monarch's fall from power. The showcases in the centre of the room are full of the elegance and exquisite workmanship that went hand-in-hand with the technical development of the watch. At the end stands a majestic row of *grandfather clocks* (properly 'long-case') of which the grandest must be the walnut one of 1705 by John May, closely rivalled by the *sea-weed marquetry clock* alongside, by George Stratford.

It is worth timing your visit for the morning, to hear these marvellous time-pieces chime the hour to best effect. Turn right and you will meet the *earliest electric clock*. Its date will surprise you. Not far away is the extraordinary *gas-operated clock*, its principle both ingenious and very, very simple. Do not miss the *marine chronometers*. These transformed navigation from an exercise in guesswork to a science, and in their development Britain led the world. The most beautiful and complex example is by Howells & Pennington, of the late C17. Everything is interestingly captioned, and an inexpensive illustrated short guide is available.

--- *the essentials* ---

Underground Bank (Central, Northern Lines), Moorgate (Circle, Metropolitan, Northern Lines). **Open** Mon-Fri 0930-1700. **Toilets. Public telephones. Shopping** sales desk. **Publications. Photography** hand-held cameras only. **Research** library.

■ COMMONWEALTH INSTITUTE

Kensington High Street W8 6NQ. Tel 603 4535
Admission *free*

The Commonwealth Institute was opened by the Queen in 1962 to replace the old Imperial Institute, which had been opened by Queen Victoria in South Kensington in 1893 but of which only the Queen's Tower in Imperial College Road remains. The new building next to Holland Park is a remarkable piece of architecture, with a five-peaked roof covered in green copper. The interior is just as stunning, with an open plan of three floors, all visible from a central dais which acts as as orientation point. It is designed to be the cultural centre of the Commonwealth, and its colourful and imaginative displays are as entertaining as they are educational.

On the **first level** the galleries are dedicated to *Australasia* - the diorama of an actual Australian sheep station reproduced in minuted detail is fascinating - the *Indian Sub-continent, Canada* and the *Pacific and Atlantic islands.* Then on the **middle level** is the new display for the *African countries,* looking at the history of the Dark Continent as well as the development of the Commonwealth constituent nations in it. On the **top floor** in the newly completed *Caribbean Gallery*, representing an area much smaller than Africa but, according to the detailed display, as diverse. On this level too are the Far East countries, the Mediterranean members of the Commonwealth, and closer to Britain still, the Isle of Man and the Channel Islands, where Britain's first postbox was erected according to a special display.

Temporary exhibitions are mounted in the art galleries on the middle floor - there are sometimes admission charges for these - and there is also a cinema, a theatre, a library and a small gallery with monthly exhibitions by young Commonwealth artists. On the ground floor is a bookshop and a restaurant. The Commonwealth Institute is truly international, with each member nation contributing in some way, many of them financially. All Commonwealth High Commissioners in London serve on the board of governors, alongside the British Foreign and Commonwealth Secretary-General. There is a lively and active education department with a continuous programme of events, and a new Friends organisation which offers a range of benefits in return for an annual membership subscription. (ST)

Commonwealth Institute, main galleries.

the essentials

Underground High Street Kensington (Circle, District Lines). **Open** Mon-Sat 1000-1730, Sun 1400-1700. **Cloakroom** schools only. **Toilets. Parking. Public telephones. For the disabled** access, toilets. **Refreshments** restaurant, snacks. **Shopping** bookshop. **Publications. Photography** apply to Press Office. **Educational facilities. Visitors' services** lectures, guided tours for groups by prior arrangement. **Research** library.

■ CORAM FOUNDATION FOR CHILDREN

40 Brunswick Square WC1N 1AZ. Tel 278 2424
Admission *charge*

The Foundling Hospital (today the Thomas Coram Foundation for Children) was established by Royal Charter in 1739, to care for London's huge and growing population of abandoned children. Its original buildings are no more, but the Foundation lives on in premises dating from 1937. So strong was the feeling for the origins of this remarkable institution that, when its present home was built, outstanding features of the original building were carefully recreated.

Hogarth, Captain Thomas Coram (1740), founder of the Foundling Hospital.

The long association of the hospital with the arts began with William Hogarth, who was one of its first Governors. He devised a scheme whereby artists of the day were encouraged to present works to attract visitors (and donations). Another benefactor was the great Handel, who gave many performances in the chapel, including some of the first English performances of his Messiah.

As you enter, at the foot of the fine staircase is a model of the Foundling Hospital as it was, dominated by Benjamin West's *Suffer Little Children*. Other notable pictures hang on the stairs. At the top, as you reach the landing, you come face to face with a masterpiece, Hogarth's portrait of *Captain Thomas Coram*. This alone is worth your visit: it is one of Hogarth's greatest achievements and a worthy monument to this kindly sea-captain who conceived the idea of the hospital and gave many years of his life to working for it. Resplendent in his scarlet coat, rosy of feature with the globe at his feet, he holds in his hand the Seal of the Royal Charter which crowned his efforts.

To the right is the **Court Room Lobby**, with another famous Hogarth *The March of the Guards to Finchley*, won by the hospital in a lottery. It takes an effort to remember that this is no historical reconstruction, but a piece of vivid on-the-spot reportage! From here you enter the magnificent **Court Room** from the original building, its red walls enriched with white-and-gilt plasterwork, and hung with the gifts of the hospital's patrons. At the end is yet another fine Hogarth, *The Infant Moses presented to Pharoah's Daughter*, who is somewhat unexpectedly a typical 'English-rose'. The sculpture over the fireplace is by Rysbrack. Do not miss *Charterhouse* by the twenty-one-year-old Gainsborough among the roundel scenes of London charitable buildings, or the showcases, one of which displays with appealing informality royal signatures from Henry VII to William IV.

Return to the landing and cross to the **Picture Gallery**, another handsome (though plainer) room, with a *Raphael cartoon* and, in front of it, the keyboard of the organ which Handel presented to the chapel. A showcase nearby contains the fair copy of the *Messiah* which Handel left to the hospital in his will. The large portrait of *George II* in Garter Robes by Shackleton was much disliked by His Majesty because, he said, it make him look like a frog. The showcase by the window contains the Royal Charter and Seal which are seen in Coram's portrait.

Before you leave, stand again before Captain Coram. No one can miss the affection which Hogarth had for his subject. The transparent goodness which he portrayed permeates the foundation to this day. The admission charge is very small — a donation, large or small, will say 'thank you' to these two great and kindly men. It is advisable to check beforehand that the rooms are open.

the essentials

Underground Russell Square (Piccadilly Line). **Open** Mon-Fri 1000-1600 (closed for special events). **Toilets. Public telephones. For the disabled** parking. **Shopping** sales desk. **Publications. Photography.**

■ CORPORATION OF LONDON PERMANENT COLLECTION

Guildhall Library, Aldermanbury EC2P 2EJ. Tel 606 3030 ext 2856
Admission *prior application*

The Corporation of London has accumulated its collection of works of art over three centuries; its first commission was to John Michael Wright in 1670 for portraits of the Judges appointed to assess property claims arising from the Great Fire. These were followed by Royal portraits: *William III and Mary II* by Jan Van der Vaart, and *George II and Queen Caroline* by Charles Jervas. In 1764 *George III* presented portraits of himself and *Queen Charlotte* by the Scottish artist Allan Ramsay. In 1783 the Corporation commissioned John Singleton Copley to commemorate the British victory over the French and Spanish the previous year; *The Defeat of the Floating Batteries at Gibraltar* measures 18 x 25 feet, took more than seven years to complete and includes over 20 portraits of British and Hanoverian commanders.

When Guildhall Art Gallery opened in 1886, the Corporation already owned almost 300 works of art, many of them portraits (of Royalty, naval and military heroes and City dignitaries) and commemorative or historical subjects. The new gallery's popularity attracted further gifts and bequests, of which one of the most important was the collection bequeathed in 1902 by Charles Gassiot: it comprised 127 works by Alma-Tadema, Constable, Landseer, Millais, Tissot and other major C19 artists.

The collection has since continued to grow by gift and purchase. As well as historical subjects, portraits dating from the C16 onwards, C18, C19 and C20 topographical paintings and watercolours and C19 landscape and genre pictures, it also includes a small group of works by Pre-Raphaelite and related artists. A recent acquisition is a sheet of studies by William Holman Hunt for his picture *The Eve of St Agnes* (itself acquired in 1924). Among the most popular pictures are *Israel in Egypt* by E J Poynter and Rossetti's *La Ghirlandata, My First Sermon* and *My Second Sermon* by J E Millais and Tissot's *Too Early* and *The Last Evening.*

Of modern pictures, the most significant are those by Sir Matthew Smith, whose studio collection of over 1,000 paintings, water colours, pencil drawings and sketchbooks was presented by his friend and model Mrs Mary Keene. A selection of this material is permanently displayed at **Barbican Art Gallery** [EC2Y 8DS] and is the only part of the Corporation's collection to be publicly available without appointment. However, the proposed redevelopment of the **Guildhall Art Gallery** [King Street EC2 2EJ] virtually destroyed by enemy action in 1941 (the surviving structure houses at present a programme of temporary exhibitions) gives hope that much of the collection may be permanently displayed there in the future.

Items from the collection are hung at numerous locations, including Guildhall, the Mansion House, the Old Bailey, the halls of several Livery companies, schools and colleges; many are frequently loaned to exhibitions at other museums and galleries. It should be noted that pictures can be made available only by prior appointment, depending on accessibility. A new catalogue will

| 1 | Corporation of London Permanent Collection: |
| 2 | 1. Ford, Sir Henry Irving as Hamlet;
2. Tissot, The last Evening. |

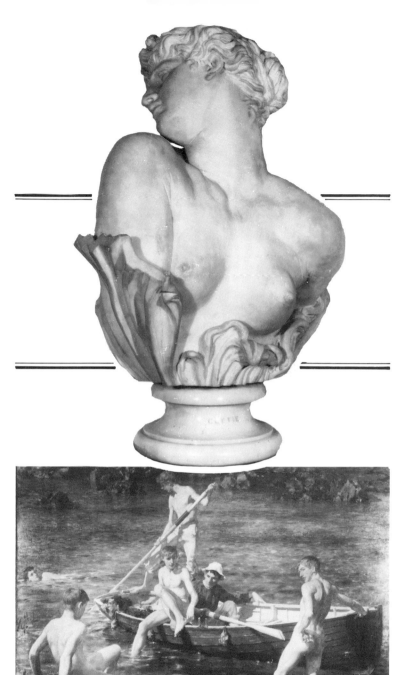

| 1 | Corporation of London Permanent Collection: |
| 2 | 1. Watts, Clytie;
2. Tuke, Ruby, Gold and Malachite. |

include reproductions of all pictures in the collection except the Matthew Smith material which , it is hoped, will form the subject of a future separate publication. The Corporation's collection also includes over 30,000 prints, drawings and watercolours, which are accessible in the **Guildhall Library Print Room.** (VK)

■ COURTAULD INSTITUTE GALLERIES

Somerset House, The Strand WC2R 0RN.   Tel 872 0220
Admission *charge*

The Courtauld Institute Galleries contain one of the finest collections of Impressionist and Post-Impressionist paintings outside France. Among the renowned works on view are Manet's *A Bar at the Folies-Bergère*, Renoir's *La Loge* and Cézanne's *La Montagne Sainte-Victoire*.

In 1932 Samuel Courtauld, industrialist and art patron, offered his London residence, Home House, 20 Portman Square and his remarkable art collection, to the University of London for the establishment of an Institute of Art within the University. His intention was that the teaching of Art History should be carried out in proximity to fine works of art. He was supported in this undertaking by Viscount Lee of Fareham and Sir Robert Witt. Samuel Courtauld's collection of Impressionist and Post-Impressionist paintings, purchased between 1922 and 1936, form the nucleus of a teaching collection which has been enlarged through subsequent bequests. These include Roger Fry's collection of pictures and other works of art by the Bloomsbury Group and the Omega Workshops, bequeathed in 1934; the collections of Italian Renaissance paintings and other Old Master paintings and objets d'art of Viscount Lee of Fareham (1947) and

Courtauld Institute Galleries, Somerset House, North Block, Strand façade.

Courtauld Institute Galleries: Manet, A Bar at the Folies-Bergère.

Mark Gambier-Parry (1966) and the William Spooner bequest which includes important examples of English landscape watercolours (1967). In 1978 Count Antoine Seilern's collection of Renaissance and Baroque paintings, the Princes Gate Collection, named after his address in Kensington, was bequeathed to the University. It was seen for the first time by the general public in 1981.

The collections were moved from Home House to the new Courtauld Institute Galleries, Woburn Square, in 1958, and remained there until December 1989. In the intervening years the collections had almost doubled in size, and both the Courtauld Institute of Art (qv) and the Galleries needed more space for teaching and for the display of the collections. A new home, the North Block of Somerset House, was provided after the successful completion of negotiations between the University and the Department of the Environment, and the Institute moved there in October 1989.

It is particularly appropriate that the *Fine Rooms* at Somerset House in the North Block, built by the Royal Architect, Sir William Chambers, from 1776-80, should now be occupied by the Courtauld. Originally designed to house the Royal Society, the Royal Academy of Arts, and the Society of Antiquaries, within a much larger government office development (the first of its kind in Britain, and most of it completed by 1796: later additions on West side by Sir Robert Smirke and Sir James Pennethorne), the Fine Rooms, with their elegant plaster ceilings, painted decorations, and distinguished neo-classical architecture, were vacated by the learned societies by the 1850s, to be occupied in part by the Registrar General for over 100 years until the early 1970s. Although some restoration work was completed in the 1970s, and several temporary exhibitions were held in them, they remained tenantless for almost twenty years until completely refurbished and adapted to their new use between 1987-89.

The Courtauld Collections are approached at ground level by the **West entrance** on the right of the main triple-arched entrance way from The Strand; the East entrance serves the Courtauld Institute of Art. To the right of the main vestibule is a bookshop (with cloakrooms and coffee shop on the lower ground floors), and visitors may ascend to the main suite of galleries on the first floor either by lift (to the left of the main staircase) or by the magnificent spiral staircase itself, which is known as the 'Rowlandson Staircase' after a famous watercolour by Thomas Rowlandson (1756-1827) showing revellers toppling down the staircase during a party.

On the **first floor** there is a suite of six galleries, with the three larger galleries (1-3) on the North range; the collections are hung in a broadly chronological sequence: Gallery 1 (formerly the Royal Academy Antique Academy) and Gallery 2 (Royal Academy Council and Assembly Room) are devoted to Italian Renaissance C15 and C16 art, with examples of North European art, drawn primarily from the Princes Gate and Lee Collections. Among the chief attractions in **Gallery 1** are the Botticelli (and assistants) *Holy Trinity* (c1500), the Giovanni Bellini *Assassination of S. Peter Martyr* (1509), and Lucas Cranach's *Adam and Eve* (1526); whilst at the East end stand two magnificent marriage-chests (*cassoni*), which celebrate the Morelli-Nerli marriage of 1472, and are remarkable for their completeness, having kept their *spalliere* (backboards); between these *cassoni* hangs Pierino del Vaga's unfinished *The Holy Family*. **Gallery 2** contains C16 and early C17 paintings, notably Albertinelli's *The Creation* (c1513-15), Palma Vecchio's *Venus in a Landscape* (c1520), two Parmigianinos, and a wall of Rubenses, including the modello and sketches for the great Baroque altarpiece *Descent from the Cross* (c1611) in Antwerp Cathedral. **Gallery 3** (Society of Antiquaries' Meeting Room) continues the Rubens display, with a fine group of his oil sketches including *The Bounty of James I triumphing over Avarice*, a modello for one of the virtues ornamenting the corners of the ceiling of the Banqueting House, Whitehall (qv); Rubens's copies after Raphael and Titian, as well as work by his distinguished pupil and assistant, Sir Anthony Van Dyck. Rubens's late *Landscape by Moonlight* (c 1635-40), once owned by Sir Joshua Reynolds, inspired both Gainsborough and Constable. **Gallery 4** (Royal Society and Society of Antiquaries' Joint Ante Room) takes us into the C18 with oil sketches by G B Tiepolo for the monastery church at Aranjuez, his last great commission (1767-69); and landscapes by Guardi, Magnasco, and Jean Barbault (1749). **Gallery 5** (Royal Society Meeting Room) and **Gallery 6** (Royal Academy Ante Room): contain the famous Courtauld Impressionist and Post-Impressionist paintings, supplemented by C19 pictures from the Princes Gate Collection. All the major artists are represented, beginning with Boudin, Daumier, and three Manets – his copy of the large *Déjeuner sur l'Herbe* (Musée d'Orsay), *A Bar at the Folies-Bergère* (1881-2), his last great masterpiece, which he made for Commandant Lejosne, and a charming sketch, *Marguerite de Conflans at the Ball*; works by Monet, Degas, Renoir, Pissarro, and Sisley, show the different facets of urban and country life chosen by individual Impressionists: from Renoir's sparkling *La Loge* (1874), Degas' *Two Dancers on Stage* (1874), to Monet's *Autumn Effect at Argenteuil* (1873) and Pissarro's *Lordship Lane Station,* painted at Dulwich in 1871, while Pissarro was living in London as a refugee from the Franco-Prussian War. Nine works by Cézanne illustrate key stages in his development, from the *Etang des Soeurs*, painted while under the tutorship of Pissarro at Osny in the 1870s, to the late *Route Tournante* c1900-1906. Gauguin is represented by three paintings, including two major Tahitian works of 1897: *Nevermore* and *Te Rerioa (The Dream)*, while van Gogh's *Self-Portrait with Bandaged Ear* and *Peach Blossom in the Crau* date from his Arles period and show his vivid response to Provençal landscape and the art of Japan. There are also important works by Seurat, Toulouse-Lautrec, Bonnard, Vuillard, and Modigliani.

Courtauld Institute Galleries: Parmigianino, Virgin and Child.

Second Floor: approached by the West Staircase, **Gallery 7** (Ante Room to Great Room) houses C17 and C18 portraits by Lely, Gainsborough (of *Mrs Gainsborough*), Allan Ramsay, George Romney, Tilly Kettle, and Sir William Beechey; to the left is the elaborate Medal Cabinet, designed by Sir William Chambers in 1767-68 for the 1st Earl of Charlemont's Dublin house, and made of mahogany, sandalwood, and boxwood, with ormolu mounts; to the right, a glass display case contains C18 Huguenot silver by three generations of the Courtauld family, who first settled in London after the Revocation of the Edict of Nantes (1685) in about 1690. The silver is on long loan from Courtaulds plc. **Gallery 8** (The Great Room): from 1780 until 1837 this vast room was used to show the Royal Academy's Summer Exhibitions, it is now subdivided by screens at right angles to the peripheral walls, so as to form discrete areas. These will contain some small thematic displays, e.g. Rubens and the Bible, Approaches to Impressionism, Roger Fry and the Omega Workshops, which will be changed from time to time; whilst above the Royal Academy 'Line' (the moulding set at 7' 1½" – 2.35 m. – from floor level), are hung some of the larger works such as Kokoschka's *Prometheus Triptych*, commissioned by Count Seilern in 1950 for his Princes Gate house. **Galleries 9** and **10** are devoted to late C19 and C20 art, ranging from Sickert to Ben Nicholson, Ivon Hitchens, and John Hoyland, drawn largely from the collections of

Courtauld Institute Galleries: Rubens, The Bounty of James I triumphing over Avarice.

Roger Fry, Alastair and Diana Hunter, and Lillian Browse. **Gallery 11** (Royal Academy School of Painting) contains Italian and Netherlandish art of the C14, C15 and C16 from the Gambier-Parry and Princes Gate Collections, mainly small gold-ground panel paintings such as the exquisite Bernardo Daddi triptych of 1338, the Master of Flémalle *Deposition*, the Estouteville Triptych (c 1360-75), and works by Simone Martini, Fra Angelico, Lorenzo Monaco, Pieter Breugel, and Massys, as well as medieval ivories.

The showcases in Galleries 1, 2, and 3, contain displays of Italian maiolica, German and Venetian C15 and C16 glass, Islamic metalwork, Limoges enamel and West European metalwork (mainly from the Gambier-Parry collection).

The **Prints and Drawings Exhibition Gallery** on the Ground Floor

(East entrance) is custom-built for the display of prints, drawings and textiles. It is intended to show changing exhibitions drawn from the permanent collections, as well as loan exhibitions, from time to time. The Courtauld Collections contain magnificent Old Master drawings by Mantegna, Michelangelo, Breugel, Rubens, Rembrandt, and the Tiepolos, among others of the first rank, principally in the Witt and Princes Gate Collections; but there is a fine collection of C18 and C19 English watercolours from the Spooner Collection, not forgetting some 25,000 Old Master prints which were bequeathed by Sir Robert Witt. Visitors will also be able to study items from the prints and drawings collections by prior appointment. (DF)

───────────────────── *the essentials* ───────── ──────

Underground Temple (Circle, District Lines), Covent Garden (Piccadilly Line). **BR** Charing Cross, Waterloo. **Open** Mon-Sat 1000-1800, Sun 1400-1800. **Cloakroom. Toilets. Public telephones. For the disabled** access. **Shopping** bookshop. **Publications. Photography** charge. **Visitors' services** guided tours by arrangement, lectures. **Staff opinion** apply at sales desk.

■ COURTAULD INSTITUTE OF ART

Somerset House, The Strand WC2R 0RN.   Tel 872 0220
Admission *prior application*

The Institute, part of the University of London, was founded in 1931 to establish the study of art history as an academic discipline and introduce the honours degree in the history of European art and architecture. It possesses two great photographic reference libraries, now housed on the ground floor and in the vaults of Somerset House.

The **Witt Library** comprises the most complete catalogue of Western Painting in the world. This unique archive, founded by Sir Robert Witt at the end of the C19, contains almost 1,500,000 reproductions by over 50,000 artists from c1200 to the present day. As such, it is an invaluable resource for both art historians and dealers.

A checklist of painters represented in the Witt was published in 1978. This is available for consultation at the library or it can be purchased. The Witt is a reference library but photographs can be ordered, or inexpensive photocopies can be made on the premises. There are also a number of useful card indexes including a Portrait Card Index and a Masters and Followers Card Index.

The collection of reproductions consists largely of black-and-white photographs of varying quality, mounted on grey card and filed in 'Witt boxes'. These are grouped in national schools and shelved alphabetically by artist; paintings before drawings. Photographic material is gleaned from exhibition catalogues, periodicals and sale catalogues. Information concerning artist, subject, medium, date, etc appears on the mounts. The library does not exclude works of questionable attribution. Thus a tradition has evolved over the years of connoisseurs appending their own comments and suggestions regarding the dating, attribution, provenance, etc to the mounts of such 'problematic' works. These annotations are considered so valuable that they are being included in a computerized programme of the entire holdings of the Witt. The Computer Index will operate as an information retrieval system enabling researchers to gain access to images according to categories such as 'subject matter', 'date', 'patronage', and 'location'.

The **Conway Library** is organised along the same lines as the Witt. It contains over 800,000 high quality black-and-white photographs of Architecture, Sculpture, Illuminated manuscripts, Medieval wall and panel painting, Stained glass, Metal work and Architectural drawings and publications. In addition, there is a Byzantine collection with reproductions of Monuments, Manuscripts, Mosaics and Wall and panel paintings.

Lord Conway began his collection at the turn of the century with cuttings taken from published books and pamphlets. Today the Conway Library holds the negatives for most of the photographs in the collection, and supplies many of the photographs used by publishers.

In 1962 the Conway Library purchased the *Garrison Collection.* This is a highly specialised collection of photographs of Italian Medieval panel paintings, frescoes, mosaics and manuscript illuminations, and there is also a selection of bibliographic and reference material.

The Conway Library is open to students and teachers from institutions in Britain and abroad. Members of the public are admitted at the discretion of the Director. Visitors should go in the first instance to the Conway General Office on the ground floor where they will be given a plan of the rooms and a list of their contents (WH).

──────────────── *the essentials* ────────────────

Underground Temple (Circle, District Lines), Covent Garden (Piccadilly Line). **Open** ☐ Witt Library: Mon-Fri 1000-1900 (University term); 1000-1800 (Vacation). ☐ Conway Library as Witt except that it closes at 1800 during University term. **Toilets. Public telephones. For the disabled** access. **Refreshments** snacks. **Shopping** sales desk. **Publications. Photography. Research** library. **Staff opinion.**

■ COURT DRESS COLLECTION

State Apartments, Kensington Palace W8 4PX.   Tel 937 9561
Admission *charge*

The exhibition is on the 'garden floor' of the wing of Kensington Palace open to the public: upstairs are the magnificent State Apartments. A joint ticket admits the visitor to both. The apartments housing the exhibition of dress worn at Court (by men and women) were occupied from 1818 by the Duke and Duchess of Kent and their daughter the Princess Victoria who lived here until her accession as Queen in 1837. Later on, the Duke and Duchess of Teck made their London home at Kensington Palace from 1867 to 1883 and their daughter Princess Mary, who later became Queen Mary, was born here. You may visit the room which is reputed to be that in which the Princess Victoria was born, the *Red Saloon*, where Queen Victoria held her Accession Council on the morning of 20 June 1837, and the early C19 *staircase hall*. All have been carefully restored to appear as they may have been at various dates during the C19.

The exhibition displays *dresses* and *uniforms* dating from the mid C18 onwards. They come from the collection (over 400 items, from the reign of Queen Victoria to the 1950s) on loan to the Queen from Mr and Mrs Aubrey Bowden, and from museums and private individuals throughout the British Isles. The Historic Royal Palaces Agency is in charge of it. These delicate exhibits are shown in a secure air-conditioned environment, with carefully-controlled light, and they are changed from time to time. The dresses and uniforms are mounted on specially-designed figures. They are in chronological sequence and the furnishings add to the atmosphere of the period to which they belong.

	2	Court Dress Collection:
1		1. Uniform (2nd Class) of HM Household, c1910; 2. Superintendent, Royal Mews c1912, Lady in Court dress c1910; Ambassador c1910; 3 Court dress, 1912; King's Bodyguard for
	3	Scotland (Royal Company of Archers), 1912.

The style of the dresses worn at Court generally followed the fashionable line of ladies' formal costume. However, certain additions were demanded at Court — feather and veil headdresses, gloves, a bouquet, a fan and a train — a length of material fastened either to the waist or shoulders, usually the most stunning feature of the whole dress. Court uniform, worn by high-ranking Court and government officials such as ambassadors, did not follow fashion. The style of many remained unaltered for decades, with lace, silk hose, buckled shoes and swords worn on the most formal Court occasions. The exhibition offers a fascinating and glittering insight in the history of dress and social life through two centuries.

─────────── *the essentials* ───────────

Underground Queensway (Central Line) High Street Kensington (Circle, District Lines) **Open** Mon-Sat 0900-1700, Sun 1300-1700. **Toilets. For the disabled** access (not to State Apartments), toilets. **Shopping** sales desk. **Publications. Educational facilities.**

■ CRAFTS COUNCIL COLLECTION
12 Waterloo Place SW1Y 4AU. Tel 930 4811
Admission *free*

The Crafts Council maintains its collection as a ready source of material for loan exhibitions for museums, art centres, libraries and other organisations wishing either to mount special exhibitions or to augment their own displays of the finest contemporary British *craftworks*. It covers ceramics, glass, jewellery, textiles, books, lettering, metalwork, furniture, toys and wood work. The collection is thus of its nature dispersed, apart from the residue in store, available for borrowing, but for those interested in the current craft scene the Council operates a Library and Information Centre, which will provide details of where craft exhibitions, and specific items of the collection, can currently be seen.

From time to time exhibitions are mounted at the **Crafts Council Gallery** in Waterloo Place drawn from the permanent collection or from other sources.

the essentials

Underground Piccadilly Circus (Bakerloo, Piccadilly Lines). **Open** Tue-Sat 1000-1700, Sun 1400-1700. **Toilets. For the disabled** access, lift, toilets. **Refreshments** coffee bar, snacks. **Shopping. Publications. Photography. Educational facilities. Visitors' services** films, lectures. **Research** library, information centre.

■ CRICKET MEMORIAL GALLERY

Lord's Ground, St John's Wood Road NW8 8QN.   Tel 289 1611
Admission *charge*

A must for all cricket enthusiasts, the Memorial Gallery was opened in 1952 in the old rackets courts at Lord's. This unique collection brings to life some of the great characters and achievements of our cricketing past. Here are the *Ashes* fought for in Test Matches between England and Australia since 1883 when two Melbourne ladies presented the victorious England side with the ashes of a bail in a tiny urn. A less famous relic is the ball which the Middlesex man Albert Trott drove over the Pavilion in 1899, a feat still unmatched. Nearby is *W.G. Grace's bat* with which he hit his hundredth century and the pads, blazers and caps of Victor Trumper, Don Bradman and Jack Hobbs.

To complement these and other curiosities is a superbly illustrated *panel display* outlining the development of the game from its rudimentary beginnings some 300 years ago, when teams of sheepfarmers played with a ball of wool, a sheepfold's wicket-gate and a shepherd's crook. Later sections are devoted to the international game. On the upper floor are *cricketing portraits* and objects d'art including Ruskin Spear's large oil study of *Freddie Truman*, R. Hannaford's *Sir Donald Bradman*, a bronze statuette of *Alec Bedser* by David Hynne and some unlikely Staffordshire porcelain figures of cricketers.

The guided tour of the Cricket Club and grounds is highly recommended. Included is a visit to the ***Long Room*** in the Pavilion, normally open only to members of the Club, where a splendid view of the pitch can be seen through its panoramic glass front. Notice on the floor hundreds of *stud marks* made over the years by fine and famous cricketers as they emerged from their dressing room to face the field. (MG)

the essentials

Underground St John's Wood (Jubilee Line). **Open** Cricket season Mon-Sat 1030-1500 or by appointment. **Toilets** nearby. **Public telephones** nearby. **For the disabled** limited access. **Refreshments** restaurant, snacks nearby. **Shopping** sales desk. **Publications. Educational facilities. Visitors' services** films, lectures, guided tours by arrangement. **Research** library.

Crown Jewels: **1.** St Edward's Crown; **2.** Imperial Crown; **3.** The Sovereign's Orb; **4.** Golden spurs and bracelets.

■ CROWN JEWELS

Tower of London, Tower Hill EC3N 4AB. Tel 709 0765
Admission *charge*

For a nation renowned for its pageantry, the heart must be the regalia of the greatest pageant of all, the Coronation. Britain's Crown Jewels are kept in our most ancient royal palace, the Tower of London, amid intense security, and carry with them all the legend and romance of the ancient nation. Here are the swords, the rings, the orbs and sceptres and the crowns of the British monarchy, in a new super-safe underground display. But most of the regalia is not as old as many believe, for the jewels were seized by Cromwell after the execution of Charles I in 1649 and either sold or melted down, so that a new set had to be made for the coronation of Charles II in 1661. Most of our sovereigns have been crowned with *St Edward's Crown,* which may have been refurbished from the crown of Edward the Confessor (1043-1066).

The *Imperial State Crown* is probably the best known, substituted for the heavy St Edward's Crown - which weighs an ounce under five pounds - at the end of the ceremony and worn on subsequent State Occasions. It was originally made for Queen Victoria and has some of the world's most fabulous jewels set in it: the Black Prince's Ruby, given to Edward III's heir by Pedro the Cruel of Spain in 1367, and worn by Henry V at the Battle of Agincourt in 1415; the Stuart Sapphire, taken into exile by the abdicating James II in 1688 and only restored when his last remaining descendant died in 1807; the four long pearl drops are traditionally called 'Queen Elizabeth I's earrings', but were probably separate pearls at one time owned by her. The frame incorporates more than 3,500 precious stones, mainly diamonds, but not - as many think - the famous Koh-i-Noor, or Mountain of Light. This fabulous diamond, which probably dates back to the C17 (although the legend goes back some 3,000 years), is in the present *Queen Mother's crown* and is traditionally worn by a King's consort - it is said to bring good luck to a woman who wears it and bad luck to a man.

Also displayed are the *Sceptre with the Cross*, with its huge 530-carat diamond, the *Great Sword of State*, and the *Exeter Salt*, hall-marked c1630, set with rubies, sapphires, emeralds and amethysts, given to Charles II by the City of Exeter. (ST)

---
the essentials

Underground Tower Hill (Circle, District Lines). **Open** 1 March-31 Oct Mon-Sat 0930-1745, Sun 1400-1745, Nov-Feb Mon-Sat 0930-1630 (Crown Jewels closed Feb) **Toilets. Public telephones. For the disabled** limited access, toilets. **Shopping** gifts sales desk. **Publications. Educational facilities. Visitors' services** guided tours.

■ CUMING MUSEUM

155-157 Walworth Road SE17 1RS.   Tel 703 6514 ext 32
Admission *free*

The museum occupies the first floor of the Newington District Library and is based on the general collection started by Richard Cuming, a local boy, in 1782, with later additions by his son. The collection was acquired in 1902 by the predecessors of the present Borough of Southwark. It now includes *pilgrim badges* and other relics from Chaucer's time; the *water pump* from Marshalsea Debtors' Prison, and the Dog and Pot *ironmongers' sign* and other items associated with Dickens's childhood and working life; also the *family prayer book* and *electrical generator* of the eminent scientist Michael Faraday (1791-1867) who was born in the district; and pieces demonstrating the skills of the *Doulton pottery* designer George Tinworth (1843-1913).

A permanent display illustrates the story of the local community from its prehistoric origins through its hey-day as a small market town by London Bridge, when the (stuffed) *dancing bear* would have been popular, to the present.

An attempt to create a 'British Museum in Miniature' was abandoned after 1941 when a wartime bomb damaged its premises, and the museum remained closed for 17 years. A special theme is London superstitions through the ages, seen through the **Lovett collection of charms and amulets** to ward off evil and sickness. Also important are geological and ethnographical specimens in the reserve collection which have been the subject of learned articles in technical journals.

---
the essentials

Underground Elephant and Castle (Bakerloo, Northern Lines). **Open** Thur 1000-1900, Mon-Wed, Fri 1000-1730, Sat 1000-1700. **Shopping** sales desk. **Photography. Educational facilities. Visitors' services** lectures, guided tours by arrangement. **Research** library.

■ HM CUSTOMS AND EXCISE MUSEUM AND EXHIBITION

Custom House, Lower Thames Street EC3R 6EE.   Tel 865 5574
Admission *free*

In the Georgian London Custom House there are displays of the history and present work of HM Customs and Excise. Topics covered include famous staff such as Chaucer, Tom Paine and Robert Burns; smuggling and concealments in the C19; drug smuggling today and the link with America (signatures of John Paul Jones and the Commission of Boston Excise officers).

Also covered are the history of Excise, King Charles II's payments to his mistress Nell Gwynne, the taxes on windows, glass and ships' sails and today's duties on oil, alcohol and gambling. There is a collection of overseas Customs uniforms, and badges from foreign countries including Europe, Russia and America. (MJRD)

the essentials

Underground Monument (Circle, District Lines). **Open** Mon-Fri 1000-1600. **Photography** by arrangement. **Educational facilities** by arrangement. **Visitors' services** guided tours. **Research** by arrangement.

■ CUTTY SARK

King William Walk, Greenwich SE10 9HT.   Tel 858 3445
Admission *charge*

Of composite iron and wood construction the Cutty Sark is the most famous great sailing clipper. Launched at Dumbarton, Scotland, in 1869 the ship was in competition with steam from the start. At the outset (1870-77) she worked as a tea-clipper, and it was then that she won her enduring fame, with the fastest voyage from China to England in 1871, completed in 107 days with a crew of 28 hands. Subsequently she was engaged in the Australian wool trade (1883-95) during the twilight years of the sailing-ship era. The name, which is derived from Robert Burns's 'Tam O'Shanter', is represented by the figurehead which wears the short chemise, or 'cutty sark' mentioned in the poem.

In permanent dry dock since 1954, the ship is both an historical relic of great beauty and a museum containing a wide range of artefacts connected with the sailing era. Above decks is the impressive and complex array of rigging, masts and general paraphernalia that is characteristic of sail, while below decks are the exhibits that have been collected from a number of other ships. The figureheads, known as the Long John Silver Collection, a nickname derived from the eye-patch worn by its owner, are outstanding examples of woodcarving art of the period. Reconstructions of the ship's history as a tea clipper and wool carrier can be seen with tea chests and bales of wool stacked as they would have been as its cargo. There are prints, paintings, drawings, brass instruments and much more on display which gives the visitor a chance to savour and appreciate the atmosphere, excitement and discomfort of life aboard a classic of its time.

the essentials

BR Greenwich (from Charing Cross Station). **Boats** from Westminster or Tower Piers. **Open** Mon-Sat 1030-1700, Sun 1200-1700. **For the disabled** limited access. **Shopping.** **Publications. Photography. Educational facilities.**

■ DARWIN MUSEUM

Down House, Luxted Road, Downe, Orpington BR6 7JT. Tel (0689) 59119
Admission *charge*

Charles Darwin's reputation as a naturalist was established early in life with the publication of the results of his work on board HMS Beagle in the South Atlantic. But it was in the quiet country village of Downe, Kent, that he spent forty productive years, writing a host of books including the immensely influential (and controversial) 'On the Origin of Species by means of Natural Selection', 1859.

The museum occupies the house where he lived from 1842 to 1882. The centre-piece is the ***Old Study*** where nearly all Darwin's scientific work was done. The appearance of the room is as it was during his lifetime with the original tables, armchair, writing-board and other items in their usual places. Other rooms are devoted to re-creating and recording Darwin's lifestyle, with memorabilia and objects which he owned or which were familiar to him. In the ***New Study*** is a display case which shows the stages of the Darwinian theory of evolution over the centuries, leading to his final conclusions regarding the common origin of life-forms. The ***Drawing***

Down House, the home of Charles Darwin from 1842 to 1882.

Room, added to the house in 1858, and now furnished as it was in his lifetime,. with the grand piano, chaise longue and bureau, evokes a comfortable domesticity. This was not the original drawing room when the family moved in — that is now the ***Charles Darwin Room***, containing various showcases, pictures and photographs of episodes throughout his varied and busy life.

It was Darwin's habit to do much of his thinking during his daily perambulation around the pleasant garden, and for this he devised a special route leading to Sandwalk Wood and back to the house; the visitor can still follow in his footsteps. Also in the **garden** is the *Worm Stone* which Darwin enjoyed using to observe how long it took for worms to undermine objects placed in soil.

―――――――――――――――――――――― *the essentials* ――――――――――――――――――――――

BR Bromley South (from Victoria Station) then **Bus** 146 (not Sun). **Open** Sat,Sun,Tue,Wed, Thur 1300-1800. **Cloakroom. Toilets. Parking. For the disabled** access, toilet (ladies). **Shopping** sales desk. **Publications. Photography. Research** library.

■ DESIGN MUSEUM
Butlers Wharf, Shad Thames SE1 2YD. Tel 403 6933 (407 6261)
Admission *charge*

The first of its kind in the world, the Design Museum is devoted to promoting the history, theory, process and practice of design in mass-produced consumer products.

The museum takes a stage further the work of the Boilerhouse Project at the Victoria and Albert Museum, where since 1981 the Project promoted an awareness of the past, present and future of design by involving the public and industry in a series of exhibitions covering a varied range of subjects.

In a riverside location, by Tower Bridge, the museum offers a permanent study collection of noteworthy design from the industrial revolution to the present day. Space is also dedicated to temporary thematic exhibitions, with special areas devoted to graphics and to new and speculative product designs; study facilities and resources are available to schools and colleges.

—————————— *the essentials* ——————————

Underground Tower Hill (Circle, District Lines), London Bridge (Northern Line). **Ferry shuttle** from Tower Pier to Butlers Wharf Pier. **Open** Tue-Sun 1130-1830 **Cloakroom. Toilets. Public telephones. For the disabled** access, toilets. **Refreshments** restaurant, snacks. **Publications. Educational facilities. Visitors' services** guided tours. **Research** library.

■ DICKENS HOUSE MUSEUM AND LIBRARY
48 Doughty Street WC1N 2LF. Tel 405 2127
Admission *charge*

It was in this early C19 house, where he lived from 1837-9, that Charles Dickens (1812-70) established his fame, working on three novels, 'The Pickwick Papers', 'Oliver Twist' and 'Nicholas Nickleby'. Saved from demolition in 1923 by the Dickens Fellowship, it is now a place of pilgrimage from all over the world, and contains not only the ***Dickens Library***, one of the most comprehensive in the world, but also a vast collection of Dickens memorabilia.

As well as many pieces of furniture including his famous desk and chair, paintings and letters, there are articles as diverse as his personal lemon squeezer, his razor set, a model of him made entirely from icing sugar and the velvet-covered reading-desk which Dickens took with him on his travels giving readings in England and America.

Some rooms in the house have been reconstructed with immense attention to detail, and give a clear picture of the house as it must have been with the Dickens family in residence. Do not miss Dickens's ***Drawing Room***, reconstructed as it may be supposed it was at the completion of 'Nicholas Nickleby' in September 1839.

The Suzannet Rooms, formerly Dickens' bedroom and drawing room, are filled with the collection of the Comte and Comtesse Alain de Suzannet, and also offer space for occasional exhibitions. The back bedroom on the second floor contains relics of Dickens's life in the theatre, and of Mary Hogarth, his sister-in-law, who died

Dickens House, the author's home from 1837 to 1839.

in the room in 1837, aged 17 years. In the basement are the Library, and, and, at the back, still room, wash-house and wine-cellar. (IO)

──────────── *the essentials* ────────────
Underground Russell Square (Piccadilly Line). **Open** Mon-Sat 0900-1700. **Shopping** sales desk. **Educational facilities. Research** library.

■ DULWICH PICTURE GALLERY

College Road SE21 7AD.   Tel 693 5254
Admission *charge*

This delightful gallery in a quiet village setting four miles south of Trafalgar Square contains one of Britain's finest collections of Old Master paintings. Here are works by Rembrandt, Van Dyck, Claude and Poussin, an exceptional assembly of C17 Dutch art and splendid portraits by Gainsborough and Reynolds.

The building itself was designed by Sir John Soane (1735-1837) and opened in 1814, the first public art gallery in Britain and an outstanding example of neoclassicism at its most ingenious. The oldest part of the gallery's collection dates from the early C17 when Edward Alleyn, an actor of Shakespeare's time, founded Dulwich College (now a well-known public school) and bequeathed his 39 paintings to the Foundation. The most substantial bequest, though, came in the early C19 from Sir Francis Bourgeois, a landscape painter, who had inherited paintings bought by his friend Noel Desenfans for the King of Poland. The latter was forced to abdicate in 1795 and his treasures eventually found a permanent home at Dulwich.

There are twelve galleries and a mausoleum, the latter an eerie chamber containing the sarcophagi of Bourgeois, Desenfans and Mrs Desenfans. From the entrance hall, which displays items relating to the history of the collection, turn left and proceed to **Gallery I** at the far end of the gallery. The several Gainsboroughs here include *Mrs Moodey and her Children* and *The Linley Sisters* (c1772), Elizabeth and Mary, daughters of the musician Thomas Linley. A prepossessing duo: Elizabeth, the standing figure, eloped to France with the playwright Sheridan at the time this portrait was painted. Their brother, *Thomas Linley the Younger*, was a brilliant violinist and composer of whom Mozart thought that, had he lived longer, he might have become one of the 'greatest ornaments of the musical world.'

The next four galleries contain a selection of the grandest works from different Schools. See in **Gallery II** Van Dyck's *Emmanuel Philibert of Savoy* painted in Sicily in 1624, the year the sitter died of the plague. A powerful contrast is wrought between the Prince's delicate features and his sturdy military apparel. On the opposite wall is Hobbema's *Wooded Landscape with Water-mill* (C17) beautifully composed and full of fascinating activity. **Gallery III** contains Murillo's celebrated *Flower Girl* (c1670), one of four works by the artist in the collection; the girl's costume has been variously identified as Andalusian, Moorish and Gipsy. In **Gallery IV** is Poussin's masterpiece *The Triumph of David* (C17), in which the celebrations following David's victory over Goliath are expounded with the utmost pictorial logic. The warm glow of Cuyp's sunsets pervades **Gallery VI** where six paintings by this fine Dutch landscapist are to be seen. Other C17 Dutch paintings by Wouvermans, Wynants and the Van de Veldes appear in **Gallery VII** as well as a splendid view of *Westminster and the Thames* by the obscure Flemish artist Cornelius Bol. Beyond the mausoleum is a room containing a number of sketches by Rubens for murals, tapestries and altarpieces. *Ceres and her Nymphs* (c1625), representing the Roman

1	Dulwich Picture Gallery:
2	1. The building by Sir John Soane; 2. Murillo, A Flower Girl.

goddess of Harvest naked with cornucopia, displays the full relish of abundant form so characteristic of this artist's work, and contrasts with the atmospheric poetry of Watteau's *Les Plaisirs du Bal*.

In **Gallery IX**, among paintings of the British School, is Canaletto's *Old Walton Bridge over the Thames* (1754). The uncertain glory of English summer weather is beautifully evoked in a scene which includes, in the foreground, the artist himself, his patron Thomas Hollis, a friend (Thomas Brand), a manservant and a small dog called Malta. Nearby is a fine portrait of *An Unknown Couple in a Landscape* (1750s) by Gainsborough, a conversation piece in the manner of the well-known 'Mr and Mrs Andrews' in the National Gallery (qv). **Gallery XI** contains what is perhaps the masterpiece of the collection, Rembrandt's *Girl at a Window* (1645), a magnetic portrait of a child who probably served in the artist's household. It seems to demand and yet consistently defy interpretation. Its only possible rival is Claude Lorrain's magnificent *Landscape with Jacob, Laban and his Daughters* (1676) in **Gallery XII**. Ostensibly a biblical narrative, its real subject is a landscape suffused with light and enchantment. Notice the small white sails of boats depicted in the distance.

In recent years the Dulwich Picture Gallery has received much deserved attention. Various exhibitions of its paintings have been held in England and abroad culminating in an exhibition in Washington and Los Angeles in 1985-6 suitably titled 'Collection for a King'. Temporary exhibitions are often held in the gallery which also offers numerous facilities for the visitor. (MG)

---
the essentials

BR West Dulwich (from Victoria Station). **Open** Tue-Sat 1100-1700, Sun 1400-1700. **Toilets.** **Parking** ample in street. **For the disabled** access. **Shoppping** sales desk. **Publications.** **Educational facilities. Visitors' services** guided tours Sat, Sun 1500, lectures.

■ EPPING FOREST MUSEUM
Rangers Road, Chingford E4 7QH.   Tel 529 4923
Admission *charge*

The large half-timbered pub not far from Chingford Station, on the edge of Epping Forest, might have been erected in 1882 especially to dwarf its neighbour, the so-called Queen Elizabeth's Hunting Lodge — 'so-called' because it was in fact built in 1543 for her father Henry VIII. Its purpose was to act as a grandstand from which the Monarch could watch in safety the hunting laid on for his amusement in the forest, for centuries a 'royal chase' or wild game reserve.

Its three floors house the Corporation of London's Epping Forest Museum, opened in 1895 to improve the 'tone' of visitors to the forest. The **ground floor** offers displays about forest management, past and present, trees, flora and fauna, and how timber-framed houses were put together. The **first floor**, reached by the sturdy staircase up which the Virgin Queen is said to have ridden her charger, displays aspects of the forest as a royal chase, with more birds and beasts. Note the sparrowhawk, with its hood, and the mantraps for unwary poachers. The **top floor**, where the royal party would have watched the sport below, is of great achitectural interest, with its lofty beamed roof. Here you will find a large showcase containing the ***Lister Collection*** of stuffed birds — owls of many kinds including the majestic Eagle Owl, certainly not one to meet on a dark night . . .

Back downstairs, you can buy many publications about Epping Forest, including suggested walks in this giant among London's public open spaces.

Epping Forest Museum.

the essentials

BR Chingford (from Liverpool Street Station). **Open** Wed-Sun 1400-1800 (closing at dusk if earlier). **Parking. For the disabled** access to ground floor only. **Shopping. Publications. Photography. Educational facilities. Visitors' services** lectures, guided tours by prior arrangement.

■ ERITH MUSEUM

Erith Library, Walnut Tree Road, Erith DA8 1RA.   Tel (0322) 526574
Admission *free*

This is one of the two museums within the Local Studies Section of the London Borough of Bexley — the other is the Bexley Museum (qv). It concentrates on the Erith community in the east of London, south of the River Thames. Displays cover the archaeology and geology of the area; also Lesnes Abbey, founded in 1178 (its remains are set in a woodland park famous for its daffodils in Spring); a model of the Great Harry (a warship fitted in 1513 in the naval dockyard founded by Henry VII at Erith); an Edwardian kitchen and prints and photos of old times.

─────────────────── *the essentials* ───────────────────
BR Erith (from Charing Cross Station). **Open** Mon, Wed, Sat 1400-1700. **Shopping** sales desk. **Photography. Educational facilities. Visitors' services** films, lectures, guided tours by prior arrangement. **Research** library.

■ FARADAY MUSEUM

The Royal Institution, 21 Albermarle Street W1X 4BS.   Tel 409 2992
Admission *charge*

Michael Faraday (1791-1867) was a pioneer in the fields of electricity and magnetism and the links between the two. This museum commemorates his many achievements. It is situated in the basement of the Royal Institution on the site of the laboratories where Faraday carried out much of his work. His original *laboratory* has been restored. There are many original and copied examples of his *instruments* as well as personal belongings. A full explanation of Faraday's work is provided.

In addition, upon special application, a smaller exhibition can be seen upstairs. It illustrates the history of the Royal Institution from its foundation in 1799 for 'the improvement of life through demonstration'. There are cases devoted to the work of major scientists. Among these are Sir Humphry Davy (1778-1829), Faraday's first teacher and the inventor of the miners' safety lamp, and Thomas Young (1773-1829) who first propounded the wave theory of light, and is also famous for deciphering the Rosetta Stone, which can be seen at the British Museum (qv). (IO)

─────────────────── *the essentials* ───────────────────
Underground Green Park (Jubilee, Piccadilly, Victoria Lines). **Open** Tue, Thur 1300-1600. **Cloakroom. Toilets. Public telephones. For the disabled** access, lift. **Shopping** sales desk. **Publications. Photography** on request. **Educational services** on request. **Visitors' services** guided tours by arrangement. **Research** library.

■ FAWCETT LIBRARY

City of London Polytechnic, Old Castle Street E1 7NT.   Tel 283 1030 ext 570
Admission *charge*

This is Britain's main reference and lending collection on women, with over 50,000 books, pamphlets and leaflets, more than 700 periodical titles, about 400 boxes of papers on organisations and individuals, large quantities of newspaper cuttings, and substantial collections of photographs, autograph letters, campaign badges and posters. The subject range is wide from women's suffrage to employment and education, prostitution, women and the church, fashion, women in politics, women writers, artists, musicians, engineers, doctors, birth control, abortion, violence against women, matriarchy, cooking etc. Most of the material relates to Great Britain, but there are substantial holdings on other countries.

It began life as the library of the London and National Society for Women's Service (now the Fawcett Society), the direct descendant of the London Society for Women's Suffrage, founded in 1867. The society was the centre of the non-militant campaign for women's suffrage under the leadership of Millicent Garrett Fawcett, and over the years accumulated a certain amount on the campaign and

Fawcett Library: 'Women's Lib', 1913.

related issues. In the 1920s the Society decided to organise this material for the use of members, and in 1926 Vera Douie was appointed as the first librarian — a post which she held for the next 41 years during which she transformed the collection from a small society library into a major national research resource.

Over the years the library acquired a number of other smaller collections, including the **Cavendish Bentinck** and **Edward Wright Libraries** (originally suffrage collections with a high proportion of old and rare books), the **Sadd Brown Library** (on women in the Commonwealth), and the library of the **Josephine Butler Society** (formerly the Association for Moral and Social Hygiene).

─────────────── *the essentials* ───────────────

Underground Aldgate East (District, Metropolitan Lines). **Open** Mon 1300-2030 (term), 1000-1700 (vacation), Tue-Fri 1000-1700. **For the disabled** access. **Shopping** sales desk. **Publications. Photography. Visitors' services** lectures, guided tours by prior arrangement. **Research** library.

■ FENTON HOUSE

Windmill Hill NW3 6RT.   Tel 435 3471
Admission *charge*

Built in 1693, this is one of Hampstead's earliest, largest and architecturally most distinguished buildings, rightly in the care of the National Trust. Its formal very English walled gardens are a delight in summer, with an almost country air. But it is for its contents that the house is famous. First, almost every room on two of the three floors contains fine examples of English C18 furniture, in just the kind of surroundings in which they are at home and seen at their best. Then, there is a remarkable array of porcelain — Chinese, English of all the main kinds and, particularly precious, Meissen figures including Commedia dell'Arte characters by the virtuoso J J Kaendler. Do not miss the exquisite Scaramouche, hands on hips, and Harlequin in his checks.

But the great attraction's the **Benton-Fletcher collection of keyboard instruments.** Often of the grandest and most beautiful workmanship, these are everywhere throughout the house. The first that you meet is in the Dining Room, a great harpsichord by Burkat Shudi and John Broadwood, made in London in 1769. This was the largest type of its day. In the Porcelain Room, the black and red instrument is an 'outsider', made in Antwerp in 1612 by Johannes Ruckers, and lent by the Queen. Upstairs in the Blue Porcelain Room is another famous harpsichord, the *two-manual Kirckman* made in London in 1777. The servants' attics, too, are given over to instruments. Note the rare and most decoratively painted virginals.

As the donor wished, as many as possible are kept in first-class playing condition and can be used (by arrangement) for study and practice. But it is a pity that the ordinary music-lover (unless he is very lucky in timing his arrival) cannot hear these marvellous exhibits, even on tape and in the privacy of headphones, as is enterprisingly done elsewhere. This would enhance the interest of an already fascinating collection.

Fenton House: C17 harpsichord.

the essentials

Underground Hampstead (Northern Line). **Open** Apr-Oct Sat-Wed 1100-1800, Mar Sat, Sun 1400-1800. **Toilets. For the disabled** access to ground floor. **Photography.**

■ FLAXMAN GALLERY

University College London, Gower Street WC1 6BT.   Tel 387 7050
Admission *free*

Located under the central dome of University College, this gallery contains plaster casts of the celebrated English sculptor John Flaxman (1755-1826). Flaxman, whose work epitomises the simplicity and grandeur of the neoclassical style, enjoyed a considerable reputation in his day both as a sculptor and as an illustrator.

The casts contained in this collection are the models for many of Flaxman's most important monuments. Bequeathed to University College by the sculptor's sister-in-law Maria Denman in 1847, they were installed in the appropriate setting of a small classical rotunda and unveiled to the public in 1857.

Flaxman Gallery, in its fine neoclassical architectural setting by William Wilkins.

To complement the casts are a number of display cases containing documents and photographs relating to the history of the gallery. (MG)

the essentials

Underground Euston, Warren Street (Northern, Victoria Lines), Euston Square (Circle, Metropolitan). **Open** Mon-Fri 1000-1700. **For the disabled** access by prior arrangement. **Publications.**

■ FLORENCE NIGHTINGALE MUSEUM

St Thomas' Hospital, 2 Lambeth Palace Road SE1 7EW.   Tel 620 0374
Admission *charge*

Florence Nightingale was born in 1820 at Florence. Her successful campaign to improve nursing care for the wounded of the Crimean War made her a national heroine. Her prized possessions, memorabilia and costume create a personal setting for the story of this celebrated and often controversial figure. A life-sized recreated ward at the Crimea is the centre-piece, whilst an audio-visual display takes the Museum beyond its four walls. A Resource Centre invites research

Florence Nightingale Museum: Crimean scene.

into the long, varied and influential life of one of the C19's most extraordinary women.

────── *the essentials* ──────

Underground Westminster (Circle, District Lines), Waterloo (Bakerloo, Northern Lines). **Open** Tue-Sat 1000-1600, Sun 1000-1600. **Toilets. For the disabled** toilets. **Shopping** gift shop. **Educational facilities** by prior arrangement. **Photography. Research** library, computer centre. **Staff opinion.**

■ FORTY HALL

Forty Hill, Enfield EN2 9HA.   Tel 363 8196
Admission free

It was in 1629 that Sir Nicholas Raynton, a wealthy haberdasher who was to become Lord Mayor of London, began his country seat, classical in style, four-square and handsome in red-brick with stone facings, just outside Enfield. After various vicissitudes it passed in 1951 to the care of Enfield Council, who restored it magnificently and maintain it so today. Before you enter, turn and survey the extraordinary view across the small lake, with its wildfowl, to what seems a limitless prospect of rural parkland. Yet miles of crowded north London are within little more than a stone's throw.

Within, you meet a series of fine rooms, distinguished by beautifully-restored Jacobean strap-work ceilings and finely-carved white-painted decorations. Fine clocks abound. In the **Raynton Room** Sir Nicholas himself, in skull-cap, ruff, gold-embroidered gloves and chains, looks down from over the attractively-painted fireplace. Note the handsome classical C18 open screen. Ascend the Staircase, pausing to view the giant Cedar of Lebanon framed in the window. Upstairs are more pieces of period furniture and, to the left, two rooms given over to a survey of packaging across the years, full of the instant nostalgia of the household everyday. The corner room, by the way, has by far the prettiest of all the house's ceilings. Other rooms contain items of local interest including early plastic products in Bakelite.

Forty Hall, across the lake.

The former stable buildings, redbrick around a spacious courtyard, contain an exhibition hall for temporary exhibitions, a banqueting hall available for receptions and an excellent cafeteria which also serves light lunches.

──────────── *the essentials* ────────────

BR Enfield Town (from Liverpool Street Station) then **Bus** 191, 231, W8. **Open** Tue-Sun Summer 1000-1800, Winter 1000-1700. **For the disabled** access to ground floor, toilets. **Refreshments** snacks. **Shopping** sales desk. **Photography. Visitors' services** guided tours by prior arrangement.

■ FREUD MUSEUM

20 Maresfield Gardens NW3 5SX.   Tel 435 2002
Admission *charge*

This Museum aims to celebrate one of the most influential figures of modern times. In 1938 Sigmund Freud (1856-1939), a refugee from Nazi-occupied Vienna, transferred his entire domestic and working environment to this house. He resumed work until his death here a year later. Freud's extraordinary collection of *Egyptian, Greek, Roman and Oriental antiquities*, his working library and papers, and his fine furniture including the *famous desk and couch*, are all here. These rooms were Freud's laboratory – the site of his discoveries about the human psyche – and they offer insights into the sources and nature of his achievements as the founder of psychoanalysis.

This beautiful, historic and dramatic environment was maintained and bequeathed by Anna Freud (1895-1982), whose pioneering development of her father's work is also represented. The museum is developing as a research archive, educational resource and cultural centre.

──────────── *the essentials* ────────────

Underground Finchley Road (Jubilee, Metropolitan Lines). **Open** Wed-Sun 1200-1700. **Toilets. Shopping** sales desk. **Publications. Visitors' services** archive films, guided tours, temporary exhibitions.

Freud Museum:

1. The famous couch; 2. Armchair; 3. Part of the rich library brought from Vienna;
4. Desk and collection of antiquities.

■ GEFFRYE MUSEUM

Kingsland Road E2 8EA. Tel 739 9893
Admission *free*

The Geffrye Museum,in the heart of London's East End,is a series of room settings displaying the style and artefacts of living in London from Elizabethan times to the 1930s, set in a row of early C18 almshouses. Its collections of furniture and woodwork, which are constantly being enriched, rival those in much better known institutions.

Sir Robert Geffrye was Lord Mayor of London in the last year of Charles II's reign, and he bequeathed money to build almshouses for the poor. In 1712 the site in Shoreditch was bought for £200, and the pretty terrace, with a chapel at its centre, was finished three years later. The almshouses were converted into a museum by the London County Council and opened as such in 1914. It is now run under the auspices of the Inner London Education Authority and educational activities are organised in connection with the collections.

The Geffrye is the least complicated of museums. After entering at the left-hand end, where there is a *Georgian Street* with real shopfronts and doorways, one walks the length of the terrace whose interior is arranged in a chronological series of room settings. But first, from the Georgian street, be sure to go into the woodworker's shop where his work room is arranged as if he were in the middle of turning a furniture leg on his primitive lathe, his other tools scattered about. Next is an open-hearth kitchen of the same period, cluttered with the many implements of C18 cooking.

The room settings start with an *Elizabethan Room* of about 1600, followed by a *Stuart Room* and so on through the reigns and styles of William and Mary, Queen Anne, the Georgian period, the Regency and Queen Victoria. At the end of the ground floor arrangements are the *Voysey Room*, an art nouveau family parlour of about 1900, and an area for temporary exhibitions. The newest arrangements are on the first floor, two rooms of the 1930s. Between the Queen Anne and Early Georgian Rooms is the original tiny chapel of the almshouses, now completely restored to its original appearance.

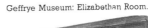
Geffrye Museum: Elizabethan Room.

The Geffrye is the educational museum at its best. Its scale is assimilable, its displays approachable, and its contents immediately apparent. Above all, it is welcoming and homely. (ST)

——————————————— *the essentials* ———————————————

Underground Bethnal Green (Central Line). **Open** Tue-Sat 1000-1700, Sun 1400-1700. **Toilets. For the disabled** access, toilets. **Refreshments** snacks. **Shopping** sales desk. **Publications. Photography** by arrangement. **Educational facilities. Visitors' services** guided tours by arrangement. **Research** library.

■ GIPSY MOTH IV

King William Walk, Greenwich SE10 9HT. Tel 858 3445
Admission *charge*

In this 54-foot ketch, minute compared to the 921-ton Cutty Sark nearby, Francis Chichester sailed single-handed round the world in 1966-7; a feat recognised by the Queen when she knighted him at Greenwich with the sword with which the first Elizabeth knighted Francis Drake. In these cramped quarters you see the ingenious design and sophisticated technology which made this epic one-man voyage possible. Such journeys are now almost commonplace, but Sir Francis was a pioneer, and his cockleshell vessel is still something to wonder at.

---
the essentials

BR Greenwich (from Charing Cross Station). **Boats** from Westminster or Tower Piers. **Open** May-Sept, Mon-Sat 1030-1800. **Photography.**

■ GORDON MUSEUM

Guy's Hospital, St Thomas' Street EC1 9RT.   Tel 955 4358
Admission *prior application*

The Museum is a collection of specimens illustrating all aspects of pathology with unique C19 wax models showing anatomic dissections, dermatological conditions and a few pathological conditions. There is also a small collection of historical instruments and the original specimens of Hodgkin, Bright, Addison and Gull. Access is restricted to the medical and ancillary professions.

---
the essentials

Underground London Bridge (Northern Line). **Open** Mon-Fri 0900-1700. **Photography** by special permission. **Research** medical personnel only.

■ GRANGE MUSEUM OF LOCAL HISTORY

Neasden Lane NW10 1QB.   Tel 452 8311
Admission *free*

The museum illustrates different aspects of past life in the Wembley, Kingsbury and Willesden areas, nowadays all part of the London Borough of Brent. Much of the material on display dates from the last hundred years or so, and shows how the area changed from countryside to suburban London., There are two period rooms — a *Victorian Parlour* and a *1930s Lounge* — and a complete *Edwardian draper's shop* from Willesden High Road.

The collections are particularly rich in domestic equipment, clothing and personal items, games and pastimes. The museum is increasingly collecting examples of local manufacture such as telephones and stamp vending machines made by Associated Automation, Smith's clocks, Dallmeyer lenses and packaging for locally produced food and drink. The collection also has what remains of the items assembled by George Titus Barham of Wembley and by the Wembley History Society with a large amount of material on the British Empire Exhibition held at Wembley in 1924-5.

New displays include a corner of a 1930s office, a selection from the fine collection of C19 and C20 ladies' clothing and accessories, and a section dealing with farming and gardening in the area, housed in the conservatory at the rear of the museum. Here a cottage garden has been recreated with herbs and old species of roses.

---
the essentials

Underground Neasden (Jubilee Line). **Open** Mon-Fri 1200-1700, Wed 1200-2000, Sat 1000-1700. **Toilets. Parking. For the disabled** limited access. **Shopping** sales desk. **Photography** on application. **Educational facilities. Visitors' services** lectures, guided tours for parties by prior arrangement. **Research** library.

■ GREENWICH BOROUGH MUSEUM

232 Plumstead High Street SE18 1JL. Tel 855 3240
Admission *free*

The present collecting policy of the museum covers the natural and human history of the London Borough of Greenwich. For historical reasons the collections have a strong bias towards the Woolwich and Plumstead areas, and towards natural history and archaeology. Some of these collections, notably butterflies, fossils, minerals, and shells, contain specimens from throughout the British Isles and other parts of the world. The archaeological collections

Greenwich Borough Museum: Woolwich kiln wares.

include important material from nearby Lesnes Abbey and from a complete C17 stoneware kiln site in Woolwich, the earliest of its kind so far discovered in Europe.

The Borough's archive and photography collections are held at the Woodlands Art Gallery (qv).

─────────────── *the essentials* ───────────────

BR Plumstead (from Charing Cross Station). **Open** Mon 1400-2000, Tue, Thur, Fri, Sat 1000-1300, 1400-1700. **For the disabled** access to first floor. **Shopping** sales desk. **Photography** by arrangement. **Educational facilities.**

■ GUARDS MUSEUM

Wellington Barracks, Birdcage Walk SW1E 6HQ.   Tel 930 4466 ext 3271
Admission *charge*

The Museum, in a purpose-built home beside Wellington Barracks, tells the story of the five Regiments of Foot Guards in peace and war, over almost 350 years, right up to the Falklands Campaign and it contains more than 30 chronologically arranged displays.

The almost frighteningly realistic tableau which greets the visitor on entry recreates a critical moment of the *Battle of Alma* (1854), the first of the Crimean War. The Colour Party of the First Battalion the Scots Fusilier Guards has been isolated, but stands firm with great bravery as a rallying point. The Queen's Colour is held aloft by Lieutenant R.J. Lindsay, who subsequently received the Victorian Cross. Other

Guards Museum: the Scots Guards Colours at the Battle of Alma (1854, Crimean War).

remarkable figures include a Musketeer with the 'Twelve Apostles' at the ready, and a Pikeman of the Coldstream Guards. A further reminder of Crimean courage is the 'pepperpot' revolver of Major G.I. Goodlake VC.

The section dealing with World War I (1914-18) underlines the grim fact that in the trenches the Brigade of Guards alone had 14,563 killed and 28,398 wounded. The World War II display includes personal mementoes such as the fur-lined flying jacket worn by Field Marshal Lord Alexander in Italy and North Africa.

—— *the essentials* ——

Underground St James's Park (Circle, District Lines). **Open** Mon-Thur, Sat-Sun 1000-1600.**Toilets. For the disabled** facilities. **Shopping.**

■ GUINNESS WORLD OF RECORDS

The Trocadero, Coventry Street W1V 7FA.   Tel 439 7331
Admission *charge*

The exhibition, a visual display of the world renowned 'Guinness Book of Records', brings together some of the more extraordinary and fascinating world records that are published in the book. The exhibits — which range from the tallest man to the smallest insect — are arranged like the book in various sections: the Animal Kingdom, Entertainment, the Human World and so on.

As soon as one enters the exhibition, one is immediately confronted with a wax model of the tallest man ever, Robert Wadlow. One can compare him with familiar objects such as a door and a table. Just next to him is the smallest lady ever — a dramatic contrast. Next is the world's heaviest man — another waxwork. He is placed on a scale, showing his weight in kilograms. There are similar scales nearby on which the public can match his weight.

In the next gallery the emphasis is still very much on human achievements. There are more waxworks on a rotating platform and visual displays to accompany these. There are some splendid life-size models of a Blue Whale's jaw and a man on 28-foot-high stilts. In the entertainments section there is a 1950s-style juke-box that plays five record-breaking singles. (FS)

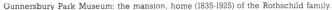

the essentials

Underground Piccadilly Circus (Bakerloo, Piccadilly Lines). **Open** daily 1000-2200. **Toilets. For the disabled** lifts. **Publications. Photography. Educational facilities.**

■ GUNNERSBURY PARK MUSEUM

Gunnersbury Park W3 8LQ.   Tel 992 1612
Admission *free*

This collection is predominantly locally orientated, with sections on archaeology, history, and topography. In the entrance hall is the Stanhope printing press, dating from 1804, and the earliest surviving example of its type. There is also an excellent transport display, including two *carriages* formerly owned by the Rothschild family,

Gunnersbury Park Museum: the mansion, home (1835-1925) of the Rothschild family.

a recently restored *Hansom cab*, a *tandem tricycle*, and a *motorcycle* dating from about 1899. As well as displaying items from its

Gunnersbury Park Museum: archaeological display.

own collection, the museum holds regular temporary exhibitions on a wide range of subjects including the work of local artists and crafts people. (IO)

Gunnersbury Park Museum: Posting chariot, C19.

the essentials

Underground Acton Town (District, Piccadilly Lines). **Open** Mar-Oct Mon-Fri 1300-1700, Sat-Sun 1400-1800, Nov-Feb Mon-Fri 1300-1600, Sat-Sun 1400-1600. **Toilets** in the Park. **Parking. For the disabled** access but help needed. **Refreshments** snacks. **Shopping** sales desk. **Publications. Photography** by appointment. **Educational facilities** by appointment. **Visitors' services** films, guided tours, lectures by prior arrangement.

■ HACKNEY MUSEUM

Central Hall, Mare Street E8 1HE.   Tel 986 6914
Admission *free*

This young museum reflects the history of Hackney, its growth from village to multiracial inner-city borough, and the origins, beliefs and activities of those who live and work there today. Fifteen exhibitions a year illustrate these themes, together with permanent displays which include Matchbox toys, workhouse boot buttons, a shop counter and a giant effigy of Sita.

──────────────── *the essentials* ────────────────
Underground Bethnal Green (Central Line). **Open** Tue-Fri 1000-1230, 1330-1700, Sat 1300-1700. **Toilets. For the disabled** access, toilets. **Shopping. Publications. Photography** no flash. **Educational facilities. Visitors' services** guided tours by arrangement. **Staff opinion.**

■ HAM HOUSE

Ham Street, Richmond TW10 7RS   Tel 940 1950
Admission *charge*

Ham House, from the gardens.

In 1678 the diarist John Evelyn wrote: 'The House is furnished like a great Prince's, the park with Flower Gardens, Orangeries, Groves, Avenues, Courts, Statues, Perspectives, Fountains, Aviaries and all this at the banks of the sweetest River in the World, must needs be admired'. His subject was Ham House, and it can be admired today much as it could 300 years ago. Owned by the National Trust but administered by the Victoria and Albert, Ham House was built on the Thames near Richmond, Surrey, in 1610, but now stands as it did when it was the home of the Duke and Duchess of Lauderdale during the reign of Charles II. Then, it was seen as the epitome of the avant-garde — it even had double-glazed windows — now it is a unique monument to Restoration Baroque taste. Inventories of the house survive and the interior has been restored as closely as possible to its pristine arrangements, with the furniture and pictures or appropriate substitutes from the V&A's own collections, placed in their original positions.

The *magnificent staircase*, which actually predates the Lauderdales

Ham House: The Great Hall.

by some 35 years but was of a style most popular in their day, is perhaps the centrepiece, and it has been completely regilded. Below, in the basement, the kitchen has been restored to precisely the way it would have looked as lunch was being prepared during the Duchess's time. At the other end of the social scale, and on the first floor, is the room prepared for the visit of Charles 1's queen, Henrietta Maria, and although it has not been possible to replace all the furniture as it was, there is a model. Not to be missed on the first floor is the **Cabinet of Miniatures**, formerly the servants' room, which has the finest *collection of miniature portraits* in the country outside the V&A including three by the Tudor master limners, Hilliard and Oliver; these portraits used to be on open display in the C17, but now the room has been made subtly secure. The walls of the house are covered with paintings by such artists as Lely, Van Dyck and Kneller.

The **gardens** which so delighted Evelyn have also been restored by the National Trust, with the beautiful *Cherry Garden* and the *Orangery* which is now partly a refreshment room. Tucked away among the outbuildings look for the *Ice House*, which was built in about 1800 as an early refrigerator. Entrance to the gardens is free. (ST).

──────────────── *the essentials* ────────────────

Underground Richmond (District Line) then **Bus** 65,71. **Open** Tue-Sun 1100-1700. **Toilets.** **Parking. For the disabled** access, toilets. **Refreshments** restaurant. **Shopping. Publications. Photography. Visitors' services** guided tours by arrangement.

■ HAMMERSMITH AND FULHAM LOCAL HISTORY COLLECTIONS

● Hammersmith Central Library, Shepherd's Bush Road W6 7AT.
  Tel 748 3020 ext 3812
● ● Fulham Library, 598 Fulham Road SW6 5NX.   Tel 748 3020 ext 3875
Admission *prior application*

Two Local History Collections, under the control of the Borough Archivist, are housed in two of the Borough's libraries. Each collection, administered by a Local History Librarian, contains books, maps, ephemera, photographs and paintings relating to the history of the two halves of the London Borough of Hammersmith and Fulham. The photographs and paintings are generally of topographical views of the borough. The ***photographic collections***, which span the period from the late 1860s to date, are housed at Hammersmith Central Library and Fulham Library and contain approximately 20,000 and 19,000 items respectively, including the work of Mrs Albert Broom, Sir Frank Short and Emery Walker.

Most of the framed ***paintings***, about 400 in all, are stored at Fulham Library where there is also a small collection of Fulham Pottery and pieces made by C.I.C. Bailey, the Martin Brothers and William De Morgan. The ***Cecil French Bequest***, given to Fulham in 1954, containing works by Burne-Jones, Lord Leighton, Waterhouse and Alma-Tadema is currently on loan to Leighton House (qv). The majority of the other paintings in the collections are by lesser-known local artists.

As there is no public access to either collection would-be visitors are advised to telephone in advance so that the items they wish to see (which are filed by subject eg bridges, Shepherd's Bush Green, churches, Fulham Broadway) can be quickly made available. Copies of many of the photographs can be supplied, orders normally taking 7-14 days to complete. (CB)

──────────────── *the essentials* ────────────────

Underground ● Hammersmith (District, Piccadilly Lines). ● ● Parsons Green (District Line). **Open** Mon, Tue, Thur 0915-1700, Sat 0915-1300, 1400-1700. **Shopping** sales desk. **Photography** by prior arrangement, charge. **Educational facilities** by prior arrangement. **Visitors' services** guided tour by prior arrangement.

■ HARROW MUSEUM AND HERITAGE CENTRE

Headstone Manor Recreation Ground, Pinner View, Harrow HA2 6PX.
Tel 861 2626
Admission *free*

In the early stages of an ambitious development scheme, its home is an impressive group of buildings. Headstone Manor itself stands islanded within a water-filled moat. A manor house in the Middle Ages when it belonged to the See of Canterbury, it became subsequently a farmhouse up until World War II. It contains a 1930s kitchen and sitting room and a display of bygone agricultural implements. Extensive restoration is in hand; across the moat the same applies to the frame of an attractive timber barn. Opposite is the magnificent *Great Barn* built in 1506. Used at present for events, special exhibitions and refreshments, it also houses Victorian roomsets destined in due course to go to the Manor House. When complete, the whole complex will recreate the former enclosed C19 farmyard. Meanwhile the Barn's majestic timbered interior justifies a visit.

──────────────── *the essentials* ────────────────

BR Headstone Lane (from Euston Station). **Open** Wed-Fri 1230-1700, Sat, Sun and Bank Holidays 1030-1700, closing at dusk in winter. **Toilets. Parking. Refreshments. Public telephones. For the disabled** facilities. **Publications. Photography. Visitors' services** lectures, talks by arrangement.

■ HARROW SCHOOL OLD SPEECH ROOM GALLERY

High Street, Harrow-on-the-Hill, Harrow HA1 3HP   Tel 869 1205
Admission *free*

The treasures of Sir Winston Churchill's old school include valuable books, natural history exhibits, assorted 'Harroviana' and major choice collections of antiquities. Note, especially, the C4 BC Apulian krater, the Ptolemaic mummy-case head, the pre-printing *Decretals* published at Mainz in 1473, the *'Vinegar' Bible* of 1717, and, most delicately beautiful, the C15 Rouen *Book of Hours*. The pictures include an oil of Venice by Sir Winston Churchill, a romantic portrait of Byron (an Old Harrovian) by the American W.E. West, one of John Sayer (also a pupil) by Romney and works by almost all the leading C19 watercolourists.

──────────────── *the essentials* ────────────────

Underground Harrow-on-the-Hill (Metropolitan Line). **Open** daily (except Wed) in termtime 1430-1700, during much of the school holidays Mon-Fri 1430-1700. **Shopping** sales desk. **Photography** no flash. **Educational facilities. Visitors' services** guided tours of Harrow School by prior arrangement.

Harrow School Old Speech Room Gallery: Greek vase collection.

HERALDS' MUSEUM

Tower of London, Tower Hill, EC3N 4AB. Tel 236 9857
Admission *free* (included in ticket to Tower of London).

The Heralds' Museum is the world's only sizeable museum entirely
devoted to heraldry. When it opened in 1980 the heralds were able

Heralds' Museum: a Herald in Coronation Uniform.

to show for the first time some of the magnificent collection which
they had built up over the centuries. Heraldry was first widely used
in Western Europe, on seals and shields, during the C12. The main
aim of the Museum is to explain in simple terms what heraldry is
all about, to show its development through the centuries, and to
display some of the best heraldic exhibits to be found in this
country. There are rolls and manuscripts. Brilliantly coloured
examples are exhibited, some dating back to Tudor times. Also
on show are weapons, helmets and pictures relating to jousts and
tournaments, at which the heralds once officiated.

Heraldry can be applied to almost any artefacts, so on show are
engraved glass and beautiful gold and silver from many centuries,
each exhibit being engraved or enamelled with the arms of its
owner. Textiles and porcelain feature as well, some dating back
to early times, some modern. Particular emphasis is laid on modern
examples to show that heraldry is very much alive today. Each year
part of the exhibition is changed to highlight various aspects of
heraldry.

The permanent exhibits include crowns and crests of past Knights of the Garter, carved in wood and then richly coloured and gilded and many shields painted with the arms of former Heralds. Adding even more colour are banners showing the arms of various famous men, and the figure of a herald in uniform. He stands complete with sword, hat, jewel and a tabard heavily embroidered with gold thread, as worn at the great Ceremonies of State, such as the Opening of Parliament. (SB)

---
the essentials

Underground Tower Hill (Circle, District Lines). **Open** Mon-Sat 0930-1745, Sun 1400-1730. **For the disabled** toilets within the Tower. **Refreshments** snacks within the Tower. **Shopping. Publications. Staff Opinion.**

■ HERITAGE MOTOR MUSEUM

Syon Park, Brentford TW8 8JF. Tel 560 1378
Admission *charge*

Approximately 120 historic cars are on view at any one time out of the approximately 300 vehicles owned by the British Motor Industry Heritage Trust. These represent nearly a century of British motoring. The earliest is a *3-Wheeled Wolseley* (1895) and other curiosities include early and record-breaking Jaguars and several interesting prototypes which never reached production.

Many famous names and types familiar to generations of motorists can be seen and closely inspected, ranging from the eminently practical and reliable mass-produced *Bullnose* Morris and Austin *Seven* of the 1920s to the more exotic Daimlers and Jaguars available only to the fortunate few. Among the other famous marques on show are examples produced by Lanchester, Morris, Austin, Daimler, Alvis, Leyland, Wolseley, Rover, Jaguar, MG, Riley, Standard and

Heritage Motor Museum

Triumph, a list of names some of which, unfortunately, have disappeared following the various amalgamations that have taken place over the years, but which fortunately can still be seen today in their original form if not always original condition. Among the most popular exhibits is the unique *Leyland Straight 8* (1927), *Jaguar D-Type* (1953), *MG Old No. 1* — the first one (1925) and *MG Record Breakers*.

These are only a fraction of the superbly restored and absorbing exhibits that are on display and such is the variety it would be difficult to highlight any particular model. Every taste is catered for whether it is racing, technical development or coachwork, equipment used in servicing and other motoring memorabilia. No commercial vehicles are on show at Syon Park. These are held at the British Commercial Vehicle Museum, Leyland, Lancs, Tel (0772) 45101.

─────────── *the essentials* ───────────
Underground Gunnersbury (District Line) then **Bus** 237,267. **Open** daily Mar-Oct 1000-1730, Nov-Feb 1000-1600. **Toilets. Parking. Public telephones. For the disabled** access. **Shopping** bookshop. **Visitors' services** by prior arrangement

■ HOGARTH'S HOUSE

Hogarth Lane, Great West Road W4 2QN.   Tel 994 6757
Admission *free*

Now situated on a busy main road, this 'little country box by the Thames' was chosen by the painter William Hogarth (1697-1764) because of its quiet location. He lived there from 1749 until his death. The collection consists mainly of engravings, including his most famous series *A Harlot's Progress, Marriage à la Mode,* and *Industry and Idleness.* Other items include a wooden box in which he is reputed to have kept his engraving tools, and two lead urns that used to be by the front gate, and were given to Hogarth by the actor David Garrick. The garden is attractive and still contains a mulberry tree dating from Hogarth's time. (IO)

Hogarth's House: interior.

─────────── *the essentials* ───────────
Underground Turnham Green (District Line). **Open** Apr-Sept Mon, Wed-Sat 1100-1800, Sun 1400-1800 (Sept closed first 2 weeks), Oct-Mar Mon, Wed-Sat 1000-1600, Sun 1400-1600 (Dec closed last 3 weeks). **For the disabled** access to ground floor only. **Shopping** sales desk. **Publications. Photography. Visitors' services** guided tours on request.

■ HORNIMAN MUSEUM

London Road, Forest Hill SE23 3PQ. Tel 699 2339
Admission *free*

How is a Navajo sand painting made? What is a sarrusophone? Who was Punch? These were the sort of questions which fascinated the Victorian tea magnate Frederick Horniman throughout his extensive travels especially in what we now know as the Third World.

He made natural history collections to start with, and kept them in his house at Forest Hill. They grew, and he began to invite friends and acquaintances to have private views of them, which were so successful that he decided to open his collections to the public. But they had grown too big for the house, and even for the one next door too, and on their site he built his impressive art nouveau museum in 1897, presenting it to London four years later, answering all the above questions and thousands more.

The Horniman is divided into three sections: ethnography, musical instruments and natural history. The ***ethnographic displays*** are perhaps the most fascinating, tracing man's development through his arts and crafts. The sand painting, which must not be missed, was made in the museum by an actual Navajo medicine man, but of particular interest in the permanent display is the section dedicated to the Egyptians, with mummies and an actual grave dating from 3000BC and reassembled exactly as it was found.

The world-class collection of 6,000 ***musical instruments*** from every continent contains both folk and art instruments including, from Europe, the renowned Dolmetsch and Carse Collections. You can now also listen to the instruments on a Soundline Walkman guide.

The huge ***natural history section*** is dominated by a mighty walrus, almost as big as a small car, and the live exhibits in the extensive aquarium and vivarium almost require a separate visit to do it justice.

The Horniman has a great many educational activities, and there can be few South London school children for whom it has not been part of school life. A colourful new guide includes ideas on things to do as well as a full-size mask to cut out. There are also short courses, lectures and workshops for adults as well as an extensive ***Library***.

Horniman Museum: the Walrus, mounted in 1870 and part of the collection since 1893.

Horniman Museum: Figure of a priest, painted wood C18, Japan; Topeng dance mask from Java, late C19.

─────────────── *the essentials* ───────────────
BR Forest Hill (from Charing Cross Station). **Open** Mon-Sat 1030-1800, Sun 1400-1800. **Cloakroom. Toilets. For the disabled** access, toilets. **Refreshments** snacks. **Shopping. Photography** no flash. **Educational facilities. Visitors' services** lectures, films. **Research** library.

■ HUNTERIAN MUSEUM

Royal College of Surgeons of England, Lincoln's Inn Fields WC2A 3PN.
Tel 405 3474
Admission *prior application*

The museum is not just a collection of anatomical teaching specimens; it shows development from the simplest organisms to the most highly developed animals. When John Hunter, an outstanding research surgeon and teacher, died in 1793 there were nearly 14,000 items in his private collection comprising normal structure and pathological specimens, fossils, stuffed animals and undissected materials. This passed into the safekeeping of the Company of Surgeons (later the Royal College of Surgeons), who twice enlarged the viewing area to accommodate additional material. The collections illustrate Hunter's views on aspects of comparative anatomy, physiology and pathology including the results of his experiments. There are three main sections. One includes examples of how the body can adapt or compensate for accidental damage or environmental changes. Another section deals with changes caused by disease, accident or congenital deformities and the third illustrates reproduction, development of the human foetus and multiple births.

Also on display are the skeleton of a tall man (7ft 8in), a small dwarf (21″ only) and those of some of the most infamous convicted murderers of the C19, the results of anatomical experiments, and early experiments in transplants and grafts. It must be emphasised that access is by written application to the Curator only, and restricted to the medical and ancillary professions, veterinary surgeons and biologists.

─────────────── *the essentials* ───────────────
Underground Holborn (Central, Piccadilly Lines). **Open** Mon-Fri 1000-1700 (closed Aug). **For the disabled** limited access. **Shopping** sales desk. **Publications.**

■ IMPERIAL WAR MUSEUM

Lambeth Road SE1 6HZ. Tel 735 8922
Admission *charge*

The Imperial War Museum is a unique institution concerned with the story of war in our century. Founded in 1917, the museum's terms of reference now extend to all conflicts involving British or Commonwealth troops from 1914 to the present day. Military exhibits such as aircraft, tanks, artillery, medals and equipment are central to the museum but there are also extensive collections of works of art, photographs, documents, books, film and sound recordings illustrating land, sea and air warfare and life on the home front.

The past ten years have seen a major expansion of the museum with the acquisition and development of three outstations. In 1976, Duxford Airfield, a former Battle of Britain fighter station, first opened regularly to the public. Now an important regional and national attraction, Duxford houses well over 80 aircraft along with many other exhibits ranging from armoured fighting vehicles to a midget submarine. In 1978 the museum assumed responsibility for maintenance of the cruiser HMS Belfast (qv), the first warship since the Victory to be preserved for the nation. In 1984 the Prime Minister Mrs Margaret Thatcher opened the restored Cabinet War Rooms (qv).

Innovative displays film, sound recordings and state-of-the-art interactive video technology, and a wealth of exhibits tell thematically the story of C20 conflict.

Imperial War Museum, with massive 15″ guns from the battleships Ramillies and Resolution.

The spectacular *Large Exhibits Gallery* offers dramatic views of more than fifty of the museum's most historically significant large items – the Sopwith 'Camel' veteran of dogfight-days above the

Imperial War Museum: The Large Exhibits Gallery.

Western Front; its successor the 'Spitfire', the P51D 'Mustang', FW190; 'Churchill', 'Sherman', 'Grant' and 'Jagdpanther' tanks; a Biber submarine and an Italian human torpedo; V1 and V2 weapons, and 'Thunderbird' and 'Polaris' missiles. Computerized lighting enhances the display's visual drama, and interactive videos around the gallery provide archive film footage of many exhibits.

Providing more detailed background information are audio-visual displays on general topics like the Battles of Britain and the Atlantic, the Eastern Front and missiles and rocket weaponry.

The Blitz experience recreates what it was like to be caught in the street in an air raid. The ground shakes, smoke fills the air and even the smell is authentic and convincing. Yet another 'experience' awaits the visitor as a 'Tommy' in the Flanders trenches of the First World War.

A glimpse of how a British C-in-C in the field lived and worked in World War II is found in the three campaign caravans used by Field Marshal Viscount Montgomery of Alamein in the Western Desert and North-east Europe.

Perhaps unexpectedly, this is one of London's most important sources for British C20 art, with works by Kennington, Paul Nash, Epstein, Sutherland, Piper, Topoloski and many more. In all, the *Department of Art* holds over 10,000 paintings, drawings, prints and sculptures in what is one of the foremost collections of British art in the world, and some 50,000 posters.

The *Department of Documents* is a repository for documentary records of all types relating to war in this century, mainly British private papers and captured foreign documents. The *Department of Exhibits and Firearms* is responsible for the museum's three-dimensional objects including uniforms, badges, medals, edged weapons, models, aircraft, boats, artillery and military vehicles. It also administers the National Collection of Modern Firearms. The *Department of Film* is one of the oldest film archives in the world with a library of more than forty million feet of film ranging from cartoons and feature films to documentaries, newsreel and unedited footage. The *Department of Photographs* is a national archive of over five million prints and negatives. The *Department of Sound Records* was set up in 1972 to collect historic sound recordings. The museum offers a wide range of educational activities for school and college groups including film shows, illustrated talks, lectures, study days, theatre in education productions, sixth form conferences, in-service courses for teachers and worksheets. Free public film shows and gallery talks are normally held at weekends and during school holidays. Programmes are available on request.

——————————————— *the essentials* ———————————————
Underground Lambeth North (Bakerloo Line). **Open** daily 1000-1800. **Cloakroom. Toilets. Public telephones. For the disabled** access, toilets. **Refreshments** licensed café. **Shopping** bookshop. **Publications. Photography** restricted. **Educational facilities. Visitors' services** films and gallery talks. **Research** library.

■ INDIA OFFICE LIBRARY AND RECORDS
197 Blackfriars Road SE1 8NG.   Tel 928 9531
Admission *free* (Prints and Drawings by appointment only)

Now part of the British Library (qv) this is one of the world's oldest and most important research institutions, with its origin in the records of the great East India Company. It holds a huge mass of material relating mainly to the Indian sub-continent and the history and culture of South East Asia with printed books, manuscripts, paintings, prints, drawings and photographs, as well as the official archives of the East India Company. Of the 28,000 *oriental manuscripts* many are of great scholastic and artistic value (including the recorded dreams of Tipu Sultan of Mysore).

Much of the Library's *collection of newspapers and periodicals* is also of historical interest, with many rare and unique titles and particularly good coverage of the C19. There is an unrivalled collection of drawings by British artists in India and the East and Persian and Indian miniatures. The large *photography collection* includes the Curzon albums. Some sculpture and antique furniture is also held.

India Office Library and Records: Lord and Lady Curzon, Hyderabad, 1902, from the Curzon albums.

───────────────────── the essentials ─────────────────────
Underground Blackfriars (Circle, District Lines), Waterloo (Bakerloo, Northern Lines). **Open** Mon-Fri 0930-1745, Sat 0930-1245. **Cloakroom. Toilets. For the disabled** access, lift, extra help available by prior arrangement. **Refreshments** vending machines. **Visitors' services** linguistic aid. **Research** library. **Staff opinion.**

■ INNS OF COURT AND CITY YEOMANRY MUSEUM

10 Stone Buildings, Lincoln's Inn WC2A 3TG.   Tel 405 8112
Admission *prior application*

The Museum's collection covers the period 1798 to today and comprises weapons, uniforms, equipment, medals, photographs and drums of the two former Regiments which go to make up the Inns of Court & City Yeomanry.

The two former Regiments were the Inns of Court Regiment (Devil's Own), formerly the Inns of Court Rifle Volunteers, and the City of London Yeomanry (the Rough Riders). The origins of the Inns of Court Regiment date back to the Napoleonic Wars, whilst the City of London Yeomanry was raised primarily out of soldiers who served with the Imperial Yeomanry during the Boer War. (R J BG)

───────────────────── the essentials ─────────────────────
Underground Chancery Lane (Central Line). **Open** Mon-Fri. **Toilets. Public telephones.**

■ IVEAGH BEQUEST

Kenwood, Hampstead Lane NW3 7JR.   Tel 348 1286
Admission *free*

Kenwood is London's very own 'stately home'. High on the northern ridge of Hampstead Heath, it owes its present aspect to William Murray, 1st Earl of Mansfield, who commissioned Robert Adam to re-model the house, and design for it interior decorations and furnishings. But for its public ownership today and for its priceless collection of Old Master paintings we must thank Edward Cecil Guinness, 1st Earl of Iveagh, who saved the Kenwood estate from speculators in 1925, and gave it to London.

Iveagh Bequest: the south front of Kenwood House, overlooking the park. Orangery on the left, Library on the right.

The house is full of treasures. Consider the paintings, which would adorn any national gallery — the deeply moving Rembrandt late *Self-Portrait*, Gainsborough's resplendent *Lady Howe*, Vermeer's coolly atmospheric *Guitar Player*, what might be called Hals's other laughing cavalier *Pieter van den Broeke*, and Bols's *Portrait of a Woman*, fine-drawn of face and ruff and 'snapped' in mid-sentence. Around stand examples of the very finest English C18 furniture, and almost every window presents a view to savour. In recent years Kenwood received some important gifts: over 1,200 *shoe buckles*, mainly C18, from Lady Maufe; part of Mrs Anne Hull Grundy fine collection of *C18 and C19 jewellery*, and a selection from E E Cook collection, notably four oil paintings by Angelica Kauffmann.

Mansfield was a friend of the poet Pope, and as Lord Chief Justice he ruled the law unchallenged for thirty-two years. His tolerance towards the disadvantaged Catholics earned him the hatred of the mob, who burned down his house. Kenwood escaped because the host of the Spaniards Inn nearby served the rioters so generously that their enthusiasm for fire-raising was doused along with their thirst! It was natural that this Scottish law-lord should employ another Scot, the young Robert Adam, lately back from Italy and almost at the peak of his fame, to up-date Kenwood in the latest taste. The great glory of Adam's Kenwood is unquestionably the *Library*, an astonishing masterpiece and one of the most successfully preserv-

1		Iveagh Bequest:
2	3	1. Rembrandt, Self-portrait; 2. Gainsborough, Mary Countess Howe; 3. The Library.

ed of all Adam interiors. You will marvel at its richness of colour, its perfection of detail and its precisely-judged proportions. Note the library steps, a triumph of practical cabinet-making which folds completely into a equally useful table.

The adjoining **Coach House** offers refreshments alongside the massive *Iveagh Family Coach*, and in fine weather in the secluded garden. In summer Sunday lunches are served in the **Old Kitchen**. There are recitals and chamber concerts in the **Orangery** and open-air symphony concerts in an idyllic lakeside setting of gently-sloping lawns.

───────────────── *the essentials* ─────────────────

Underground Golders Green (Northern Line) then **Bus** 210. **Open** daily Apr-Sept 1000-1900; Oct, Feb, Mar 1000-1700; Nov-Jan 1000-1600. **Cloakroom. Toilets. Parking. For the disabled** access, toilets. **Refreshments** restaurant, snacks. **Shopping. Publications. Photography** on application. **Educational facilities. Visitors' services** lectures, guided tours by arrangement.

■ JEWISH MUSEUM

Woburn House, Upper Woburn Place WC1H 0EP. Tel 388 4525
Admission *free*

Few peoples have a cultural and historical heritage to rival the Jewish in richness and diversity. This is abundantly evident in this collection which, though small, is full of interest and fine craftsmanship. You will hardly overlook the *Ark*, C16, intricately carved and gilden in Venice to contain the Scrolls of the Law. Around are all kinds of ceremonial objects, and *Sabbath lamps* hang from the ceiling. There are pieces of fine *silverwork,* C17 and C18 *candlesticks,* and majolica *Passover dishes.* Note the *Lord Mayor's Salver* (1702), the C8 *gold plaque,* Byzantine with a Greek inscription, and the collection of *marriage contracts* and *wedding rings.* There are many

Jewish Museum: Hanukah lamp, Polish, c1840.

nd varied tokens of the contribution made by the Jews to Britain's history and development.

─────────── *the essentials* ───────────

Underground Euston (Northern, Victoria Lines), Russell Square (Piccadilly Line). **Open** Summer Tue-Fri 1000-1600, Sun 1000-1245, Winter Fri, Sun 1000-1245. **For the disabled** access. **Shopping. Visitors' services** guided tours for groups by appointment, audio-visual programme.

■ DR JOHNSON'S HOUSE
17 Gough Square EC4A 3DE.   Tel 353 3745
Admission *charge*

The only surviving house of the many where Dr Samuel Johnson (1709-84), lexicographer and scholar, lived in London. It was in this house, built about 1700, that Johnson lived while he was writing his English Dictionary and The Rambler. Most of the objects in the house are connected with Johnson or his great biographer Boswell, including a fine ***collection of portrait prints.*** More unusual items on display are: Sir Joshua Reynolds's china *tea caddy, dish and saucer,* a pair of iron *sugar tongs* belonging to Dr Johnson, and *Johnson's will.* Particularly worth seeing is the *first edition of the Dictionary,* and the garret where it was written. The house is the only one of the period left in this part of London and is pleasantly peaceful compared to the noise and bustle of the city that surrounds it. (IO)

Dr Johnson's House: Miss Williams' Room.

─────────── *the essentials* ───────────

Underground Chancery Lane (Central Line), Blackfriars, Temple (Circle, District Lines). **Open** Mon-Sat, May-Sept 1100-1730, Oct-Apr 1100-1700. **Shopping** sales desk. **Publications** in several languages. **Photography** on application, charge.

■ KATHLEEN AND MAY

St Mary Overy Dock, Cathedral Street SE1 9DE. Tel 403 3965
Admission *charge*

This is the last surviving West Country wooden top-sail schooner. She was built at the beginning of this century near Chester for Mr John Coppack and named Lizzie May after his daughters. For many years she was employed as a general cargo carrier, being sold in 1908 to an Irish owner who renamed her Kathleen and May. The vessel was the first acquisition by the Maritime Trust, which was able to secure the ship thanks to the generosity of Sir Yue-Kong Pao, a wealthy Hong Kong shipowner, who donated £100,000. She was moved to her present berth in 1985.

The wooden top-sail schooner Kathleen and May.

---
the essentials

Underground London Bridge (Northern Line). **Open** daily 1000-1700. **Shopping** sales desk. **Publications. Photography. Visitors' services** exhibition on board.

■ KEATS HOUSE

Keats Grove NW3 2RR.   Tel 435 2062
Admission *free*

The home of the poet John Keats (1795-1821), it was originally built as a pair of semi-detached houses and from 1818 to 1820 Keats occupied the eastern house. He became engaged to Fanny Brawne whose family rented the house next door, and while here he wrote most of his greatest poetry. In 1838 the actress Eliza Chester acquired the houses, converted them into one, and added the fine drawing room. The house retains much of its original character despite extensive restoration. It was opened to the public in 1925 on the 130th anniversary of Keats's birth. The interior is decorated and furnished in the Regency style. Included in the displays are one of *Keats's love letters* to Fanny Brawne and the engagement ring which she wore until her death. The house is set in a pleasant **garden**, and it was under a plum tree here that Keats wrote the 'Ode to a Nightingale'.

Keats House: John Keats, by Joseph Severn.

the essentials

Underground Belsize Park, Hampstead (Northern Line). **Open** Mon-Sat 1000-1300, 1400-1800, Sun 1400-1700. **Toilets. Shopping. Publications. Photography. Educational facilities** limited. **Visitors' services** films, lectures, guided tours by prior arrangement. **Research** library

■ KEW BRIDGE STEAM MUSEUM

Green Dragon Lane, Kew Bridge Road TW8 0IN.   Tel 568 4757
Admission *charge*

Steam and water are the themes of the museum. Located next to the Thames, the site has been a pumping station since the early 1800s and contains the finest collection of **Cornish beam engines** in the world. These massive engines, developed for pumping out water in Cornwall's tin and copper mines, were ideally suited for

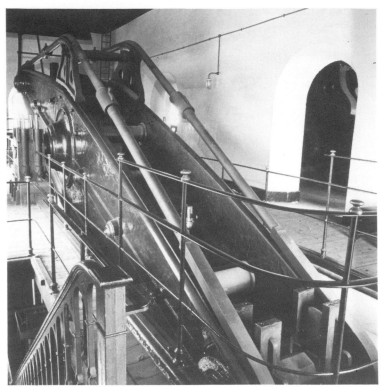

Kew Bridge Engines Trust: 90″ Cornish Beam Engines.

pumping London's drinking water. They performed efficiently and reliably for over a century, the last until 1945, and six are regularly demonstrated, under steam, as working examples. Several types can be seen including the famous *Harvey & Co 100-inch Engine* which started operations in 1871 and the 1910 *Hawthorn Davey triple expansion engine* commonly used as well for ship propulsion.

Apart from the stationary engines there are many water supply relics including a water main made of hollowed-out tree trunks, an early water meter and a pendulum counter to record the number of strokes made by a beam engine which determined payments due to Boulton and Watt, manufacturers of the engine. A 2ft gauge steam railway is in operation and gives rides. An additional delight for the steam enthusiast is a collection of steamboats, the most famous being the *Consuta,* a high-speed launch built in 1898, which became a familiar sight at the Oxford and Cambridge annual boat races and the Henley Royal Regatta when it was used by John Snagge, the BBC commentator on these events. Also often on view and fully restored is *Eva,* built for carrying umpires at the Henley Regatta from 1874.

Full-time museum staff and volunteers have specialist knowledge on all aspects concerned with steam and the handling and care of steam machinery. Lectures can be arranged for societies and educational establishments interested in steam and records of

:ngines and other related machinery can be consulted on application.

───────────────── *the essentials* ─────────────────

BR Kew Bridge (from Waterloo Station). **Open** daily (steaming at weekends) 1100-1700. **Toilets. Parking. For the disabled** limited access. **Refreshments** tea room. **Shopping** bookshop. **Publications. Photographs. Educational facilities. Visitors' services** guided tours by arrangement. **Research** by arrangement. **Staff opinion.**

■ KINGSTON UPON THAMES MUSEUM AND HERITAGE CENTRE

Fairfield West, Kingston-upon-Thames KT1 2PS.   Tel 546 5386
Admission *free*

Formed in 1980 to unify the Borough's archives, museum, archaeological and local history collections, Kingston Heritage also has a role in the promotion of visual arts by providing facilities for temporary exhibitions. It is concerned with the preservation and promotion of material of historical interest and provides an information service for tourists. Here is the ***Muybridge Photographic Collection***, of international significance. Eadweard Muybridge (1830-1904) won fame in the USA as a pioneer photographer of movement. He was born and died in Kingston, and to the town he bequeathed the *zoopraxiscope*, a moving-picture projector, and other material. Another important collection is art pottery of the late C19 and early C20, particularly *Martinware*. In the first-floor gallery is a display of local history and prehistory. Displays are changed from time to time to show different aspects of local life and what is not on show can be seen by special arrangement.

Kingston upon Thames Museum: Muybridge's zoopraxiscope.

The Borough **Archives** cover more than eight centuries of local administration. Among the records are *King John's Charter* (1209), *World War II log books*, financial and judicial reports dating from the C15 and much more. Local history interests are catered for by a wealth of books, pamphlets, Ordnance Survey maps, plans and illustrations. There is an unbroken file of local newspapers dating from 1954.

───────────────── *the essentials* ─────────────────

BR Kingston (from Waterloo Station). **Open** Mon-Sat 1000-1700. **Parking. For the disabled** access. **Shopping** sales desk. **Photography. Visitors' services** lectures, guided tours by arrangement. **Research** library.

■ LAMBETH PALACE AND LIBRARY

Lambeth Palace Road SE1 7JU. Tel 928 8282
Admission *prior application*

The Palace has been the London home of the Archbishops of Canterbury for nearly eight hundred years. In addition to many features of great historical interest, the visitor will find here an important collection of ***portraits of former Archbishops*** painted by leading artists of the day. The C17 and C18 archbishops' portraits hang on the walls of the **Guard Room**; the most notable are Lely's painting of *Sheldon*, Sir Godfrey Kneller's portrait of *Tillotson*, George Romney's of *Moore* and that by Sir Joshua Reynolds of *Secker*. A portrait of particular interest is that of *Laud* which is said to have been presented to the Archbishop by Sir Anthony van Dyck. It hung in his study in his lifetime, and on an October day during the troubled year of 1640 it fell to the ground, where Laud discovered it and noted in his diary his fear that this might be an ill-omen. He was right: shortly afterwards he was imprisoned in the Tower and later executed. Those who study the various pictures carefully will notice how the 'Canterbury Caps' worn by Laud and other C17 Archbishops, gave way in the C18 to wigs, indicating the changing fashions of the Church of England during these periods. Other portraits are to be found in the **Picture Gallery** and Great Corridor.

The other important collection is that of ***books and manuscripts*** which are housed in Lambeth Palace Library. The **Library** came into being as the result of a bequest of Archbishop Bancroft when he died in 1610. Since that time it has grown into a great national library, comprising some 3,500 volumes of manuscripts and 150,000 printed books, as well as papers and diaries belonging to well-known personalities of English history. Among its priceless treasures are the famous *Lambeth Bible* of about 1150 with superb illustrations such as that of the Tree of Jesse in rich hues of gold, blue, pink and green at the beginning of the Old Testament prophecy of Isaiah; a fine edition of Sir Thomas More's *Utopia*; King Henry VIII's treatise against Martin Luther which earned him the title of 'Defender of the Faith', complete with notes made by Archbishop Cranmer. But above all, Lambeth Palace Library is a place where scholars can study its unrivalled collection of records of the Church of England which include an almost complete sequence of registers of Archbishops of Canterbury from the late C13, as well as books and documents in its possession relating to other Christian communities overseas.

One must bear in mind that Lambeth Palace is a residence and also a busy office, and as such is open only to visitors by prior arrangement with the Bursar. The Library is open to bona fide students after they have produced a letter of introduction. Special permission is necessary for access to certain categories of manuscripts. (GH)

───────────────────────── *the essentials* ─────────────────────────

Underground Lambeth North (Bakerloo Line). **Open** ☐ Palace: Wed or Thur afternoons by arrangement with the Bursar. ☐ Library: Mon-Fri 1000-1700. **Cloakroom. Toilets. Shopping** sales desk. **Publications.**

■ LEIGHTON HOUSE

12 Holland Park Road W14 8LZ. Tel 602 3316
Admission *free*

This is one of the earliest examples of a purpose-built studio house of the Victorian age open to the public. It was the home of the highly successful painter Lord Leighton (1803-96), for the last thirty years of his life. It is the result of the collaboration between Leighton and the architect George Aitchison (1825-1910). The most spectacular room in the house is the **Arab Hall**, based on drawings of Moorish halls in Spain done by Aitchison; it combines tiles and carvings from the east with work by C19 artists, particularly the *mosaic frieze* by Walter Crane.

The collection includes *furniture, ceramics* and important *paintings* by Leighton and his contemporaries, and has recently been augmented by the **Cecil French Bequest**. This includes 53 works of art by well-known pre-C20 artists executed in oils, watercolour, chalk, pencil and other media and is part of the Hammersmith and

Leighton House: the Arab Hall.

Fulham Local History Collections (qv). The large **garden** is open from March to September, and contains examples of Leighton's *sculpture*, including his most important work, the *Athlete Wrestling with a Python*. (IO)

───────────────── *the essentials* ─────────────────

Underground High Street Kensington (Circle, District Lines). **Open** Mon-Sat 1100-1700 (until 1800 Mon-Fri during exhibitions). **Cloakroom. Toilets. For the disabled** access. **Shopping** sales desk. **Publications. Photography** by prior arrangement. **Visitors' services** guided tours by prior arrangement.
──

■ LINLEY SAMBOURNE HOUSE

18 Stafford Terrace W8 7BH.   Tel 937 0663
Admission *charge*

The home from the early 1870s of the 'Punch' political cartoonist Edward Linley Sambourne. This Victorian terraced house has been perfectly preserved in every detail to give a clear picture of upper-middle class artistic life at the end of the nineteenth century. Even

Linley Sambourne House: the Drawing Room.

nough few of the items are of great note, the comprehensive nature of the display which fills almost every room, from the well-furnished downstairs lavatory to the overcrowded drawing room, gives an unusual air of domesticity to the house. The walls are covered with a large number of photographs, and drawings by Linley Sambourne and other artists such as Kate Greenaway. The house provides a fascinating contrast with the grandeur of nearby Leighton House (qv). (IO)

──────────── *the essentials* ────────────

Underground High Street Kensington (Circle, District Lines). **Open** Mar-Oct Wed 1000-1600, Sun 1400-1700, parties at other times by arrangement.

■ LLOYD'S NELSON COLLECTION

Lloyd's of London, Lime Street EC3M 7HA.   Tel 623 7100
Admission *prior application*

Lloyd's connection with Lord Nelson dates back to 1798 when the merchant underwriters who traded there subscribed the then very large sum of £38,436 for the wounded and dependants of men killed at the Battle of the Nile. Nelson received a personal tribute in the shape of an extensive silver dinner service, some of which is in the collection together with pieces similarly acquired by him after the Battle of Copenhagen. The tradition at Lloyd's of rewarding gallantry in action began in Nelson's time and several other magnificent pieces of silver presented to sea officers have been added to the collection over the years. The naval victories of the Napoleonic war, principally Trafalgar, saw the award of many *silver vases* and *presentation swords* by Lloyd's Patriotic Fund (founded 1803), several of which are displayed. An interesting sword on show is that awarded by the City of London to Thomas Masterman Hardy for his gallant conduct as flag captain to Nelson on board HMS Victory at Trafalgar. This sword, which is of a unique design unlike the usual City presentation pieces was acquired in 1979 when it was presented to the Nelson Collection by insurance broking firms placing business at Lloyd's.

In addition to the silver and swords there are many *letters from Nelson,* mostly in his well-known left-handed script, though one was written a few days before he lost his right arm at Teneriffe in July 1797. A rare exhibit is *Nelson's Collar of the Order of the Bath* which, by special dispensation from the Crown, remained in his

Lloyd's Nelson Collection: silver gilt buckle from a Patriotic Fund sword-belt.

family's possession until 1932 when it was presented to Lloyd'.
Another feature of the collection is the *log book of HMS Euryalus*
This not only describes the daily routine of a frigate in Nelson's
fleet but contains a unique eye-witness account of Trafalgar by her
navigating officer, Frederick Ruckert, who also records receiving
Nelson's famous signal 'England expects that every man will do
his duty'. (TA)

―――――――――――――― *the essentials* ――――――――――――――

Underground Bank (Central, Northern Lines). **Open** Mon-Fri 1000-1630. **Cloakroom.**
Toilets. For the disabled lift, toilets. **Shopping** bookshop. **Publications. Photography**
by prior arrangement. **Educational facilities. Visitors' services** guided tours by prior
arrangement. **Research** by prior arrangement. **Staff opinion** by prior arrangement.

■ LONDON CAB COMPANY MUSEUM

1/3 Brixton Road SW9 6DJ.   Tel 735 7777
Admission *free*

It contains an interesting selection of some of the motor taxi cabs
that have circulated around the streets of London since 1904. The
oldest example is a *Unic* of 1907 vintage which was not withdrawn
from service until 1931. The 1932 *Beardmore* was the first taxi cab
to be fitted with front wheel brakes, while the 1938 *Austin* on show
is the first with an illuminated roof sign. The *Austin FX3* Diesel had
a relatively short life (from 1948 to 1958) and retained the open space
beside the driver, a once common feature of British taxis. There
are two post-war Beardmores on show, the later model, of which
only 49 were built before the company went into liquidation, having four doors. The extremely ugly 1967 fibreglass *Winchester*
made with Ford mechanical components is quite rare. A prototype
Metro (1969), by Cammell Laird Shipbuilders, was not put into production. The design incorporated controversial forward-hinged
passenger doors and a body constructed of fibre-glass and balsa
wood. Another prototype, this time by Lucas Electric (1975-6), was
powered by batteries and electric motors.

―――――――――――――― *the essentials* ――――――――――――――

Underground Oval (Northern Line). **Open** Mon-Fri 0900-1700, Sat 0900-1400. **Toilets.**
Public telephones. Photography. Visitors' services guided tours by arrangement.

■ LONDON DUNGEON

28/34 Tooley Street SE1 2SZ.   Tel 403 0606
Admission *charge*

It aims to present an accurate recreation of the often harsh realities
of life in times past. The effect, it must be admitted, is one of
unredeemed horror and bloodthirstiness, and is certainly not for the
squeamishly-inclined. On the outside of the building there are large
wall paintings. Once one enters, one is immediately plunged into
another era. The inside is lit by candles and in the entrance are
skulls and a skeleton. The exhibits are placed in chronological
order. All are accompanied by detailed descriptions.

A *Druid* sacrifices a victim on Stonehenge; *Boudicca* spears a
Roman soldier to death; *St George* is having his flesh rent. A
description of *Thomas Becket's* untimely death is astounding in its
detail. There is also a comprehensive survey of gruesome tortures of
the past. You witness the beheading of *Anne Boleyn* – one of Henry

VIII's wives. The horror of the *Great Plague* (1665) is shown by a room filled with stricken victims. Most of the exhibits are based on fact or myth. All are vividly represented – some are unsuitable for young children.

──────────────────── *the essentials* ────────────────────
Underground London Bridge (Northern Line). **Open** daily Apr-Sept 1000-1630, Oct-Mar 1000-1630. **Toilets. For the disabled** access, toilets. **Refreshments** snacks. **Shopping. Publications. Photography.**

■ LONDON GAS MUSEUM
British Gas plc, Twelvetrees Crescent, Bromley-by-Bow E3 3JH.
Tel 987 2000 ext 3344
Admission *prior application*

Starting with the foundation of the Gas-Light and Coke Co in 1812 the Museum explains and illustrates the evolution of an industry which changed the whole pattern of domestic life. It shows how gas was produced first from coal and then, more recently, from North Sea resources. The display includes examples down the years of fires, lighting equipment, meters, even a gas fan-heater and a waffle-maker. There are sections devoted to working conditions in the industry and gas in wartime.

──────────────────── *the essentials* ────────────────────
Underground Bromley-by-Bow (District Line). **Open** Mon-Fri 0930-1230, 1400-1600. **Cloakroom. Toilets. Parking. Public telephones. Refreshments** by arrangement. **Photography** by arrangement. **Visitors' services** guided tours by arrangement.

■ LONDON TOY AND MODEL MUSEUM
21/23 Craven Hill W2 3EN.   Tel 262 7905
Admission *charge*

An enjoyable experience for children and adults, where the toy products of a bygone age can be savoured and appreciated. Opened in 1982 by the Levy family, the museum concentrates on the models and toys of the C19 and C20. Students of social history have the chance to compare and to note what was available to children everywhere, as the collection is probably one of the most comprehensive of its kind in the world.

There is the ***Paddington Bear collection*** showing a selection of items connected with the Paddington story, early editions, puppets

London Toy and Model Museum: dolls and dolls' houses.

used in TV series, bears in all shapes and sizes, and clothes. Another gallery shows two centuries of *dolls* with the earliest, made of wood, dating from the mid-C18 and the latest from the mid-1950s. With these exhibits also goes a selection of *dolls' houses, wooden toys and optical toys.* There is also a gallery devoted to **toy road vehicles** in diecast, tinplate, white metal and plastic. They represent the output of many different countries and some are extremely rare.

Of interest to everybody are the reconstructed shops displaying the famous products of Basset-Lowke and Meccano. Their train sets, cars and model construction kits are still as desirable today as in their heyday. Another reconstructed shop illustrates a typical 1930s toyshop. And there are further displays of toy animals, toy soldiers and teddy bears. A **train room** has been set up to demonstrate several working models as well as a large range of locomotives and carriages made by German, British and American toy industries from the mid C19 to the latest in super trains. Tin toys and other items can be viewed in yet another gallery. Here is the best from such companies as Bing, Marklin, Carette, Martin and other famous names of the Victorian and Edwardian eras.

At the rear of the buildings, the **garden,** doubled in size in 1984, is another great attraction. Here children can ride on an *Orton & Spooner roundabout,* made in 1920, sail their model boats on the pond, or ride on a train.

―――――――――――――――― *the essentials* ――――――――――――――――

Underground Lancaster Gate (Central Line), Paddington (Bakerloo, Circle, District Lines), Queensway (Central Line). **Open** Tue-Sat 1000-1730, Sun and Bank Holiday Mondays 1100-1730. **Toilets. Public telephones. Refreshments. Shopping. Publications.** Photography by prior arrangement. **Educational facilities. Visitors' services** guided tours by prior arrangement.

■ LONDON TRANSPORT MUSEUM

Covent Garden WC2E 7BB. Tel 379 6344
Admission *charge*

Happily for London, London Regional Transport is obliged by law to conserve its historical vehicles and other relics. Hence this excellent museum, one of London's most interesting and intelligently planned, housed in a handsome High Victorian building left vacant when the famous fruit-and-vegetable market moved south of the Thames in the Seventies.

Under this lofty cast-iron and glass roof are horse-buses, with a replica of Shillibeer's first London bus of 1829, the mid-C19 *Knifeboard* and the later *Garden Seat*, trams, trolleybuses, and motor-buses including the *B-type* like the ones which saw service in World War I, and the classic *RT*. Rail items include the stately *L23 steam locomotive* from the world's first underground railway opened in 1863 and the City & South London *Padded Cell* car of 1890. Specially prepared video displays provide a unique record of London and its earlier forms of transport while photographs, tickets, posters vividly illustrate the changes which have taken place. There is a *tube train cab, a tram* and a *modern bus* which you can 'drive' yourself and other working displays on modern developments such as the computer-aided *Bus Control System*.

There are frequent special exhibitions, often offering glimpses of

| 1 |
| 2 |

1. London Transport Museum: Shillibeer's Bus, 1829 (replica).
2. London Transport Museum: buses and trams - a family gathering.

things to come, and a lively education department which caters specially for schools activities and young visitors, plus an energetic organization of Friends which anyone can join.

This is a must for visitors and Londoners, not only for its splendidly restored vehicles but for the way in which you can see how public transport has shaped the growth of London, and the part which it has played (and still plays) in its everyday life.

the essentials

Underground Covent Garden (Piccadilly Line). **Open** daily 1000-1800. **Cloakroom. Toilets. For the disabled** access, toilets. **Shopping. Publications. Photography** no tripods. **Educational facilities. Visitors' services** films, lectures. **Research** library.

■ LONDON ZOOLOGICAL GARDENS COLLECTIONS

Regent's Park NW1 4RY.   Tel 722 3333
Admission *charge*

Over 8,000 mammals, birds, reptiles, amphibians and fish plus quite a few thousand invertebrates live and flourish at the Zoological Gardens which have been occupying 36 acres of Regent's Park for over 160 years. The task of establishing and supporting the zoo was undertaken by the Zoological Society of London, founded in 1826 with the aim of pioneering the management, welfare, breeding and study of British and exotic animals. This highly scientific purpose remains very much the goal of the Society and has extended to over 40 conservation projects abroad.

At Regent's Park the public was first admitted in 1847 and ever since, few generations of Londoners have missed the opportunity of visiting this 'ark'. Apart from the great variety of species to be seen living in relative comfort and natural surroundings a major attraction of the zoo is the architectural merit of some of its buildings.

It is worth remembering that the original plan of the Zoological Gardens was conceived by Decimus Burton, who laid out Hyde Park and designed the Palm House at Kew. Other famous architects employed were Anthony Salvin (pupil of John Nash), and John Belcher who with Jass was responsible for the world-renowned *Mappin Terraces* which opened in 1913 as a home to the bears, goats and mountain sheep. The *Penguin Pool* (by Lubetkin of the Tecton Group) was a 'classic' of the Thirties. In recent years more attention has been aroused by the *Elephant and Rhino Pavilion* designed by Sir Hugh Casson and the *Aviary* designed by Lord Snowdon.

The zoo contains one of the finest collections of animals in the world, and its methods of display and interpretation (especially for children) are being constantly developed. Generous patronage has provided the most up-to-date accommodation for apes and monkeys (the *Sobell Pavilions)* and for small mammals (the *Charles Clore Pavilion*). The *Aquarium* is outstanding in the diversity of its exhibits and will be the first of new developments.

Of all the stars of the zoo, the most popular with all categories of visitors are the elephants, followed closely by lions, monkeys and apes. Off-spring are always much-loved and they are important too, in the context of the zoo's work in breeding and conservation.

In 1931 an 'open zoo' was established at Whipsnade Park (near Dunstable, Beds, 50km from Central London) to accommodate some of the larger animals in paddocks and to carry out further research on husbandry in captivity of breeds threatened by extinction.

---

the essentials

Underground Camden Town (Northern Line). **Open** daily Mar-Oct 0900-1800 (Sun until 1900) or dusk if earlier. Nov-Feb 1000-dusk. **Toilets. Parking. Public telephones. For the disabled** access, toilets, wheelchairs for hire. **Refreshments** restaurant, snacks. **Shopping. Photography. Visitors' services** lectures.

London Zoo:
1. Snowdon Aviary;
2. Orang-utan;
3. Elephant Pavilion;
4. Common Marmoset.

■ MADAME TUSSAUD'S WAXWORKS
Marylebone Road NW1 5LR.   Tel 935 6861
Admission *charge*

Marie Tussaud came to England from Paris in 1802. For thirty-three years she toured Britain with her show of waxworks. At the age of 74 she decided on London as its permanent home, and today it is one of London's greatest tourist attractions, drawing visitors from all over the world. Its scope is endless, ranging from Beethoven to Michael Jackson, Henry VIII to Elizabeth II.

The exhibition starts at the top and works its way down. First one arrives at the new *Garden Party* where celebrities from the world of Film, TV and Sport have gathered for an evening soirée. The *Sleeping Beauty* can be seen next. She is the oldest figure in the exhibition – made in 1765 – and has an electric mechanism beneath her dress which makes her chest rise and fall. Next one moves into the *Conservatory* to the melodies of some of the greatest Beatles hits played by *Paul McCartney*. He stands at an upright piano with the other *Beatles* – John Lennon, Ringo Starr and George Harrison – surrounding him. One now moves into the world of glittering lights and music – *The Super Stars.* Here light, sound and special effects are combined with the latest technology. *Boris Becker* lines up ready to serve with images of his defeated opponents projected onto a screen behind him. In the new *Hollywood Section* movie superstars such as *Joan Collins, Cher, Eddie Murphy* and *Michael Caine* are displayed in an appropriately glitz-and-glamour setting.

Next is the *Grand Hall*, which is one floor down. It houses the great of all kinds, past and present. *Henry VIII* is shown amongst his six wives, who are clothed in splendid, painstakingly-researched and detailed dresses. The formidable *Elizabeth I* wears a beautiful dress inlaid with pearls. The present-day Royal Family is shown in its entirety. *Thatcher, Reagan, Gorbachev* and *Lenin* are here, too.

The next section is the *Chamber of Horrors.* One walks down stairs to the entrance where a bell is being rung solemnly to announce a hanging. The garrotte, guillotine, shooting and the electric chair are some of the horrors brought to life.

The last section is the *Battle of Trafalgar.* The smoke-filled gundeck of the Victory is shown, with deafening sound-effects. The figures are authentically dishevelled and bloodstained. Everything has been carefully constructed to convey the realistic sensation of being on a cramped, filthy gundeck in the tumult of battle.

The *London Planetarium*, next to Madame Tussaud's, aims to give an insight into the Universe. Recently, it has had a *gallery* designed to show famous scientists connected with the exploration of the Universe such as Einstein and Halley. In the centre is a *scale model of the Sun* with the eight planets orbiting it — Pluto has been excluded. A winding passage leads up to the large *auditorium* beneath the large copper dome where the massive Zeiss star projector weighing two tonnes projects the night skies on to the inside of the dome. The star show (30-40 minutes) is changed every year. (FS)

1	2
3	

Madame Tussaud's:

1. Electric chair, Bruno Hauptmann, kidnapper and murderer;
2. Sleeping Beauty (Madame du Barry, mistress of Louis XV);
3. Planetarium: the Zeiss star projector.

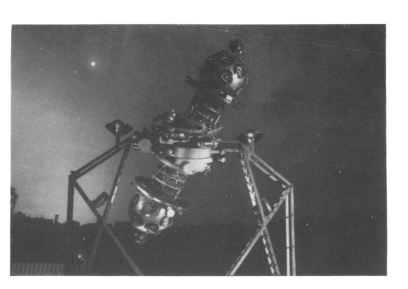

the essentials

Underground Baker Street (Bakerloo, Circle, Jubilee, Metropolitan Lines). **Open** daily Apr-Sept 1000-1800, Oct-Mar 1000-1730. **Cloakroom. Toilets. Public telephones. For the disabled** access by prior arrangement (not Planetarium). **Refreshments** cafeteria. **Shopping. Publications. Photography** allowed plus camera loan scheme. **Educational facilities.**

■ MANDER AND MITCHENSON THEATRE COLLECTION

Beckenham Place, Beckenham Place Park BR3 2BP. Tel 658 7725
Admission *prior application*

Somehow it is hard to believe that although London has been the centre of the performing arts for many centuries there has not, until recently, been found a satisfactory and permanent home for a major collection on the subject. The Mander and Mitchenson Theatre Collection, certainly unique, is soon to be opened (according to plans) to the general public in an imposing Georgian mansion set in a park owned by the Borough of Lewisham. Until recently only researchers were able to gain access to it, since it was in a private house in Venner Road, SE26, shared by the actors Raymond Mander and Joe Mitchenson who, it seems, spent all their spare time accumulating objects related to their profession. As far back as 1944 the collection was promised to the nation. It includes paintings, engravings, manuscripts, prompt copies, playbills, programmes, postcards, photographs, recordings, letters and other documents relating to all aspects of entertainment, and a fine collection of porcelain and china. The theatrical library attached to it can be consulted by researchers.

─────────────── *the essentials* ───────────────

BR Beckenham Hill (from Victoria). **Open** Mon-Fri 1000-1700. **Cloakroom. Toilets. Parking. Public telephones. Refreshments** cafeteria. **Photography** by prior arrangement. **Visitors' services** guided tours by prior arrangement. **Research** by prior arrangement.

■ MARBLE HILL HOUSE

Richmond Road, Twickenham TU1 2NL. Tel 892 5115
Admission *free*

Like many other museums in London, this house is set in the centre of a pleasant park, and provides an attractive view from the road. Built in 1724-9 for the then mistress of George II, Henrietta Howard, a fascinating character, Marble Hill was designed by the architect Roger Morris (1695-1749). As well as being a beautiful building with an interesting array of rooms grouped around a central staircase, Marble Hill contains a fine *collection of early C18 English paintings and furniture,* and an important overmantel and overdoors in their original setting, painted by G.B. Panini in 1738. The restoration of Marble Hill is well documented and of particular interest is the re-

Marble Hill House.

Hayman, Girl at Spinning Wheel.

discovery in 1984 of the remains of a *highly decorated grotto* built by Lady Suffolk in the gardens of the house.

──────────── *the essentials* ────────────

Underground Richmond (District Line) then **Bus** 90b,202,270,290. Open daily (except Fri) Feb-Oct 1000-1700, Nov-Jan 1000-1600. **Cloakroom. Toilets. Parking. For the disabled** access to ground floor, toilets. **Refreshments** snacks, meals by arrangement. **Shopping** sales desk. **Publications. Photography** on application. **Visitors' services** guided tours, lectures by appointment.

■ MARTINWARE POTTERY COLLECTION

Southall Library, Osterley Park Road UB2 4BL.   Tel 574 3412
Admission *free*

Of all the forms of English pottery, Martinware is perhaps the oddest. Produced by the Martin Brothers from 1873 until 1923, it is little-known outside experts and devotees, but it can be found in museums and collections throughout the world. They were specialist 'studio' potters of salt glazed stoneware, sticklers for uniqueness and quality of finish, doing everything themselves. Of the four brothers, Wallace the eldest was the modeller, Walter the thrower, Edwin the designer and painter, while Charles looked after distribution and the management of a tiny shop off High Holborn. The style of the Martins, who have been called the first of English studio potters, was idiosyncratic — crude and heavy, often carved, to begin with, becoming more refined in later years. Their range was wide — from architectural features to tiny birds and pots — and their creative resourcefulness inexhaustible.

The collection, housed in a room within a branch library of the Borough of Ealing, consists of around 800 pieces of various shapes and sizes. It includes the characteristic face-jugs and grotesque birds, tiles, teapots and jugs, in riotous variety, alongside photographs of the brothers, honourable odd-men-out among the long line of English craftsmen. A small selection of the Martin Brothers production can be also found at Kingston-upon-Thames Museum (qv).

──────────── *the essentials* ────────────

BR Southall (from Paddington Station). **Open** Tue, Thur, Fri 0900-1930, Wed, Sat 0900-1700. **Photography.**

■ MARX MEMORIAL LIBRARY

37a Clerkenwell Green EC1R 0DU.   Tel 253 1485
Admission *free*

London is full of reminders of the 30 years Karl Marx spent in the capital. As a German refugee he lived here from late summer 1849 until his death in March 1883, often looking for new accommodation for himself, his wife and four children, due to the impoverished circumstances in which they lived. His tomb in Highgate Cemetery (almost next to the grave of his contemporary Herbert Spencer, who wrote, inter alia, 'Socialism is slavery') has attracted many visitors, some simply to be photographed beside the huge Cornish granite plinth, dominated by Marx's head and bearing the exhortation 'Workers of all lands unite'. Understandably, Communist public figures have been the most assiduous pilgrims especially after the much-publicised visit paid by Kruschev in 1956.

However, when Mikhail Gorbachev arrived here in 1984, his first destination was the Marx Memorial Library. The choice was very likely deliberate and intended to underline the riches of this under-rated library of the left-wing movement. Besides over 100,000 books,

Marx Memorial Library.

Lenin Room.

pamphlets and periodicals connected with the author of 'Das Kapital', it houses much, much more. The 'holy of holies' is the **Lenin Room**, the very first, pokey, room where the leader of the Bolshevik Revolution spent long hours during his stay in London (April 1902-May 1903) writing and editing 'Iskra' (The Spark). Here also are specialised *collections on the Spanish Civil War, the Hunger Marches, the John Williamson Collection on US politics, the Bernal Peace Library and the James Klugmann Collection of Chartist and Radical literature.*

The two-storey building the library has occupied since 1933 has many historic connections, as has Clerkenwell. During the C19 it remained a fertile ground for the radical up-surge. The Labour Party came officially to life in the neighbourhood. The building on Clerkenwell Green started in 1737 as a charity school for Welsh children and was later let to the London Patriotic Club in 1872, where William Morris was a speaker. His banner for the Hammersmith Socialist Society still adorns the hall on the ground floor of the library. It is doubtful whether Marx himself ever took part in any debates at No. 37 although it was well patronised by his daughter Eleanor and her companion Dr. Edward Aveling. In 1892 the building became the headquarters of the Twentieth Century Press, the first socialist publishers in Britain.

the essentials

Underground Farringdon (Circle, Metropolitan Lines). **Open** Mon, Fri 1400-1800, Tue-Thur 1400-2100, Sat 1100-1300. **Cloakroom. Toilets. Shopping** sales desk. **Publications. Educational facilities. Visitors' services** films, lectures, guided tours by appointment. **Research** library.

■ MUSEUM INTERPRETATIVE CENTRE AND NATURE RESERVE

Norman Road, East Ham E6 4HN. Tel 470 4525
Admission *free*

This, like the North Woolwich Station Museum (qv), is a branch of the imaginatively-run Passmore Edwards Museum (qv). The nine-acre churchyard of St Mary Magdalene, East Ham, became a Nature Reserve in 1976, and many species of animals and plants find refuge there in various habitat areas. A marked trail and guidebook help the visitor to appreciate what is being achieved in this oasis amid densely-populated East London. A research centre, opened in 1983, houses laboratories, and fully-computerised ecological and biological records available to all for research. The display area and shop are open to the general public.

the essentials

Underground East Ham (District, Metropolitan Lines). **Open** Tue, Thur, Sat, Sun 1400-1700. **Cloakroom. Toilets. For the disabled** access, toilets. **Shopping** sales desk. **Photography. Educational facilities.**

■ MUSEUM OF ARTILLERY

The Rotunda, Repository Road SE18 4BQ. Tel 856 5533 ext 385
Admission *free*

The famous collection of artillery pieces and ammunition was founded by Captain (later Lieutenant-General Sir William) Congreve in 1778. The exhibits are in date order, tracing the development

Museum of Artillery: Nash's giant 'tent'

and interior.

of the cannon weapon from Crećy in the C14 to the C20. The building deserves an explanation. When the Allied sovereigns assembled in London in 1814 to celebrate Napoleon's abdication, John Nash designed for their accommodation in what is now St James's Park a number of huge tents. One of these was subsequently re-erected at Woolwich, encased by Nash in a more durable structure, and now, as the Rotunda, forms the picturesque home of this collection.

Each exhibit illustrates a particular phase in weapons development. Early short-barrelled mortars and the *long-barrelled gun from the Mary Rose* (which sank in 1545) represent the initial phase of the primitive but effective weapons which transformed tactics. In the next phase from the mid C16 to approximately 1850 smooth-bore ordnance cast in one piece, in iron or bronze, was given the refinements in structure, strength, range, firepower and mobility which greatly increased the importance of this arm. Included in this section is a *9-pounder gun* used at Waterloo, 1815. Further developments are shown in the exhibits which deal with the advent of the rifled barrel, breech loading, propellants, shells, etc. and the more complicated mechanism which resulted from these changes. On display is the *13-pounder field gun* used by the Royal Horse Artillery at the battle of Néry, 1914, for which three Victoria Crosses were awarded. The action is commemorated in the painting by F. Matania.

Mechanization in World War II increased speed and mobility and the guns from that period are comprehensively included in the collection. Also shown are anti-aircraft guns, a *multi-barrelled Gatling gun of 1865*, later developments in machine guns, and an extensive assortment of small arms from 1500 to 1939.

the essentials

BR Woolwich Arsenal, Woolwich Dockyard (from Charing Cross Station). **Open** Daily Summer 1300-1700, Winter 1300-1600 (except Sat). **Toilets. Parking. Refreshments** vending machines. **Shopping** sales desk. **Publications. Photography** by prior written application. **Research** library.

■ MUSEUM OF GARDEN HISTORY
St Mary-at-Lambeth, Lambeth Palace Road SE1 7JU.   Tel 261 1891
Admission *free*

The Tradescant Trust was founded in 1977 to save from demolition the historic church of St Mary-at-Lambeth and to establish there this museum of garden history, the first in the world, in memory of the two Tradescants — father and son — pre-eminent C17 gardeners, who lie in a fine tomb in the churchyard. The elder John was gardener to Robert Cecil, the first Lord Salisbury, and travelled extensively in Europe collecting plants and trees with which to stock

Museum of Garden History:
a corner of the garden with Captain Bligh's tomb in the foreground.

the gardens of Hatfield House. He later became gardener to Charles I. In his garden at Lambeth he propagated the plants collected on his travels, as did his son, who followed his father as royal gardener. John the Younger voyaged three times to Virginia, bringing back many plants, among which were the tulip-tree, the yucca and the red trumpet honeysuckle.

Both men collected 'all things strange and rare' and their house at Lambeth became the first museum open to the public. Among the many curiosities on view was the mantle of Chief Powhattan, father of Princess Pocahontas, who married John Rolfe the colonist, came to England and died at Gravesend in 1617. She had saved the life of Captain John Smith, Governor of Virginia and friend of the Tradescants. John Tradescant the Younger produced the first museum catalogue (1656) of his collection, the 'Museum Tradescantianum', a copy of which is held by the Tradescant Trust. When John died in 1662 his collection was acquired by Elias Ashmole, who with it founded the Ashmolean Museum, Oxford in 1683. In the churchyard (where also is buried Captain William Bligh of the Bounty) a replica of a C17 garden, designed by Lady Salisbury and containing trees, shrubs and flowers known to have been grown by the Tradescants, was opened by the Queen Mother in 1983. In the museum a regular programme of lectures and exhibitions take place. (RN)

---
the essentials

Underground Lambeth North (Bakerloo Line). **Open** Mon-Fri 1000-1500, Sun 1030-1700. **For the disabled** access. **Refreshments** snacks. **Shopping** sales desk. **Photography** charge. **Visitors' services** guided tours. **Lectures** by prior arrangement.

■ MUSEUM OF LONDON
150 London Wall EC2Y 5HN.   Tel 600 3699
Admission *free*

Located in a corner of the City on the southern edge of the Barbican development, the museum is probably not the kind of place you stumble across by accident. And yet it is Britain's premier social history museum and definitely the place to come to soak up the spirit of London's past.

The museum entrance is situated on the pedestrian highwalk above the busy traffic of London Wall; access is by stairs from road level. Finding the museum is not, in fact, difficult, and it is well served by public transport. Once found, first impressions of this museum register it as being unlike any other in London; the building — one of this country's largest and most ambitious new museums — was purpose-built and inside, the modern architecture and display techniques, 'period' music and relaxed ambience all contribute to a refreshingly un-museum-like atmosphere.

This is a very visual museum, enticing and inviting to the eye. The permanent displays start with pre-historic and Roman London and proceed chronologically through medieval, Tudor and Stuart, Georgian, Victorian and C20 galleries to tell the story of the evolution of London and its people over the centuries. It is also a very young museum compared with other august institutions in the capital; it was opened by the Queen in December 1976 having been created by an Act of Parliament which amalgamated two much older museums and their collections. These were the Guildhall Museum established in 1826 and the London Museum founded in 1912 which many people still remember from its Kensington Palace

Museum of London: Lord Mayor's State Coach.

days. The collections from both formed the basis of the new Museum of London collections, although since 1976 these have expanded enormously and what you see displayed in the permanent galleries constitutes only 10% of the total collections.

As you walk around the Museum, Johnson's observation that 'a man who is tired of London is tired of life', will seem increasingly true. The broad themes of London's history are all covered — housing, diet and dress, education and leisure, politics and the Church, trade and industry, religion and culture. But it is also the human story behind London's expansion and change, successes and setbacks, that is conveyed to the visitor; every object is included because it has something to contribute to the story of London, whether it be a medieval leather shoe excavated from a City site or the ceremonial splendour of the Lord Mayor's Coach. It is this interaction of objects — archaeological with social history and costume, fine and decorative arts with industrial history and ceremonial — that makes this museum colourful, accessible and alive.

Certain exhibits clearly fall into the 'top ten' category with all ages: the reconstruction of a Roman kitchen and dining room, the *collection of Jacobean jewellery* known as the 'Cheapside Hoard', the *Great Fire Experience* which recreates through visual and sound effects the Fire of 1666, the *Lord Mayor's Coach*, the C18 prison cells from Newgate Goal, Mr Bugg's late C19 grocer's shop, Selfridge's Art Deco lifts and a Woolworth's counter from the 1930s, to name but a few.

The Museum of London's collections are extensive and of national importance; the 90% not on display includes one of the finest *costume collections* in the country. In 1980 the Friends of Fashion

1	Museum of London:
2 3	1. Roman galleries; 2. Sloping ramp for wheelchairs - the disabled are not forgotten; 3. Late Stuart interior from Poyle Park, Surrey.

organization was formed to fund-raise for a special costume gallery extension where, at a future date, this superb collection can be seen by the public. The museum's Modern Department has also built up an important *collection of material relating to the Docklands* and London's commercial and industrial activities; it is hoped that permanent exhibition space will be found for this as well.

The splendid new **C18 Gallery** covers all aspects of London life from shops and slavery to science and ceramics. The gallery looks at all levels of society and highlights include a recreated façade of Newgate Gaol and stunning Spitalfields silk dresses.

The Museum's reserve collections and library are an important source of material for students and scholars of London's history. Apart from the Study Collections which cover the whole range of artefacts from Prehistory to the present day, the Department of Paintings, Prints and Drawings houses a unique collection of more than 20,000 works covering the last four hundred years and the Photographic Collection comprises some quarter of a million images from the 1840s to the 1980s. These, together with the Library, are all open to researchers by prior appointment with the appropriate department.

It is not only the galleries and exhibitions which draw visitors to the Museum of London; on Wednesday, Thursday and Friday lunchtimes at 1310 free lectures and workshops are held. Excellent speakers, including members of the museum's own staff, talk on all manner of topics connected with London history.

In addition to the permanent displays, the museum also presents a programme of changing temporary exhibitions. (PM)

────────────── *the essentials* ──────────────

Underground Barbican (Circle, Metropolitan Lines), St Paul's (Central Line). **Open** Tue-Sat 1000-1800, Sun 1400-1800. **Cloakroom. Toilets. Public telephones. For the disabled** access, toilets, ramps; tapes and Braille sheets for the blind. **Refreshments** restaurant, snacks. **Shopping. Publications. Educational facilities. Visitors' services** lectures, films. **Research** library. **Staff opinion** items must be left for inspection.

■ MUSEUM OF MANKIND

6 Burlington Gardens W1X 2EX.   Tel 437 2224
Admission *free*

The Museum of Mankind contains the exhibition centre, offices, library and store for the British Museum's (qv) Department of Ethnography. Behind the austere facade with its statues of scientific and other worthies (the building was designed in 1866-7 by Sir James Pennethorne to house London University), you might in recent years have found an Asante Palace, a corner of a Gujerati village, a Yemeni 'souk' or a bleak Arctic landscape complete with snow house, for as well as providing the usual traditional museum displays, this Museum has pioneered exhibitions in which objects are shown against reconstructions of the settings from which they came.

When the British Museum was established in 1753, among the collections of its founder Sir Hans Sloane were ethnographical objects – Eskimo snow spectacles, American Indian baskets and carrying straps, leather shoes from North Africa, an Asante-style drum from West Africa – the nucleus of a collection which today numbers some third of a million objects and is one of the finest of its kind in the world. After Sloane various 'curiosities' trickled in from the great voyages of exploration – from Captain Cook in the late C18 (the Museum's collection of such material from his voyages is the finest in the world), from T E Bowdich's mission to Ashanti in 1817, Captain Parry's 1828 expedition to the Arctic, George Vancouver's voyage (some magnificent Hawaiian featherwork). Much was presented by C19 travellers and administrators. More recently the Museum has been active in collecting properly documented material from societies whose way of life is fast being transformed. Although the Museum has many of the finest pieces of art in the world, it has never regarded itself primarily as a museum of 'primitive' art; rather it is concerned with people and their way of life, both in historical and contemporary terms. One of its strengths is that much pre-dates European contact with other peoples. The collection therefore represents many aspects of the art and life of the indigenous peoples of Africa (it is particularly notable for textiles), Australia and the Pacific Islands, North and South America and parts of Asia and Europe (the European collection is perhaps the least notable and excludes Western European folk art). Recent acquisitions have included material from Madagascar, Bolivia, the North-west Coast of America, Guatemala and Mexico.

With so much on which to draw there is a changing programme of exhibitions, some running for up to three years, others for a shorter period. Forthcoming shows may include aspects of the life of the peoples of New Guinea, Borneo, Central Africa, Palestine and the Maori of New Zealand. There is a permanent room of **Treasures** where the objects change from time to time but among them you might see a magnificent *Mourner's Dress* from Tahiti given to Captain Cook in 1774 and presented by him to the Museum.

Museum of Mankind:
1. Mourner's dress (Tahiti), presented by Captain Cook;
2. Human skull decorated with turquoise mosaic, pre-C15, Mixtec-Aztec;
3. Wood kava bowl (Hawaiian Islands), from Captain Cook's last voyage.

There is a stunning rock crystal skull from Mexico acquired in the last century (the intriguing question is whether the lines of the teeth were made on a post-Conquest jeweller's wheel or is it a unique C15 Mixtec survival), the dignified bronze head of a C12-15 Nigerian notable from Ife, dark green Maori jade ornaments, Aztec stone figures, New Guinea carvings and African masks.

The Museum has the largest **anthropological library** in Britain, one of the finest in the world, having in 1976 combined the library of the Royal Anthropological Institute (RAI) with its own. The Library is open to the public for reference and although tickets are not required, books may be borrowed only by Fellows of the RAI.

General advice and guidance with reading in anthropology should however be sought in the Students Room, which is open for enquiries and opinions on objects (Mon-Fri 1300-1645). The reserve collections are largely housed in East London where they may be made available for research on application. Some objects may be brought to the Students Room at Burlington Gardens. (MLC)

─────────────── *the essentials* ───────────────

Underground Green Park (Jubilee, Piccadilly, Victoria Lines), Piccadilly Circus (Bakerloo, Piccadilly Lines). **Open** Mon-Sat 1000-1700, Sun 1430-1800. **Cloakroom. Toilets. Public telephones. For the disabled** access, leaflet. **Shopping. Publications. Photography. Visitors' services** films, lectures. **Research** library.

■ MUSEUM OF RICHMOND

Old Town Hall, Whittaker Avenue, Richmond, Surrey TW9 1TP.   Tel 332 1141
Admission *charge*

This Museum is housed in a surviving late C19 building amid the architect Quinlan Terry's much-discussed neo-classical development adjoining Richmond Bridge. It reflects the exceptionally rich and varied history and architectural development of Old Richmond, and possesses two particularly splendid models, one of the Tudor Richmond Palace, the other of the C15 Carthusian Charterhouse of Shene. Other noteworthy items are a fine early C19 clock (in working order) from the former Workhouse, and a huge hatchment from St Anne's Church, Kew Green, bearing the arms of George III's son, the Duke of Cumberland and King of Hanover. The arts (including C18 music, tactfully subdued) are well represented and the standard of display, especially graphics, is commendably high.

─────────────── *the essentials* ───────────────

Underground Richmond (District Line). **Open** Tue 1330-1700, Wed 1330-2000, Thur and Fri 1330-1800, Sat 1000-1700. Sun June-Oct 1330-1630. **Toilets. Public telephone. For the disabled** access, toilets. **Refreshments** (not Sun). **Shopping** sales desk. **Publications. Photography** by prior arrangement. **Educational facilities** groups and parties by arrangement, in the mornings. **Research** archives, local history collections, photocopying (in same building, closed Sun). **Visitors' services** local information office in the building.

■ MUSEUM OF THE INSTITUTE OF OPHTHALMOLOGY

Judd Street WC1H 9QS.   Tel 387 9621
Admission *prior application*

This highly specialized collection belongs to the Institute of Ophthalmology, Dept of Visual Science (University of London) and consists of instruments formerly used by eye specialists in examining and correcting defects. The instruments, housed in one cabinet, date from the late C17 to the early C20 and include examples of early microscopes made by Culpeper in the 1700s which were based on the principles of the compound microscope established by the Dutch physicist Leeuwenhoek in the C17. The *ophthalmoscope* invented by Helmholtz in 1851 for examining the inside of the eye is displayed together with an original *Landolt 'C' chart* of symbols used since the 1870s for eye testing. Viewing by appointment as the collection is an historical record mainly for medical students.

---
the essentials

Underground King's Cross (Circle, Metropolitan, Northern, Piccadilly, Victoria Lines).**Open** Mon-Fri 0930-1730. **Cloakroom. Toilets. Public telephones. Photography. Research** library.

■ MUSEUM OF THE MOVING IMAGE (MOMI)
South Bank SE1 8XT.   Tel 401 2636
Admission *charge*

The Museum tells the story of movies and television from their flickering beginnings to holograms and beyond. There is a host of evocative items from Chaplin's cane to Marilyn Monroe's shimmery dress worn in the film 'Some Like It Hot'.

But the great fascination of MOMI is the technology which allows you to watch yourself fly across London or even read the evening news. A cast of professional actors guides the visitor from the silent era to modern animation; from Charlie Chaplin to the operation of a TV studio. And there are movies to be seen, over 1,000 film extracts, and a Hollywood studio with make up and wardrobe.

Museum of the Moving Image (MOMI): one of the many dazzling sections.

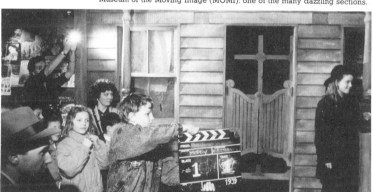

---
the essentials

Underground Waterloo (Bakerloo, Northern Lines). **Open** Tue-Sat 1000-2000, Sun and Bank Holidays June-Sept 1000-2000, Oct-May 1000-1800. **Cloakroom. Toilets. Public telephones. For the disabled** access. **Refreshments** café, restaurant, bar. **Shopping. Publications. Educational facilities.**

■ MUSEUM OF THE ORDER OF ST JOHN
St John's Gate, St John's Lane EC1M 4DA.   Tel 253 6644
Admission *donation*

St John's Gate was originally the southern entrance to the Priory of the Knights of St John of Jerusalem in Clerkenwell. The collections relate to the history of the Order of St John from the time of its foundation during the Crusades and comprise paintings, silver, furniture, ceramics, coins and medals. insignia, books and manuscripts. A highlight of the collections is a pair of *panels* from

Museum of the Order of St John: St John's Gate, view into the Old Chancery, one of the rooms on the second floor of the Gatehouse.

a late C15 Flemish triptych, showing the arms of the Order. In the same building is the **St John Ambulance Museum** which traces, through medical equipment, uniforms and personal memorabilia the development of St John Ambulance from its foundation in 1877. The Gate has connections with William Shakespeare, David Garrick and Dr Samuel Johnson. (IO)

——————————————— *the essentials* ———————————————

Underground Farringdon (Circle, Metropolitan Lines). **Open** Tue, Fri 1000-1800, Sat 1000-1600. **Cloakroom. Toilets. For the disabled** toilets. **Shopping** sales desk. **Publications. Photography. Visitors' services** guided tours and lectures by prior arrangement. **Research** library.

■ MUSEUM OF THE PHARMACEUTICAL SOCIETY

1 Lambeth High Street SE1 7JN. Tel 735 9141
Admission *prior application*

The museum is located within the offices of the Pharmaceutical Society of Great Britain, just across Lambeth Bridge on the south side of the River Thames. It displays representative material from the Historical Collection of the Society relating to the development of pharmacy. The exhibits are arranged in different locations throughout the stunning contemporary building which is the headquarters of the Society.

Examples of C17 and C18 *materia medica* — raw materials used for the preparation of drugs — and *proprietary medicines* — drugs sold under a specific brand-name — are complemented by a selection of books, prints, paintings, photographs and ephemera, relating to medical and pharmaceutical subjects and to the history of the Pharmaceutical Society. ***English Delft drug jars*** and pharmaceutical Leedsware, creamware, stoneware and earthenware, including feeders, leech jars and potlids are on display. There is also a good ***collection of mortars*** with some medieval specimens and other objects used by pharmacists, containers for storage, aids and tools for dispensing, microscopes, medicine chests, weights, scales and measures.

——————————————— *the essentials* ———————————————

Underground Lambeth North (Bakerloo Line). **Open** Mon-Fri 0900-1700. **Cloakroom. Toilets. For the disabled** access. **Photography. Research** by prior arrangement.

■ MUSEUM OF THE UNITED GRAND LODGE OF ENGLAND

Freemasons' Hall, Great Queen Street WC2B 5AZ. Tel 831 9811
Admission *free*

The Museum was formed in 1837 from a small collection of regalia
and artefacts found in a store-cupboard. From that it has grown to
be the major collection in the world of items which have had a
Masonic use or incorporate Masonic symbols in their decoration.
As might be expected a major part of the collection is concerned
with the history and development of Masonic regalia and jewels
(as Masonic medals are termed), including fine examples of C18
hand-painted and embroidered (silks, beadwork and appliqué)
aprons and sashes. The jewels follow the taste of their periods and
include fine examples of the work of the goldsmith, silversmith and
enameller. Silver and plate include presentation pieces (salvers,
candelabra etc.) from the early C19 to modern Swedish silver.
English pottery and porcelain (creamware, Sunderland Lustreware,
early Worcester, Wedgwood, Doulton etc.) with Masonic transfer
prints are well represented together with a fine collection of
Chinese export porcelain (Chi'en Lung period), *Meissen* (Kaendler
period and later), French and modern Scandinavian items.

Museum of the United Grand Lodge of England: Masonic jewels.

The large collection of engraved and enamelled drinking glasses
and decanters illustrates both the development of English glass and
Masonic symbolism from the mid-18th century, including three rare
Beilby enamelled firing glasses and a Bristol blue glass decanter
with gilt decoration c1770. Additionally there is a representative
collection of European glass, particularly strong in coloured Bohe-
mian crystal and modern Swedish glass. The collection is completed by a wide miscellany of artefacts all having Masonic
decoration, in various media, including snuff boxes, clay and briar
pipes, tobacco jars, playing cards, sun dials, fire backs, iron stands,
cuff-links and stick pins, watches and watch fobs, etc. Attached to
the museum is the 38,000-volume **Library.** This holds the most comprehensive collection of printed material on Freemasonry and can
be freely consulted, although prior arrangement with the
Librarian/Curator's Office is advisable. (JMH)

---
the essentials

Underground Holborn (Central, Piccadilly Lines). **Open** Mon-Fri 1000-1700. **Cloakroom.**
Toilets. Public telephones. For the disabled lifts. **Shopping** sales desk. **Publications.**
Photography by prior arrangement. **Visitors'** services guided tours by prior arrange-
ment. **Research** library. **Staff opinion.**

■ MUSEUM OF ZOOLOGY AND COMPARATIVE ANATOMY

University College London, Gower Street WC1E 6BT.   Tel 387 7050 ext 3564
Admission *prior application*

Of great historical and scientific interest, this teaching collection
was founded by Robert Edmund Grant, Britain's first Professor of
Zoology, in 1828. The nucleus was Grant's own personal collection of
specimens. The range covers the entire Animal Kingdom with many
items of great importance and rarity.

--- *the essentials* ---

Undergound Euston Square (Circle, Metropolitan Lines). **Open** Mon-Fri 0930-1700. **Toilets. Public telephones. Refreshments** restaurant in main College. **Photography** charges for specific items and commercial use. **Visitor's services** guided tours. **Research** by prior arrangement.

■ MUSICAL MUSEUM

368 High Street, Brentford TW8 0BD.   Tel 560 8108
Admission *charge*

A comprehensive collection of large and small historic musical instruments, predominantly self-playing, housed in a disused church.

The instruments are all in working order and a selection is
demonstrated in each guided tour by Frank Holland, the dedicated
founder of the museum. Many of the exhibits are fine period-pieces,
as well as ingenious inventions such as the automatic *Phonoliszt
Violina* (1908-12) in which three violins can play at once, in (approx-
imate) harmony. There is also the only roll-playing unit *Wurlitzer
Organ* in Europe which is played automatically from perforated
paper rolls, and a magnificent *Aeolian Duo-Art Residence Organ*.

Apart from exhibits like the Steinway Grand player-piano, on which
the performances of past 'lions of the keyboard' are authentically
reproduced, the music on offer here is, perhaps, mainly of curiosity
value, but it is astonishing to see (and hear) the ingenuity and in-
ventiveness which was lavished on these playthings of an earlier
affluent society, at the start of the home-entertainment industry.

Musical Museum:
Erard-Ampico
Grand Player piano (foreground)
and Welte and Imhof & Mukle
Orchestrions (background).

BR Kew Bridge (from Waterloo Station). **Open** Apr-Oct   Sat-Sun 1400-1700. **Shopping** sales desk. **Visitors' services** guided tours with demonstrations. **Staff opinion** given but not valuation.

■ NAAFI HISTORICAL COLLECTION

Imperial Court, Kennington Lane SE11 5QX.   Tel 735 1200
Admission *prior application*

This small museum is part of the headquarters of NAAFI or Navy, Army and Air Force Institutes. Naafi was set up in 1921 to cater for the needs of the British Forces at war and in peace and rid the Service community of profit-making camp followers. The historical collection contains items relating to all aspects of the service provided. There are photographs of clubs and shops in various parts of Britain and overseas covering the period of Naafi's existence and some of its predecessors. Other exhibits include uniforms, a delivery bicycle, a diorama of a World War I rest camp, tins of cigarettes, lists of bar prices, bakery utensils and even an official Naafi-issue Christmas pudding.

This collection is very cramped and facilities are strictly limited, but the range of exhibits is astounding and well worth a visit by anyone with a specialist interest in the history of this great institution. Please note that admission must be arranged beforehand. (IO)

Underground Kennington (Northern Line), Vauxhall (Victoria Line). **Research** photographic archives.

■ NATIONAL ARMY MUSEUM

Royal Hospital Road SW3 4HT.   Tel 730 0717
Admission *free*

Housed in a purpose-built building, it is the only museum in Great Britain which records the British Army's activities in general over the five centuries of its existence. Also included is the record of the Indian Army up to independence in 1947 and of the colonial forces. The most important of the museum's displays is the Story of the Army which begins with the Yeomen of the Guard (1485) and ends with the Falklands campaign (1982). The galleries dealing with this subject relate events up to the outbreak of the First World War, and from 1914 up to the present.

In the **basement** is the ***Weapons Gallery*** which systematically traces the development of hand-held weapons used by the British soldier from medieval times to the present. How tradition, science, invention and fashion influenced their shapes is illustrated with the help of visual aids. The weapons vary from the practical to the ornamental, but each development can be seen in its historical context with improvements, some small and some major, steadily being incorporated to provide the destructive power which the two figures in a street tableau represent with their selection of weapons currently in use.

On the **first floor** is the main display divided into two galleries. ***Gallery One*** illustrates the history of the British soldier up to the outbreak of the First World War and includes a major display of the Battle of Waterloo. Among the exhibits are the *Duke of Wellington's* *telescope,* a *French eagle and standard* captured at Waterloo (1815) and *the skeleton of Marengo*, Napoleon's favourite horse.

Gallery Two extends the period from 1914 until today. Lifelike reconstructions of soldiers in barracks and on the battlefield are set against realistic backgrounds from the trenches of the Western Front (1914-18), the North-West Frontier in India (1920s and 1930s), the Western Desert and the jungles of Burma in the Second World War and the mountains overlooking Port Stanley (1982).

The **Uniform Gallery** on the **second floor** contains a selection from the largest collection of *military uniforms* in the world, comprising more than 20,000 items. There, too, the visitor will see *badges, medals* and *insignia*. These uniforms are distinctive emblems of the British Army as it changed from the colour and style of the 'Redcoats' known throughout the world to the now universal combat dress by way of the familiar 'khaki' and its derivatives, adopted by the Army for service in India and the Boer War. Adjacent to the Uniform Gallery is the **Art Gallery** where there is a selection of C17, C18 and C19 paintings by Gainsborough, Reynolds, Romney and others of famous names in military history such as General Burgoyne, Sir John Moore, the Duke of Wellington and the Earl of Cardigan. Scenes of battles and camp life are displayed on the corridors and staircases of the museum together with standards, pennants, colours and flags.

There are excellent facilities for the student of military history, armed with a reader's ticket (obtainable on writing to the Director), to consult an extremely comprehensive — sometimes very rare — range of books, manuscripts, prints, maps, drawings and photographs. The Department of Education exists to help students and teachers make the best use of the facilities. Talks, films, worksheets, facsimiles of historical documents and public lectures are all available.

─────────────── **the essentials** ───────────────

Underground Sloane Square (Circle, District Lines). **Open** Mon-Sat 1000-1730, Sun 1400-1730. **Toilets. Parking. Public telephones. For the disabled** access, toilets. **Refreshments** snacks, light lunches. **Shopping. Publications. Photography** no flash. **Educational facilities. Visitors' services** films, lectures. **Research** library.

■ NATIONAL ART LIBRARY

V&A, Cromwell Road SW7 2RL. Tel 589 6371 ext 331
Admission *donation*

The National Art Library is a part of the V&A which actually predates the museum, for it was founded in 1837, 15 years before the South Kensington Museum to which it moved in 1857, and which was to become the Victoria and Albert Museum.

By the time of the move to South Kensington in 1851 there were 6,000 books mostly covering the principles and practice of fine art for the benefit of the students at the School of Design (later the Royal College of Art). Now there are over one million books and manuscripts, studied each year by about 40,000 readers — any visitor to the V&A can use the library, no reader's ticket is required, except for access to the Special Collections.

Not only is the library a vast lexicon of the history of art, it is also a magnificent collection of some of the most beautiful volumes and illustrations ever made. There is Margaret of Foix's *Book of Hours* of the 1470s, and a spectacularly bound Luther translation of the Bible made in 1583. Contemporary books are also collected both for their scholarship and their beauty, and there are books containing illustrations by Marx Ernst, Matisse and Bonnard among others. The National Art Library also has a unique collection of children's books, particularly those of Beatrix Potter. There are occasional free exhibitions of aspects of the library's collections. (ST)

National Art Library, within the Victoria and Albert Museum.

────────────────────── *the essentials* ──────────────────────
Underground South Kensington (Circle, District, Piccadilly Lines). **Open** Mon-Thur, 1000-1700; Sat 1000-1300, 1400-1700. **Cloakroom. For the disabled** access. **Refreshments** as V&A. **Shopping** as V&A. **Photography. Visitors' services** guided tours by appointment. **Staff opinion.**

■ NATIONAL BOOK LEAGUE COLLECTIONS

Book House, 45 East Hill SW18 2QZ.   Tel 870 9055
Admission *free*

The National Book League is unique; small but influential, it promotes literature and offers advice on the availability of all kinds of reading matter to authors, publishers and the general reader. Its collections are grouped under two main headings. The **Mark Longman Library** and Book Information Service was started in 1929 with the presentation of 200 books by Maurice Marston and assumed its present name in 1975 in memory of Mark Longman, head of the famous publishing house and a past chairman of the National Book League.

The collection consists of 8,000 books, pamphlets and bibliographies on books, the book trade and reading, supplemented by a cuttings file and 90 periodicals, most of which are kept for reference. Classification is by the Bliss Schedules. Among the library's special collections are the Perez Collections of Bookplates, the engravings of Leo Wyatt, the Diana Stanley and Arnrid Johnston collections of their illustrations, the C20 engravers collection and a collection of letters and documents relating to the C18 and C19 booktrade.

The **Centre for Children's Books** in the same building is the only specialist centre for children's books in the UK. The Current Collection holds one copy of every children's book published in the last 24 months, arranged in Dewey order with an index of authors, titles, illustrators and translators. The reference collection is a comprehensive collection of over 700 volumes relating to all aspects of children's literature including biographical works on children's authors and illustrators, supplemented by information files of cuttings and periodical references. Around 60 periodicals are taken and kept on file. The special collections include the *Signal Poetry Collection* of current poetry books for children of single poets, nursery rhymes, picture books and anthologies, the *Leslie Linder Collection* of 300 original illustrations of Beatrix Potter and present and previous award-winning children's books.

Both the Mark Longman Library and the Centre for Children's Books are accessible to anyone for reference purposes, but a preliminary telephone call is advisable because of limited study space. (MP)

the essentials

BR Wandsworth Town (from Waterloo Station) then Bus or walk (10 min). **Open** Mon-Fri 0900-1700. (Centre for Children's Books closed 1300-1400). **Photography.**

■ NATIONAL FILM ARCHIVE

21 Stephen Street W1P 1PL. Tel 255 1444
Admission *charge*

The National Film Archive and its parent, the British Film Institute, were set up in 1935, and the NFA's job is to 'select, acquire, preserve, document and make permanently available for research and study a national collection of films and television programmes exhibited or transmitted in the United Kingdom'. Apart from the specialist collection at the Imperial War Museum, it is the only national repository of film and TV material. The NFA contains 75,000 films, documentaries, newsreels, amateur films and television programmes, dating from 1895 to the present day. Because the huge collection has to be stored in various different places, mostly outside London, the NFA usually need some few days' notice depending on what is required. Three kinds of access are catered for: for the catalogue material, a very comprehensive record which is really the first enquiry point; the viewing service which will provide material to be seen on special viewers; and the extraction service for use in new productions for bona fide film producers. For the last two, charges are made. (ST)

the essentials

Underground Tottenham Court Road (Central, Northern Lines). **Open** Mon-Fri 1000-1730. **Toilets. Public telephones. For the disabled** lift. **Shopping** sales desk. **Publications. Educational facilities. Visitors' services** guided tours. **Research** library. **Staff opinion** by prior arrangement.

■ NATIONAL GALLERY

Trafalgar Square WC2N 5DN. Tel 839 3321 (839 3526)
Admission *free*

National Gallery, Trafalgar Square, by William Wilkins.

'I know of only two painters in the world' said a female admirer to Whistler, 'yourself and Velázquez'. 'Why drag in Velázquez?' answered Whistler. If the admirer had wished to expand her somewhat limited knowledge of painting, there could be no better place to do so than at the National Gallery. The collection, comprising just over 2,000 paintings, is remarkably comprehensive. It includes nearly all the major schools of Western paintings from the C12 to C19, and features the work of such great names as Leonardo, Raphael, Titian, Rubens, Rembrandt, Velázquez, Goya, Constable, Turner, Monet, Van Gogh and Picasso. The list is almost endless. Indeed one can think of no more attractive and pleasurable way to take an art history lesson than to stroll around the Gallery and to view its treasures.

The National Gallery was founded in 1824, by which time national galleries had already been established in Vienna, Paris, Amsterdam, Madrid and Berlin. The British government's reluctance to commit itself to funding its own national collection changed on the death of John Julius Angerstein — a Russian-born financier whose own notable collection of thirty-eight paintings, including works by Claude, Rubens and Rembrandt, was threatened with sale abroad. Prompted by the promised gift of two other excellent collections — that of Sir George Beaumont and the Rev Holwell-Carr — Parliament voted just £57,000 for the purchase of Angerstein's pictures and within a month the paintings were on display to the public in his house in Pall Mall. Over the next few years, however, the growth of the collection, and its popularity with visitors, demanded a purpose-built gallery. So it was, in April 1838, that the recently-crowned Queen Victoria paid her first visit to the new National Gallery building in Trafalgar Square, designed by William Wilkins. A building which has expanded over the years but whose distinctive facade has hardly changed to the present day.

What makes the National Gallery virtually unique amongst all the major museums and galleries in the world is its continuing policy of exhibiting the whole collection. Every painting, unless being treated or lent for exhibition elsewhere, or relocated owing to maintenance work, is on show to the public. The collection is divided almost equally between two floors: on the whole the main floor galleries holding the most popular and famous works (including Piero

1	National Gallery:
2	1. Piero della Francesca, Baptism of Christ; 2. Botticelli, Mars and Venus.

149

Orange Street Entrance

Orange Street Theatre

stairs down to Lower Floor Galleries

lift

22

23

21

24

Main floor

20 18

19 25 26

17

15

16

♿ **Orange Street Entrance**

Orange Street Vestibule

cloak-room

lift for disabled visitors

A

9

10

stairs down to Lower Floor Galleries

8

6

7

B

C

Lower Floor Theatre

stairs up to Main Floor Galleries

D

E

F

♿ warder-assisted wheelchair access between Lower Floor Galleries and Restaurant Corridor

G

H

☎ public telephone

toilet also for disabled visitors ♿

♂ →

stairs up to Main Floor ▶

cloakroom and information desk on main floor

150

Floor plans of the National Gallery

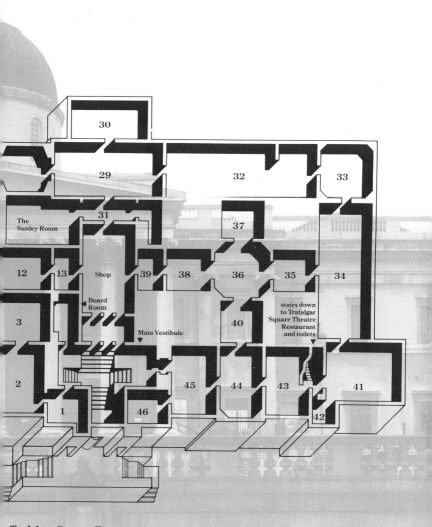

30

29   32   33

The Sunley Room

31

37

12   13   Shop   39   38   36   35   34

Board Room

3

Main Vestibule

40

stairs down to Trafalgar Square Theatre Restaurant and toilets

2   45   44   43   41

1   46   42

Trafalgar Square Entrance

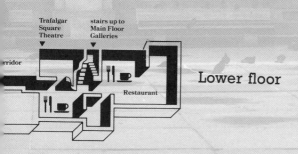

Trafalgar Square Theatre

stairs up to Main Floor Galleries

Corridor

Restaurant

Lower floor

| 1 | National Gallery: |
| 2 | 1. Van Eyck, The Arnolfini Marriage; 2. Memlinc, Virgin and Child (triptych). |

della Francesca's *Nativity*, Leonardo da Vinci's cartoon of the *Virgin and St Anne*, Titian's *Bacchus and Ariadne*, Rubens's *Le Chapeau de Paille*, Van Eyck's *Arnolfini Marriage*, *Rembrandt's Self Portrait*, Constable's *The Haywain*, Velázquez's *The Rokeby Venus*, Van Gogh's *Sunflowers*) – while the remainder of the collection forms a treasure trove in the Lower Floor Galleries. These paintings change place constantly as space must always be made to accommodate the more illustrious works from upstairs which for some reason (most often room closures) have had to be hung below. The Gallery's total range of works is exceptionally comprehensive, not just by school but also within a particular artist's own oeuvre. There are, for instance, no less than 23 Rubenses and 22 Rembrandts. The weakest aspects are C19 European Romantic art and particularly the C18 and early C19 French (although the recently purchased *Winter Landscape* by Caspar David Friedrich and the portrait of *Jacobus Blauw* by David are the only works by these artists on show in this country.

Among the **Early Italian** and **C16 Italian paintings** are masterpieces such as Piero della Francesca's *Baptism*, recently hailed as one of the most perfect paintings in the gallery. The landscape is recognisably that around San Sepolcro, Piero's home town, and painted with the same familiarity with which Constable was later to portray the Suffolk countryside of his youth; Uccello's *Battle of San Romano*, where the careful arrangement of men, horses and lances illustrates the artist's obsession with linear perspective; Botticelli's *Mystic Nativity*, a curiously structured painting which is perhaps a personal prayer for peace, symbolised by the olive branches held by all except the Holy Family; Leonardo da Vinci's *Virgin of the Rocks*. This version is almost the twin of that in the Louvre, the artist having painted a copy of the original commission for the church of San Francesco Grande in Milan. The soft colouring and modelling illustrate Leonardo's own phrase, that light and shade should blend 'without lines or borders, in the manner of smoke', hence the term 'sfumato'; Raphael's *Pope Julius II*. The compassion and dignity of this portrait speaks eloquently of the sitter who was to die a year later. According to the art historian Vasari, the likeness was so convincing that all who saw it were intimidated; Mantegna's *Agony in the Garden*, a scene which was painted with equal intensity by the artist's brother in law, Giovanni Bellini, and which is also on show in the Gallery; Titian's *Bacchus and Ariadne*, which was revealed in its true colours after cleaning in 1969. Finally, Bronzino's *Allegory with Venus and Cupid*. This curious scene of Venus disarming Cupid, witnessed by Envy, Pleasure and Time, has for long puzzled scholars as to its true meaning. Suffice to say that the harshly delineated and distorted figures indicate the that the rules of proportion, soft handling and naturalism known to the painters of the High Renaissance were already beginning to be broken by Mannerist artists such as Bronzino.

With the **Dutch, Flemish** and **Early Northern masters** (most of which are in the Northern extension opened in 1973) the visitor can study the northern Renaissance. Here works such as Van Eyck's *The Arnolfini Marriage*, – the world's most famous pictorial marriage certificate – and Van der Weyden's pensive but frustratingly incomplete study of the Magdalen reading, Dieric Bout's *Entombent* and Hans Holbein's renowned portrait of *The Ambassadors*, complement the paintings from the warm South. One of these Northern works, a religious triptych by Hans Memlinc, has a curious link with England. Memlinc worked mainly in Bruges, where he may have met the Englishman Sir John Donne who had come to Bruges in 1468 to witness the marriage between Margaret of York, Edward IV's sister,

154

National Gallery: 1. Bronzino, An Allegory.
2. Van Gogh, Chair and Pipe.
3. Seurat, Bathers at Asnières (detail),

155

and Charles the Bold, Duke of Burgundy. Donne probably commissioned this triptych from Memlinc on that occasion, as both he and his wife are portrayed wearing the Yorkist collar of roses with King Edward's pendant. Works by Rubens, Van Dyck, Rembrandt, Vermeer, de Hoogh and Ruysdael provide a visual feast to linger over. Contemporary tastes may find much of Rubens's work somewhat indigestible; however it is worth savouring, in particular the powerful yet tender *Samson and Delilah*, painted by the artist shortly after his return from Rome. The dramatic lighting, deep shadows and muscular figures are souvenirs of his study of Caravaggio and Michelangelo. One of the Rubens's greatest admirers was the English *King Charles I*, whose portrait by Van Dyck hangs in the Gallery. There are also two notable acquisitions by Van Dyck, the *Lords Stuart* and the *Balbi Children*. Although the painting bears close resemblance to Titian's portrait of the Emperor Charles V on horseback (Madrid, Prado) the composition is more likely to have derived from the classical statue of Marcus Aurelius in Rome which Van Dyck would have seen on his travels in 1621. Of the 22 Rembrandts in the collection, it is hard for the visitor to single out just one for close study. The two self-portraits – one revealing a confident young man of 34 years, the other a tired and dispirited old figure of 63 – or his loving portrayal of his mistress *Hendrijke Stoffels*, or the severe and uncompromising features of his old patroness *Margaretha de Geer,* or even the eerie stillness of his deeply shadowed *Nativity*; they all evoke an artistic confidence which speaks across the centuries. It is hard also to resist the charm of the other paintings in the Dutch school; Cuyp's placidly chewing cows, Vermeer's steely calm interior showing a lady at the virginals, and Ruysdael's mighty land and sky scapes, each having a seductive appeal of their own.

Among **Italian paintings after 1600** will be found Caravaggio's *Supper at Emmaus* and Luca Giordano's *Perseus turning Phineas and his companions to stone.* Claude and Poussin give way to Chardin and Boucher. Canaletto and Tiepolo lead to Velázquez, Murillo and Goya or Turner, Constable, Reynolds and Gainsborough. Impressionist gems – Monet's *Gare St Lazare*, Degas' *Woman Drying Herself*, Manet's *Music in the Tuileries Gardens*, Van Gogh's *Chair and Pipe* and *Sunflowers*, both Seurat's and Cézanne's *Bathers* – as well as Picasso's *Still-Life* and Matisse's portrait of *Greta Moll.*

Two or three exhibitions a year are designed to complement the collection and to give a deeper understanding of its works. Often one or two, or perhaps a group of paintings are singled out and rehung with accompanying text or video to draw attention to their particular qualities. These displays are sometimes part of a series. Loan Exhibitions are somewhat larger, including about 40 works from other galleries. A notable example was 'French Paintings from Russia' with works from the Hermitage Museum in Leningrad and the Pushkin Museum in Moscow, most on show in this country for the first time. But perhaps the most popular exhibitions are those in the Artist's Eye series. Here a contemporary artist is invited to select paintings from the collection and display them alongside examples of his own work. The 'eyes' have belonged to Anthony Caro, Richard Hamilton, Howard Hodgkin, R B Kitaj, David Hockney, Francis Bacon, Patrick Caulfield, Lucien Freud and Bridget Riley!

National Gallery: Hans Holbein, The Ambassadors

Behind the 'No Entry' signs at the Gallery many activities take place which are not often seen or appreciated by most visitors. A relatively small (for a gallery of international standing) team of specialists work towards the paintings' research, conservation and presentation. There are several curatorial staff, including the Director, who each hold responsibility for a different school of painting. These keepers up-date the extremely precise and detailed text catalogues covering every work in the collection. They also devise exhibitions and write the accompanying catalogues and audio-visual presentations. The department whose work is perhaps the most fascinating is that of *Conservation*. There are two sections, known as the Upper and Lower studios — partly because they are on two floors, but also because Lower Conservation deals with the structure and support of the paintings, while Upper Conservation is responsible for the cleaning and restoring of their upper parts, the grounds and paint layers. The two sections work closely with each other and with the *Scientific Department*, who use some of the most sophisticated equipment in the world to analyse the paintings' structure and monitor the environment in which they are kept. Analysis of pigments, paint mediums and colour changes is the Department's speciality. An annual Technical Bulletin is produced by the restorers and scientists, which lists the works cleaned and highlights some of the more interesting cases or facts they have revealed. But one department which the visitor has most contact with is that of *Education*. A team of full-time and part-time members of staff provide a wide range of services to adults and children. There are guided tours and lectures, tape/slide and video programmes, quizzes for children, talks for school groups, specialist tours and even gently didactic exhibitions.

The National Gallery has a **_Library_** which is open to scholars by appointment only. It contains approximately 25,000 books and subscribes to over 100 periodical titles. It is not a comprehensive art library, but its aim is to complement the paintings in the Collection. In 1985 the Gallery received two remarkable gifts – a £50m Endowment Trust from J Paul Getty Jr for the purchase of paintings and the financing of a whole new extension by the Sainsbury brothers. The extension, currently being built to the west of the present building, by a team led by the American architect Robert Venturi, will eventually house the Renaissance collection (both Northern and Southern) as well as a special exhibition room, lecture theatre, information room and other educational facilities. With funds and space assured, the National Gallery's future looks not only secure but exciting. Above all, it can remain as a collection whose quality and variety is a constant source of surprise and delight to its 3½ million visitors who pass through the doors each year. (SB and MC)

─────────────── *the essentials* ───────────────

Underground Charing Cross (Bakerloo, Northern, Jubilee Lines), Leicester Square (Piccadilly, Northern Lines). **Open** Mon-Sat 1000-1800; Sun 1400-1800 and until 2000 on Wednesdays in June, July and August. **Cloakroom. Toilets. Public telephones. For the disabled** access, toilets, wheelchairs on request. **Refreshments** restaurant, snacks. **Shopping. Publications. Educational facilities. Visitors' services** guided tours, films, lectures. **Research** library by appoinment only. **Staff opinion** Wed 1430-1700 only.

■ NATIONAL MARITIME MUSEUM

Romney Road SE10 9NF. Tel 858 4422
Admission *charge*

This very fine museum, the largest of its kind in the world, was brought into being through an Act of Parliament in 1934 and opened to the public (as one of King George VI's first engagements of his reign) in 1937. It was used by the Admiralty during World War II and re-opened as a museum gradually from 1946 onwards. Between 1971 and 1981 it was completely remodelled, using the latest in museum display techniques, and is a mecca for sea-freaks of all ages and nationalities. It is a very fine art gallery as well.

At Greenwich, set in the beautiful and ancient Royal Park, the Museum is housed in the C17 Queen's House, flanked by colonnades linking this to C19 wings. The **Queen's House** attracts visitors

from all over the world for its beauty and unique architecture. It was designed by Inigo Jones, inspired by seeing the work of Palladio in Italy, begun in 1616 as a summer residence for Anne of Denmark, wife of King James I. However she died in 1619 when it was far from complete, and what had been built was covered with a roof of thatch and left. It was only completed — under the direction of John Webb, Jones's kinsman and sometime pupil — by 1636 for another Queen, Henrietta Maria, wife of Charles I. For her the King ordered exquisite carvings and paintings, installed lovely furniture and furnishings, had the ceilings (some of which survive) painted by artists such as the Gentileschi father and daughter and put wrought iron balustrading on the fine spiral staircase (the first unsupported staircase ever built in England – without the hitherto always-used central pole).

The **West Wing** contains the Museum's main Bookshop and the Information Desk, with the Public Visual Index of photographs of what the Museum holds, whether or not it is on public view. The ***Medal and Seal Rooms*** are small but very interesting and the ***Library and Reading Room*** (access usually only on production of a reader's ticket) are nearby. On the two upper floors are displays on the ***Royal and Merchant Navies in the C18***, the ***Nelson galleries*** which contain the Museum's greatest treasure — the uniform coat the little but very famous Admiral was wearing when he was shot at the Battle of Trafalgar on 21 October 1805. The shot hole is distinct, there are bloodstains on the lining, on the nearby breeches (cut off the fatally wounded man) and the stockings.

There is, too, the gallery on ***Captain James Cook***, whose voyages of exploration opened up the Pacific and virtually doubled the size of the known world, as well as adding much to man's knowledge of the flora, fauna and geography of the Southern Hemisphere. Not least through scientific and botanical work, and the paintings of

National Maritime Museum: looking south towards the Old Royal Observatory on the hill. On the left, the East Wing; on the right, the West Wing; in the centre, Inigo Jones's Queen's House.

Queen's House: the Great Hall.

the official artists who accompanied Cook. The discovery of the North American continent, and the birth of the United States, the development of world trade with the protection of the Royal Navy's ships, and the building of wooden vessels for war and merchant voyages are also shown here. There is an **Archaeology of the Boat gallery** with evocative fibreglass replicas of ancient craft discoveries in Britain, a major **Yachting Gallery** with a bay on Royal Yachts, and alongside the West Wing is the **Neptune Hall**, dominated by a real paddle tug, the *Reliant*, with its engines, boiler room and accommodation easily seen and even walked through. There are dioramas and displays on such as lighthouses and lifeboats, a boat building shed reconstructed, the first class cabin of a transatlantic passenger liner, and small boats from many different countries as well as Britain. Below the platform level is a gallery full of magnificent models and reconstructions on cargo handling and ports, from Roman times to the present C20. The **Barge House** contains the splendidly gilded Royal Barge of 1732

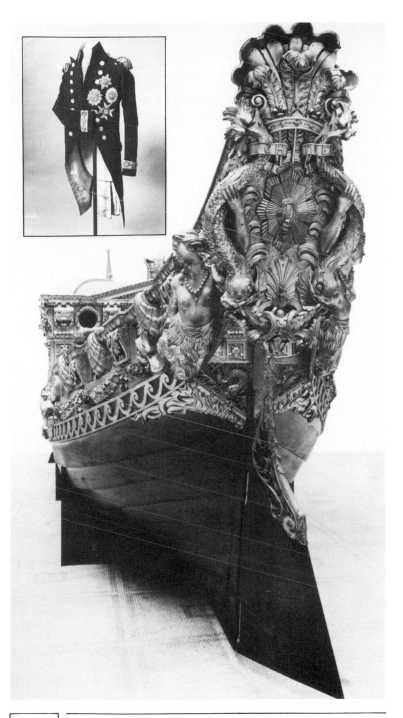

161

built for Frederick, Prince of Wales, son of George II and father of George III but never himself king (he died before his father, and the *shallop* built in 1688 for Queen Mary, wife of William II.

In 1960 the Royal Observatory, high on the hill in Greenwich Park, became the **Old Royal Observatory** and was opened by the Queen as a part of the Museum, housing the story of astronomy and navigation. The original 1675 building, designed by Sir Christopher Wren and containing one of the last unspoilt Wren interiors in England, is called Flamsteed House, after the first Astronomer Royal who lived and worked there. Some of the earlier instruments are to be seen and under the pale green 'onion' dome is the 28-inch refracting telescope still in use — as are most of the C19 instruments here — by professional and amateur astronomers. Not to be missed is the display of *chronometers* invented by John Harrison as part of finding the answer to the problem of longitude for sailors, and the *galleries of timekeepers* from early Persian astrolabes to an atomic clock.

National Maritime Museum: Old Royal Observatory, The Meridian Building.

the essentials

BR Maze Hill (from Charing Cross Station). **Docklands Light Railway** Island Gardens. **Boats** from Westminster or Tower Piers. **Open** Summer Mon-Sat 1000-1800; Sun 1400-1730; Winter Mon-Sat 1000-1700; Sun 1400-1700. **Toilets. Public telephones. For the disabled** limited access. **Refreshments** restaurant. **Shopping** bookshop. **Photography. Educational facilities. Visitors' services** films, lectures, guided tours by prior arrangement for parties. **Research** library and archives by prior arrangement. **Staff opinion.**

NATIONAL MONUMENTS RECORD

Fortress House, 23 Savile Row W1X 1AB.   Tel 734 6010
Admission *free*

The major aims of the National Monuments Record (NMR) are to survey and record historic buildings and archaeological sites, and to maintain archives which are available for consultation. The NMR is the responsibility of the Royal Commission on Historical Monuments, established by Royal Warrant in 1908 (there are separate commissions for England, Scotland and Wales).

The volume of records has grown enormously as the terms of reference for the Royal Commission on Historical Monuments were successively enlarged to cover an ever-wider range, including the *National Building Record* (1941), the *Industrial Monuments Survey of England* (1981), the *National Archaeological Survey*, the record-keeping functions of the Ordnance Survey (1983), the huge *Air Photographic Library of the Department of Environment* (1984), and lately the *GLC archive on London* (1986) following the demise of that institution.

Much material of the NMR, which is the most important source of documentary records on England on a county and parochial basis, is readily available on open shelves for immediate reference, but prior notice must always be given to obtain access to stored documents. Research facilities are excellent but even to casual visitors the NMR has much to offer, especially to those with an inquisitive mind, who will be able to indulge to the full their curiosity and nostalgia for times past.

National Monuments Record: 65 Cheapside, London in 1891.

the essentials

Underground Piccadilly Circus (Bakerloo, Piccadilly Lines). **Open** Mon-Fri 1000-1730.
Toilets. For the disabled access.

■ NATIONAL PORTRAIT GALLERY

St Martin's Place WC2H 0HE. Tel 930 1552
Admission *free*

The only English gallery whose first requirement is the eminence of the sitter rather than artistic merit, the National Portrait Gallery was founded in 1856 to 'acquire portraits of men distinguished in the history of this country'. The early intake was strong on politics and literature, less so on science and industry, and over-cautious about the recent past. Scholarship has always been of a high order, but of recent years presentation and coverage have greatly improved. Rehanging, which includes admirable thumbnail biographies and historical labels, and refurbishment, are still very much in progress.

Perhaps 1,000 of the total collection, now about 8,000, is on exhibition (items in reserve can usually be seen on application to Information Desk). Up to the C19, paintings predominate, though there are notable drawings, miniatures, busts and engravings. Thereafter photography plays an increasing role, especially in the newly-opened C20 rooms, which now pay due tribute to recent and contemporary personalities. Artistic quality is variable; the great do not always sit to great artists. The superlative rubs shoulders with the adequate, or even inadequate: Holbein's *Henry VIII* (the Chatsworth cartoon), with Taylor's *Shakespeare* (the Chandos portrait). But the gallery offers a unique illustrated Who's Who of the national achievement, from Henry VII to Thatcher, from Purcell to 'pop'. It is hung by period: C16-18 on 2nd floor, C19 on 1st, C20 on ground floor.

From the entrance, the shop on the left, *Margaret Thatcher* by Moynihan on right; up the steps and take the lift to 2nd floor, **Room 1** (The Tudors), where the collection begins. For an outline of the late medieval English portraiture, see the display on the half-landing below. What follows is a selection of major and popular items, which takes the visitor through the main rooms in sequence. *Sir Thomas More*, though only a copy, retains much of the impact of Holbein's original (New York, Frick Collection):his autograph whole-length drawing of *Henry VIII* is menacing,even in the dim

National Portrait Gallery:
Sir Walter Raleigh by
Nicholas Hilliard.

light necessary for its preservation. *Shakespeare*, the National Portrait Gallery's first acquisition, is flanked by three portraits of *Elizabeth I*, newly crowned, in mid-reign, austere and delicately coloured, and as an old woman, painted c1592 for her champion Sir Henry Lee. Note the miniatures, among them a flamboyant Hilliard of *Raleigh*. In **Room 2** is *William Harvey*, discoverer of the circulation of the blood, painted by Mytens. His portrait of *Charles I* is almost apologetic by contrast with Rubens's study of the art collector *Arundel*.

Through the next room with the earliest miniature of *Oliver Cromwell* by the miniaturist Samuel Cooper, one of the greatest

National Portrait Gallery: HM Queen Elizabeth II by Pietro Annigoni.

of all British portrait painters, to *Mr and Mrs Pepys*. Her bust, a cast from her monument, illuminates the distaff side of that famous marriage. Nearby are *Newton* and *Wren*, both by Kneller, and a room of his 'Kit-Cat' portraits. Hudson's majestic *Handel*, in a splendid carved frame, was painted in 1756. The terra-cotta busts 'extremely like' are Roubiliac, the greatest sculptor of his day: *Robert Walpole*, a solid Roman senator; *Hogarth*, half pugnacious, half sad — there was once a companion-piece of his dog, too — and a patrician marble of *Lord Chesterfield*. Hogarth and Chesterfield are in **Room 9**, where *Reynolds's* young self-portrait looks forward to the golden age of British painting and some of its finest portraits: his whimsical *Sterne; Warren Hastings* (in **Room 10**), chilling but exquisite, and Gainsborough's *Garrick* and *J.C. 'London' Bach*, both painted with affectionate brilliance. On, past *Captain Cook*, painted on his last voyage by Webber, a Swiss topographical artist who sailed with him and survived, and Wilton's compelling, though posthumous, bust of *James Wolfe*. On the landing, some spectacular Jacobites.

The newly refurbished Rooms 12-15 display the opulent and tumultuous years of the Regency in an appropriately sumptuous setting, dominated in **Room 12** by *Nelson, Wellington* and George Romney's *Emma, Lady Hamilton*. In **Room 13** are an array of Romantic poets including *Wordsworth, Coleridge, Byron, Shelley* and

Keats. **Room 14** features some figures who transformed Brita
through its industrial revolution – *Humphrey Davy, James Watt* an.

National Portrait Gallery: Oliver Cromwell, by Samuel Cooper.

Richard Arkwright – and **Room 15** displays the Gallery's largest picture, George Hayter's huge *House of Commons*, 1833.

Down the stairs to the C19. Facing you is Hayter's young *Queen Victoria* in the robes in which she began a reign that lasted to 1901. Here are the *Brontë Sisters* by Branwell, Maclise's *Dickens, Peel, Gladstone, Disraeli, Salisbury*; Mrs Cameron's photographs of *Tennyson* and *Carlyle*, a daguerreotype of *Mrs Beaton*, and the lovely *Ellen Terry*, by Watts, 'Choosing' between vanity (red camellias) and innocence (violets). *Gilbert and Sullivan*, and *Oscar Wilde* take you through the Edwardians at the far end of the corridor to the Royal Landing. Lord Snowdon's delightful photograph of the *Princess of Wales holding Prince William* (the youngest sitter?) joins Bryan Organ's earlier portraits of *Prince Charles* and his then fiancée.

A short flight of stairs leads to the ground floor and C20 rooms. Beresford's tranquil photograph of *Virginia Woolf*, 1902, is in the Cameron tradition. Much of the impetus of portraiture between the wars undeniably passed to the media, to the action photograph. Many of the 500 images accommodated on revolving screens are for the press; there is a video of *Amy Johnson*'s dramatic flight. But the art of the portrait painter was not altogether obliterated. Grant's *Vanessa Bell* and Robert's *Maynard Keynes and wife* demonstrate its beauty; Sickert's *Churchill* and his *Beaverbrook*, its power. Works

National Portrait Gallery: Princess of Wales, by Bryan Organ.

like *Paul McCartney* and *Sebastian Coe* give hope that the interest of younger artists is returning to the portrait.

The National Portrait Gallery has rather outgrown the present building, a neo-Italianate palazzo (architect Ewan Christian), the gift in 1896 of W.H. Alexander, a Victorian philanthropist. Adjacent sites are under investigation; meanwhile pressure has been relieved and the regions served by the opening of 'out-stations' at two National Trust houses, Montacute, near Yeovil, for the C16, and Beningbrough, near York, for the C18. (JFK)

--- *the essentials* ---

Underground Charing Cross (Bakerloo, Northern, Jubilee Lines). **Open** Mon-Fri 1000-1700, Sat 1000-1800, Sun 1400-1800. **Cloakroom. Toilets. Photography** by prior arrangement. **Educational facilities. Visitors' services** lectures, guided tours by arrangement.

■ NATIONAL PORTRAIT GALLERY ARCHIVE AND LIBRARY

The Mill, 72 Molesworth Street, Lewisham SE13 7EW.   Tel 318 2888
Admission *prior application*

The departments are housed in a watermill built in 1828. The **Archive** is perhaps the largest collection of British portrait engravings ever assembled; it comprises several hundred thousand items. It is essentially a working collection, invaluable to researchers interested in the appearance, and portrayals, of past figures. A mass of reference photographs of portraits of all kinds (even the photographs!) provides a visual record which includes items which the National Portrait Gallery does not itself possess, logging their whereabouts in a vast card-index system of approaching one million entries.

The **Library** comprises some 30,000 volumes, including annotated sale-catalogues going back to the C18. Large sections are devoted to family history, heraldry, costume history and biography; collections of engravings, lithographs, mezzotints and caricatures show not only how the subjects actually looked, but how they were regarded by their contemporaries. Of special interest are the 200 notebooks of the National Portrait Gallery's first director, Sir George Scharf, all the more valuable for now being available on microfilm.

Both Archive and Library play an important part in the daily scholarly activity of the National Portrait Gallery. Equally, they are regularly used by accredited scholars and researchers from all over the world.

---
the essentials

BR Lewisham (from Charing Cross, Waterloo, London Bridge Stations). **Open** Mon-Fri 0930-1300, 1400-1700. **Toilets. Staff opinion** on portraits of British sitters: send photograph.

■ NATIONAL POSTAL MUSEUM

King Edward Street EC1A 1LP.   Tel 239 5420
Admission *free*

The Museum was formed in 1965 following the donation to the nation of the outstanding collection of Mr Reginald M Phillips of Brighton. This collection, which had gained the Grand Prix at the London International Stamp Exhibition in 1960, is probably the finest collection of Victorian stamps put together by a private collector. To this, the Post Office has added its own extensive collection of registration sheets, proofs, dies and artwork to form the most comprehensive research facility for British Stamps. In addition to these collections, the Museum holds the Post Office UPU Collection of stamps which have been received from time to time from the Universal Postal Union. This collection is virtually complete as a world-wide collection since 1900.

The Museum puts on several exhibitions each year. Each presentation shows a different facet of Post Office History and regular visits will help students to understand how the British Post Office has developed over the 350 years since it became a public body. Although stamps themselves are the prime part of the Museum's Collections, it also holds many small three-dimensional items including stamp boxes, weighing scales and models.

National Postal Museum. Inset, Penny Black.

At the Museum, the only complete sheet of the *Penny Blacks* is held. This sheet of 240 stamps is a unique part of the philatelic heritage of Great Britain and is the proof sheet taken from the printing plate in 1840 before the main print run of the world's first stamp. School visits are welcome by prior arrangement and the parties are not only given a conducted tour of the main exhibit, but are shown a film in the *Museum Cinema* and are given the opportunity of answering a questionnaire which, if answered correctly, gains a certificate from the Museum. Research facilities are provided for students and advanced collectors, with access to the museum *Library* and reproduction facilities. The Museum's collection is far too extensive for permanent display, only some 25% of the total collection is permanently on view, but the balance is available on request. Material not on display may be examined subject to prior notification.

the essentials

Underground St Paul's (Central Line). **Open** Mon-Thur 1000-1630, Fri 1000-1600. **For the disabled** access by arrangement. **Shopping** books, postcards. **Publications. Photography** by arrangement. **Visitors' services** guided tours, films, talks, by arrangement. **Research** by arrangement. **Staff opinion** given but not valuation.

■ NATIONAL SOUND ARCHIVE

29 Exhibition Road SW7 2AS.   Tel 589 6603
Admission *free*

National Sound Archive.

Formerly the British Institute of Recorded Sound and now part of the British Library (qv), the National Sound Archive serves as the national centre for the study of recorded sound. It aims to be comprehensive with special responsibility to British recording and includes classical and popular music of all kinds, jazz, international folk and ethnic music, wildlife sounds, drama including the entire repertoires of the National Theatre, the Royal Shakespeare Companyand selected live recordings of other English stage companies, and spoken poetry and other literature. There is a permanent exhibition illustrating the history of recorded sound.

The Archive is the principal public reference point for the *BBC Sound Archives*, acquires around 80% of all commercially-issued discs and has an extensive live recording programme of its own. It is playing a central role in the compilation of a **National Discography** and currently holds over a million items on carriers ranging from primitive wax cylinders to compact discs. Seasons of talks and discussions, a free listening service (by appointment) and a full reference library facility are open to the public.

the essentials

Underground South Kensington (Circle, District, Piccadilly Lines), **Open** Mon-Fri 1000-1730 (2100 Thur) **Toilets. For the disabled** by prior arrangement for individuals. **Publications. Educational facilities. Visitors' services** listening by appointment, lectures, videos. **Research** library. **Staff opinion.**

170

■ NATURAL HISTORY MUSEUM

Cromwell Road SW7 5BD.   Tel 938 9123
Admission *charge* (free at certain times)

This Museum, an international centre for reference and study in naming and classifying the natural world, houses one of the world's largest collections of animals, plants, fossils and minerals – in all, more than 65 million specimens.

Its original name the British Museum (Natural History) bears testimony to the fact that until fairly recently it was part of the British Museum (qv). Nowadays it incorporates the former Geological Museum and includes the outstation Zoological Museum at Tring (53 km from Central London, Tel. 044 282 4141). In recent years many of the older biological displays, reflecting the traditional scientific division of Zoology, Palaeontology, Entomology and Botany, have been replaced by thematic exhibitions which incorporate interactive devices and computer games in addition to video programmes.

A word of warning: the museum's public galleries total about 20,000m² so only the indefatigable will try to see everything in one visit. It is far better to concentrate on one exhibition at a time and make further visits if you can. Visitors are given a plan of the galleries with up-to-date information on changes in the exhibitions, temporary exhibitions and other events. There is also a full-colour souvenir guide available from the bookshop to the left of the main entrance and each month the museum issues a leaflet describing forthcoming lectures, films and exhibitions.

Natural History Museum, architect Alfred Waterhouse.

Natural History Museum: the Central Hall; the giant Diplodocus.

The two-fold function of the museum is essentially public education and scientific research. Visitors to the museum will be more conscious of the first than of the second 'behind-the-scenes' aspect. The museum is, in fact, a giant archive or 'data-bank' of accurately named and classified specimens. The care and maintenance of this natural history treasure trove is entrusted to the five scientific departments of *Zoology, Entomology, Palaeontology, Botany* and *Mineralogy.*

The main entrance leads into the **Central Hall** which is devoted to the spectacular *dinosaurs* such as Diplodocus and Iguanodon. Along the left-hand side of the hall, a video programme 'Dinosaurs and their living relatives' and a series of exhibits invite the visitor to learn about the evolutionary link between the dinosaurs and present-day birds and reptiles.

The *Hall of Human Biology* was the first of the new-style exhibitions. Opened in 1977 it covers selected topics dealing with our physical and mental development, and ranges from cells, chromosomes, conception and birth to learning, understanding our surroundings and problems of visual perception. *Introducing Ecology* is an abbreviated version of a larger exhibition opened in 1978. It presents some of the basic ideas of ecology – energy transformations, food chains, food webs and ecosystems – using specimens, dioramas and models. Visitors can use a computer game to follow step-by-step a real-life ecological problem. This will be superseded by a new permanent exhibition on ecology to open at the end of 1990. Two other exhibitions are Origin of Species (opened in 1981) and Man's Place in Evolution. *Origin of Species* presents a modern view of Darwin's classic work on natural selection. It introduces the visitor to the idea of 'species' and shows how Darwin answered the question 'How do new species evolve?' The main ideas presented in the exhibition are drawn together in the 'Natural Selection' computer game. Specimens from the museum collections illustrate variation,

Natural History Museum: part of the exhibition "Man's Place in Evolution".

mimicry and the remarkable camouflage of the peppered moth. *Man's Place in Evolution* sets out the story of our new evolution and our relationship with other primates.

In 1989 a new gallery was opened devoted to the world of **Creepy-Crawlies** (this is the title of the exhibition). The Arthropod kingdom is the most numerous and diverse on earth, with as many as 80 million specimens living in the air, on the land and in the sea. It includes everything from insects, spiders and crabs to centipedes and millipedes. The exhibition includes a full-size house, complete with uninvited inhabitants such as flour mites and carpet beetles. There is also a six-metre-high termite mound. Many interactive displays help the visitor to understand the vital role of arthropods within the ecosystem.

The display *British Natural History* illustrates the animals and plants of seven typical habitats found in the British Isles and includes about 2,000 species ranging in size from the grey seal and red deer to insects and other invertebrates. British birds are displayed separately at the end of the **Bird Gallery** on the ground floor. Visitors with more than a passing interest in natural history can also obtain information on over 800 local societies and naturalists' trust and can consult the index of reference literature. Other exhibitions cover bird, marine invertebrates and arachnids (spiders, scorpions etc).

The popular full-size model of the *Blue Whale*, in the former Whale Hall, continues to be the centre-piece of the gallery since the exhibition has been extended by bringing some land mammals together with the aquatic mammals, illustrating the theme of 'Mammal Diversity'. Representatives of the principal orders of mammals, including a fine group of 'big cats' are displayed in another gallery. The **Rowland Ward Pavilion** comprises three large dioramas (scenes) of African mammals. Elsewhere there are displays of Chi-Chi (the giant panda), the Coelacanth (a 'living fossil' fish from the Indian Ocean) and reptiles, amphibians and fishes.

Natural History Museum: the exhibition 'The Origin of Species' shows Darwin in his study at Down House, Kent.

One of the most comprehensive collections of minerals in the world is on display in the **Mineral Gallery,** including impressive large crystal groups, gemstones and carved stones. Meteorites – extra terrestrial samples of the Solar System – are displayed in the **Meteorite Pavilion.**

A new development is a **Discovery Centre** where visitors, particularly younger ones, will be able to have direct contact with a range of specimens and to carry out experiments and observations with help from museum staff.

The adjoining Building, in Exhibition Road, formerly the Geological Museum, displays the collections of the British Geological Survey and is, effectively, the National Museum of Earth Science. In recent years it has purchased unusual gems, mainly uncommon varieties of well-known gems, gem-quality versions of ordinary rock-forming minerals, and transparent minerals not normally cut for use as gems, such as fluorite and zinc blende. The result is the **Gemstone Collection,** a Mecca for gemmologists, by whom it is set above any other collection in the world for scope and variety. It is difficult to choose amongst so many outstanding objects, but recommended are the following: the priceless and unique *fibrolite,* the perfect large *peridot* of exceptional colour, the *orange sapphire,* the splendid collection of *tourmalines* displaying the extraordinary range and subtlety of colour characteristics of this gem, the *opals,* and the diamond-encrusted *Murchison Snuff Box* presented to Sir Roderick Murchison by Czar Alexander II for his geological researches in Russia.

An imposing rock-face at the west end of the Main Hall contains the entrance to the exhibition **The Story of the Earth.** Highlights are: the *Moon rock,* an exceptional specimen of the primordial crust embodying in the one sample visible evidence of all the main events in the Moon's history, on long-term loan through the generosity of NASA; the *tracking panorama* – a moving scenario of the first 1,000 million years of the Earth's history from the molten primordial Earth to the point at which life originated; the *animated model of the Surtsey volcano;* the *film of volcanic products* with spectacular eruption sequences; and the *earthquake machine,* a section of floor which is shaken by hydraulic rams to the exact wave pattern of an earthquake of magnitude 4 on the Richter scale, the shaking accompanying a graphic description of the Great Alaskan Earthquake of 1964.

The exhibition ***Britain's Offshore Oil and Gas*** looks at all aspects of the North Sea oil and gas industry. It takes the form of an oil platform with the displays on two decks explaining the role of nature and man in the formation and exploration of the deep sea reserves. An innovative and award winning vertically projected video show adds to the realism and visitors can look down on the turbulent seas below. Computer games and models help to complete the picture of the exciting life experienced offshore.

The geological history of the British Isles is seen as a sequence of relatively tranquil periods, when layers of sediment were deposited in the region, interrupted by violent distortion of the strata by periodic continental collisions, and the layout of the exhibition ***Britain before Man*** follows this, the bays corresponding to the tranquil periods. A tracking panorama with stills, *Britain from the Beginning,* summarises the geological history of the British Isles and the exhibition concludes with a *diorama of a Neanderthal family* terrified at the approach of a hunting party of modern man.

The exhibition ***Treasures of the Earth*** aims to tell about the many mineral and rock commodities which, after processing or smelting and fabrication, become part of the accoutrements of civilisation surrounding us in everyday life. After seeing a scene-setting film, one enters a sectioned house full of sectioned objects which contain elements and commodities that can be related to ore deposits in the section of the Earth's crust. Thirty-five different commodities vital to industrial societies are the subjects of 20 visitor-operated data-banks producing words and pictures on television screens dealing with all aspects of materials from their origin to their uses and reserves. A 'treasury' and a hands-on 'rock-garden' of raw, processed and manufactured objects back up the information modules.

Upwards of 2,000 selected fossils are displayed according to their ages, from Precambrian to Pleistocene, in the ***British Fossils*** exhibition, intended to enable fossil collectors to identify their material even where they know only where their fossils were found. Back-up displays tell the story of fossils, their character and preservation and how to go about collecting them.

A fine lecture theatre forms part of an education department pursuing a variety of activities in adult, secondary and primary education, and arranging specialist courses and field excursions as well as lectures, demonstrations and films for the general public.

The museum is committed to a continuing programme of evaluation of the exhibition and to improvements in visitor facilities; some sections of the galleries may therefore be temporarily closed. Such closures will be indicated on the information panel at the main entrance.

--- *the essentials* ---

Underground South Kensington (Circle, District, Piccadilly Lines). **Open** Mon-Sat 1000-1800, Sun 1300-1800. **Cloakroom. Toilets. Public telephones. For the disabled** access, toilets. **Refreshments** snacks, cafeteria. **Shopping** bookshop. **Publications** in several languages. **Photography. Educational facilities. Visitors' services** films, lectures. **Research** library.

■ NEWSPAPER LIBRARY

Colindale Avenue NW9 5HE.   Tel 323 7353
Admission *reader's pass* (see British Library)

This is the British Library (qv) national collection of newspapers and holds well over half a million volumes and parcels and 120,000 reels of microfilm. The collection includes national and provincial British daily and weekly newspapers as well as some periodicals and large collections of Commonwealth and foreign newspapers. The UK collections are very comprehensive from about 1840 onwards.

Newspaper Library: Daily Mirror, 1912; Daily Graphic, 1908: Mrs Pankhurst cross-examines Lloyd George.

The collection originated in 1762 when George III presented to the British Museum George Thomason's collection of tracts of the English Civil War and Commonwealth period. Thomason, a bookseller, foresaw the future value of such ephemera and had amassed some 22,000 items, including 7,000 numbers of editions of newspapers. The collection includes many rarities such as *The Mafeking Mail* special siege slip 1899-1900 published during the defence of Mafeking on such materials as wrapping paper, and many oddities such as *The Matrimonial Post*, published from 1860 to 1955, the forerunner of the computer dating service.

Today the Newspaper Library is an important central source of information for researchers and journalists and for other newspaper libraries and archives. Microfilming is increasingly used to safeguard this valuable but fragile material for the future. The Reading Room is open to adults (over 21) with a reader's pass. Facilities are available for using typewriters, tape recorders and microfilm reading machines. The main collection at Colindale is supported by other newspaper collections at the Round Reading Room of the British Library in Great Russell Street, where the *Burney collection* is held; at the India Office Library and Records (qv) and the Oriental Collections building (qv).

Underground Colindale (Northern Line). **Open** Mon-Sat 1000-1645. **Cloakroom. Toilets. Parking. Public telephones. For the disabled** lift. **Refreshments** vending machines. **Photography** by appointment. **Visitors' services** guided tours by arrangement, some linguistic aid. **Staff opinion.**

◼ NORTH WOOLWICH STATION MUSEUM
Pier Road E16 2JJ.   Tel 474 7244
Admission *free*

Opened in September 1984 in the Old Station building at North Woolwich, which was carefully restored to its pre-1914 appearance, the museum includes three exhibition galleries telling the story of the Great Eastern Railway, linking London with the ports and towns of East Anglia. The network included the North Woolwich Railway which played an important part in the development of East London. There are old photographs, models, relics, and a completely restored and furnished booking-office, but the centre-piece of the museum is the steam locomotive *Coffee Pot* (No. 229), built in 1876 and restored to its 1910 condition, which used to shunt goods trains at nearby Canning Town. This museum is part of the Passmore Edwards Museum (qv).

Underground Stratford (Central Line) and then **Bus** 69. **Open** Mon-Sat 1000-1700, Sun 1400-1700. **Toilets. For the disabled** access, toilets. **Shopping** sales desk. **Photography** by request. **Educational facilities.**

◼ ODONTOLOGICAL MUSEUM
Royal College of Surgeons of England, 35-43 Lincoln's Inn Fields WC2A 3PN. Tel 405 3474 ext 75
Admission *prior application*

Developed under the guidance of Sir Frank Colyer, who was its curator for many years, the museum is housed at the Royal College of Surgeons of England. Its purpose is to preserve objects that are important in the history of odontology and its application to dentistry. It also contains a large number of skulls of mammals, including one of the finest collections of comparative pathology in the world. The exhibits provide a visual aid to teaching and the museum is normally only open to students and teachers from dental schools, medical schools and universities.

Only a small sample of the collections is displayed (the remainder is accessible, and permission can usually be obtained for research workers who wish to study it) as three-quarters of the material is in storage. Important historical pieces are strongly represented in the form of old extraction instruments and early types of artificial teeth and dentures. There are examples of 'phossy jaw' produced by the yellow phosphorus used in the manufacture of matches in the C19 which led to the famous 'Match Girls Strike' by workers at the Bryant and May factory in the 1880s. Among the curiosities is the denture made in Italy for Caroline of Brunswick-Wolfenbüttel, Queen to George IV.

Underground Holborn (Central, Piccadilly Lines). **Open** Mon-Fri 1000-1700. **Cloakroom. Toilets. Public telephones. For the disabled** access, toilets. **Publications. Photography. Visitors' services** guided tours by arrangement. **Research** access to stored specimens.

■ OLD ST THOMAS' OPERATING THEATRE

Chapter House, St Thomas Street SE1 9RY. Tel 407 7600 ext 2739
Admission *charge*

London has many surprises for the discerning visitor. Where else can one find at the top of a Wren church a C19 operating theatre which still retains most of the original fixtures when it was first built? We owe the rediscovery of the theatre to a famous surgeon with a passion for history. In 1956 Russell Brock (later Lord Brock) while reading through the archives of the Old St Thomas' Hospital by London Bridge, became convinced that the operating theatre for women used from 1821 to 1862 (when the hospital vacated the site where it has stood since 1225 and moved to Lambeth) could be located in a part of the old building which had been sealed off. His intuition proved to be correct.

Old Operating Theatre.

Now the place, carefully restored to its original form, can be visited by anyone interested in seeing how surgeons used to perform their gruesome work in front of their students, before Joseph Lister's revolutionary introduction of antiseptic surgery. There are further attractions. Before the operating theatre was placed in the loft of St Thomas' parish church, rebuilt by Sir Christopher Wren in 1702, this was used for drying and storing medical herbs. A small exhibition is mounted to show the activities of the apothecary, responsible for supplying vital medicines. Another exhibition is devoted to Florence Nightingale, the famous reformer of hospital nursing, whom St Thomas' Hospital honoured by naming a school and home for nurses after her.

Just a word of warning. To reach the entrance to the museum visitors have to climb a very steep and narrow spiral staircase used for entry and exit. Particularly dangerous is the exit, since the door from the exhibition opens directly without warning on to the first step of the stairs. Care is needed, but this is still a very worthwhile expedition.

---
the essentials

Underground London Bridge (Northern Line). **Open** Mon, Wed, Fri 1230-1600. **Photography. Visitors' services** guided tours for groups by prior arrangement. **Staff opinion.**

■ ORIENTAL COLLECTIONS

14 Store Street WC1E 7DG.   Tel 323 7642
Admission *reader's pass* (see British Library)

This is the home of the British Library's collections covering the
languages and literature of Asia and northern Africa. With over a
half million books, 40,000 manuscripts and other items, the collection is both a modern working library and a classical archive serving scholars and researchers from all over the world.

The collection includes many priceless treasures, such as *Chinese
oracle bones* of the Shang period (second millenium BC), which
provide evidence for the earliest form of Chinese Characters, several C8 Buddhist charms from Japan, which are the world's earliest
printed texts datable with any certainty, and the Chinese *Diamond
Sutra* of 868, the world's earliest printed book, on view in the British
Library (qv) exhibition galleries. Some 360 languages are represented within five main groups: Judaeo-Christian, Islamic, South-
Asian, South-east Asian and Far Eastern.

1	Oriental Collections:
	1. A dog-headed demon, from the Wonders of Creation, late C16; 2. Woodcut from
2	the Album of Mountain Landscape with Kyoka poems, published in 1804.

The material form of the collections is also important with items on papyrus, paper, vellum, silk, palm-leaf, birch-bark, bone, ivory, copper plate, other metals and various kinds of cloth. The forms of presentation also vary with items in codex form (ie like a normal book), in scrolls, in concertina folds or even in the form of fans.

the essentials

Underground Tottenham Court Road (Central, Northern Lines). **Open** Mon-Fri 0930-1700; Sat 0930-1300. **Cloakroom. Toilets. For the disabled** access, lift by prior arrangement. **Publications. Photography** by arrangement. **Educational facilities. Visitors' services** guided tours by arrangement, photographic services, typing room. **Research** library. **Staff opinion.**

■ ORLEANS HOUSE GALLERY

Riverside, Twickenham TW1 3DJ.   Tel 892 0221

Admission *free*

Orleans House Gallery, the Octagon.

Orleans House had a fascinating history. Built for James Johnston in 1710, it was enlarged in 1720 when the Octagon — a real masterpiece of architecture designed by James Gibbs — was added. The house took its name from Louis-Philippe, Duc d'Orleans, who leased the place from 1815-17. The house itself has, sadly, disappeared, but the Octagon survived, thanks to the timely action of Mrs Basil Ionides who on her death, in 1962, donated the estate together with a rich collection of works of art to the local authority. The ***Ionides Collection*** housed at Orleans House Gallery includes oils by Samuel Scott, William Marlow and George Hilditch, watercolours by Peter de Wint, Joseph Farington and Augustin Heckel and many fine engravings of Richmond and the surrounding area.

The gallery has a continuous programme of exhibitions of works from the Ionides Collection and the Richmond upon Thames Art and Local History collections. Few galleries are more fortunate in their setting. The walk from Richmond on the Twickenham bank of the Thames, past Marble Hill House (qv), is indeed a treat not to be missed.

the essentials

Underground Richmond (District Line) then Bus 90b,202,270,290. **Open** Apr-Sep Tue-Sat 1300-1730, Sun 1400-1730, Oct-Mar Tue-Sat 1300-1630, Sun 1400-1630. **Cloakroom. Toilets. Parking. For the disabled** access to ground floor and Octagon, toilets. **Shopping** sales desk. **Publications. Photography** by application. **Visitors's services** guided tours on request.

■ OSTERLEY PARK HOUSE

Isleworth TW7 2RL.   Tel 560 3918
Admission *charge*

Osterley Park House.

'Oh! the palace of palaces!' wrote Horace Walpole of Osterley Park House in 1773. 'There is a hall, library, breakfast room, eating room, all chef d'oeuvre of Adam, a gallery one hundred and thirty feet long, and a drawing room worthy of Eve before the Fall'. The house was then the home of the Child family, whose banking firm eventually became Williams and Glyn's Bank. It is now a National Trust property, administered by the Victoria and Albert Museum (qv) who have restored it as near as possible to the interior that Walpole, who lived at nearby Strawberry Hill, so much admired. Osterley Park House was already a distinguished Elizabethan mansion when the Child family commissioned the architect Robert Adam to transform it into a fashionable C18 villa; it stands today as perhaps the finest surviving example of Adam's work.

Re-created as a temple to the arts, the house has the finest interior design and furnishing that the third quarter of the C18 could provide, and perhaps the most stunning example of Adam's brilliance is the *library ceiling*, a multi-coloured masterpiece of plasterwork now restored to its original hues. Still on the ground floor, the antechamber of the State Apartment has become the tapestry room housing the French Gobelins *tapestries* which in startlingly well-preserved colours represent the Elements by relating the Loves of the Gods. In the State Bechamber itself is the *Osterley State Bed*, painstakingly restored by the V&A's textiles conservators. Adam designed it as a Temple of Venus, with velvet and silk hangings and garlands of silk flowers decorating the domed canopy.

The National Trust has also restored the grounds, open free of charge all the year round. The architect William Chambers, who designed Somerset House, helped lay out the pleasure gardens, and designed the charming Doric temple. Adam was responsible for the semi-circular greenhouse. The parkland is bordered by a serpentine lake, near whose cedars is the concealed mound of the ice-house. (ST)

---
the essentials

Underground Osterley (Piccadilly Line). **Open** Tue-Sun 1100-1700. **Cloakroom. Toilets. Parking. Refreshments** cafeteria (Apr-Sept). **Shopping** sales desk. **Publications. Photography** no tripod. **Educational facilities** through the V&A. **Visitors' services** guided tours by arrangement through the V&A. **Research** by arrangement through the V&A.

■ PASSMORE EDWARDS MUSEUM

Romford Road E15 4LZ. Tel 519 4296
Admission *free*

Passmore Edwards Museum.

This modest-sized but intelligently-run museum was opened at the turn of the century to conserve and display the heritage of the country of Essex and in particular that part which is now Newham. It covers archaeology, biology, geology and, of course, local history. The central **Hall**, adorned with a pool, contains cases of many kinds of British mammals. Other displays comprise products of the famous *Bow porcelain* factory (including a Boxer known to at least one visiting family as 'Fancy-Pants'), costumes down the ages, items on the history of the Great Eastern Railway, and agricultural bygones from rural Essex. The Passmore Edwards Museum group also includes the North Woolwich Station Museum (qv) and the Museum Interpretative Centre and Nature Reserve (qv).

──────────── *the essentials* ────────────

Underground Stratford (Central Line). **Open** Mon-Fri 1000-1800, Sat 1000-1700, Sun 1400-1700. **For the disabled** access to lower floor only. **Shopping** sales desk. **Photography** by request. **Educational facilities.**

■ PAVLOVA MEMORIAL MUSEUM

Ivy House, North End Road NW11 7HU.
Admission *free*

Close to the top entrance to Golders Hill Park and almost opposite the Bull and Bush stands Ivy House, the London home of Anna Pavlova from 1912 to her death early in 1931. The small museum collection upstairs is the only one in the world devoted to this legendary figure. In the studio overlooking the grounds and lake, where Pavlova kept her tame swans, there are photographs, periodicals and other memorabilia, including a fitted travelling trunk used on tour, the dressing-table from the Palace Theatre (the great dancer is pictured seated at it), and a life-mask from her early thirties. A modest memorial to a hugely influential talent.

──────────── *the essentials* ────────────

Underground Golders Green (Northern Line). **Open** Sat 1400-1700. **Toilets. Public telephones. Shopping** sales desk. **Photography. Visitors' services** guided tours by arrangement. **Research** by arrangement.

■ PERCIVAL DAVID FOUNDATION OF CHINESE ART

53 Gordon Square WC1H 0PD. Tel 387 3909
Admission *free*

This impressive collection of Chinese ceramics which is administered for London University by the School of Oriental and African Studies is located in what was previously a spacious private house in Bloomsbury. Sir Percival David (1892-1964) was a scholar and a Governor of the School of Oriental and African Studies who, in 1950, bequeathed his collection of 1,400 ceramic pieces and unique library to the University. He was a discriminating collector and many of the items on display were once in the possession of

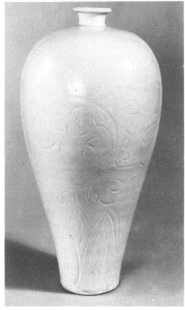

1	2
3	4

Percival David Foundation:
1. Porcelain dish decorated in famille rose enamels in Ku yüeh style (1736-95); 2. Olive green celadon glaze box (Song, 960-1279); 3. Crackled blue grey glaze vase (Song dynasty); 4. Mei-p'ing vase, C11-C12.

Chinese emperors — several feature poems from the brush of Emperor Qianlong.

The galleries are arranged on three floors: the earliest dated items begin on the first floor with the white wares of the *Song period* (950-1279), displaying delicately incised and carved motifs. Later white wares include a pair of elephants bearing cloisonné incense pots and a model of a hare whose eyes are indicated by two spots of brown glaze. In cabinets nearby are fine examples of various celadon wares characterized by their greyish-green glazes. In striking contrast are the porcelains of the *Ming and Qing Dynasties* (1368-1644 and 1644-1912), to be seen on the second floor, with their brilliant yellows, greens and blues. Splendid monochrome pieces are complemented by a number of the classic Blue and White porcelains including the earliest dated examples of these, a pair of temple vases dated by a dedicatory inscription to 1351.

The **Lady David Gallery**, opened on the ground floor in honour of the wife of the founder, is an attractive display area. Normally contains a primary exhibition with examples of the majority of the wares found in the collection. In December 1985 a special exhibition was opened here to mark the fiftieth anniversary of the London International Exhibition of Chinese Art: an historic event, masterminded by Sir Percival, which opened the eyes of many Europeans to the splendours of Chinese art.

At the sales desk near the entrance a wide range of publications, catalogues, posters, colour slides and postcards are available for the scholar and souvenir hunter alike. The Foundation also houses an important Reference Library of books relating to Chinese art and culture, available only on application to the Curator of the Foundation. (MG)

--- *the essentials* ---

Underground Euston Square (Circle, Metropolitan Lines), Russell Square (Piccadilly Line). **Open** Mon 1400-1700, Tue-Fri 1030-1700, Sat 1030-1300. **Cloakroom. Toilets. For the disabled** toilets. **Shopping** sales desk. **Publications. Photography** restricted. **Visitors' services** guided tours by arrangement. **Research** library on application. **Staff opinion** by prior application.

■ PETRIE MUSEUM OF EGYPTIAN ARCHAEOLOGY

University College London, Gower Street WC1E 6BT.   Tel 387 7050 ext 617
Admission *free*

This museum contains the collection of Egyptian antiquities assembled by the eminent British archaeologist, Sir Flinders Petrie (1853-1942). Petrie, a pioneer in modern archaeology methods, was appointed the first professor of Egyptology at University College in 1892. His excavations in Egypt led to a number of spectacular discoveries, among them the palace of King Akhenaten, the Greek city of Naucratis and fragments of a colossal statue of Rameses II. The museum retains its original status as a study and teaching collection rather than a gallery of showpieces — thus the presentation is, perhaps, somewhat dry but unusually detailed.

Immediately inside the entrance are a portrait of Petrie by de László and a photograph of him on excavation (one of his students in Egypt was T.E. Lawrence, 'Lawrence of Arabia'). In a display case nearby is a *child's linen tunic*; dating from the 1st Dynasty (c3100 BC), this

Petrie Museum of Egyptian Archaeology:
1. Ebony statuette of a negress (New Kingdom, c1500 BC);
2. One of the monumental limestone lions from Koptos reconstructed by Richard Jaeschke. The pair were found in the temple at Koptos by Petrie in 1894 and date to the 1st Dynasty.

is the oldest known linen garment in the world. Nearby are two Old Kingdom *dresses* from Deshasheh. The rest of the room is devoted to the chronological display of pottery which ranges from examples of crude Neolithic wares (prior to 5000 BC) to Egyptian pottery of the Coptic, or Christian, period (284-614). A number of the latter are decorated with figures of saints, crosses and fish. Other interesting pieces include *Predynastic Gerzean wares* (c3300 BC), with their comma and checker patterning and the pottery 'mourners', bewailing the departed, which were produced during the Middle Kingdom (c2113-1786 BC). A graphic display draws attention to the monumental Archaic *Koptos Icons* now in the main cloisters of UCL.

In the following room, on the right-hand side, are 18 inscription cases containing temple *reliefs* and tomb *stelae* (upright stone slabs). A number of these are decorated with scenes of religious worship, others bear Greek, Latin and Arabic and hieroglyphic inscriptions. The *Langton Cats* are a group of faience, bronze and stone cats of great beauty, bequeathed to the museum in 1972. Further display cases in this room contain artefacts discovered on various sites and arranged chronologically. These range from flint tools and jewellery of Pre-Dynastic origin (c5000-3100 BC) to decorative glass work of the Roman period (30 BC-284). A separate exhibit among these is the *Hierakonpolis Bowl*, a large feldspar porphyry bowl of Archaic date bearing reliefs of the goddess Hathor and a jabiru bird. A case exhibits newly conserved Graeco-Roman *mummy portraits*; works of art as well as archaeological artefacts.

Downstairs are a number of miscellaneous exhibits. A series of 31 bead cases line the walls, containing a chronological display of *jewellery*; here also are a group of *metalwork figures* representing deities, kings and animals including a silver figure of the ithyphallic god Min and a silver feather from a large statue of Min from Koptos. Nearby are two cases of Predynastic objects and a number of *soul houses*, small clay dwellings where the departed can carry on their existence. One of the museum's largest relics in situ is the colossal sandstone *jackal's paw* dating from the 18th Dynasty (c1567), which was discovered on the site of the temple of Amenopolis III. Dynastic textiles, Graeco-Roman funerary portraits and metal vases complete the staircase display. In addition to the main exhibition, further material from the collection is presented in glass-topped drawers beneath the display cases. A detailed guide, postcards and slides can be purchased from the Beadle, as well as current publications concerning the collection and Egyptology, notably Petrie's biography and the story of the re-discovery and restoration of the Koptos Icons. (MG)

---

the essentials

Underground Euston Square (Circle, Metropolitan Lines). **Open** Mon-Fri 1000-1200, 1315-1700 (closed 4 weeks or more in Summer). **Cloakroom** in adjacent Library. **Toilets** in adjacent Library. **Refreshments** restaurant in main College. **Shopping** sales desk. **Publications. Visitors' services** guided tours by arrangement.

■ PHOTOGRAPHERS' GALLERY LIBRARY
5-8 Great Newport Street WC2H 7HY.   Tel 240 5511
Admission *free*

A wide range of photographers' work, British and foreign, C19 and contemporary, famous and unknown, is contained in the Reference and Slide Library. Over 15,000 slides cover the full range of the photographic medium in all disciplines including fine art, vintage prints, reportage and photo-journalism. The nucleus of the fairly comprehensive collection of books is the *collection of Norman Hall*, sometime Picture Editor of The Times. It is the only reference library in London which concentrates on the aesthetics of photography with illustrations from an international selection of books, periodicals, journals and magazines. The library, which occupies most of the first floor of the gallery, offers also a comprehensive selection on British photographers since the war.

---

the essentials

Underground Leicester Square (Northern, Piccadilly Lines). **Open** Tue-Sat 1100-1900. **Toilets. For the disabled** access, toilets. **Refreshments** snacks. **Shopping** bookshop. **Publications. Photography** on application. **Educational facilities. Visitors' services** lectures, guided tours by arrangement. **Research** library.

■ PITSHANGER MANOR MUSEUM
Mattock Lane W5 5EQ.   Tel 567 1227
Admission *free*

This from 1800 to 1810 was the country villa of Sir John Soane, architect of the Bank of England and founder of Sir John Soane's Museum (qv). It is now, after years as one of Ealing's public libraries, being restored to its full magnificence. It houses an extensive display of Martinware pottery (cf Martinware Pottery Collection) which is on loan from the Trustees of the Hull Grundy Estate.

Pitshanger Manor Museum: East front

——————————— *the essentials* ———————————
Underground Ealing Broadway (Central, District Lines). **Open** Tue-Sat 1000-1700. **Toilets.**
For the disabled partial access. **Refreshments** hot and cold drinks. **Shopping** sales desk.
Publications guidebook, postcards. **Photography. Visitors' services** group tours by
arrangement. **Research. Staff opinion.**

■ POLISH INSTITUTE AND SIKORSKI MUSEUM
20 Princes Gate SW7 1PT.   Tel 589 9249
Admission *free*

This is by far the most important museum outside Poland with over
10,000 items displayed plus a library with two branches: in London
[26 Pont Street SW1X 0AZ, Tel. 589 9249] and in Scotland [42 Cecil
Street, Glasgow G12 8RJ, Tel. (041) 339 2135] and Archives.

The collection is spread over a large elegant Victorian house on
the edge of Hyde Park, built at the time of the Great Exhibition (1851).

On entering the building the visitor is confronted with a huge red-
and-white striped *tent* taken by the Poles in the striking victory over
the Turkish army in 1621, and now mounted at the top of the staircase. In fact to some extent all the artefacts on display derive essentially from the collection of two field museums whose original
purpose was to preserve for future generations an idea of the appearance, and equipment used, of Polish soldiers fighting on
various fronts. Systematic collection began during the French campaign but items from 1939 were also brought to Britain so that a continuous period of Poland's involvement in the war can be seen.
Preserved in the museum are war standards, over 300 military
uniforms, the orders and distinctions of Generals Sikorski and
Anders, the respective Commanders-in-Chief, regimental badges
in enamel etc.

A major exhibit in a glass cabinet is *General Sikorski's uniform*
salvaged from the sea after the air disaster in Gibraltar. Another
major exhibit is the red-and-white *Polish national flag* which was
flown over the ruins of the monastery of Monte Cassino (1944).
Separate collections record the history of cavalry, artillery, and armoured units with many mementos of national and sentimental
value. Other items on display are armour from the C17, C18 water-

Polish Institute and Sikorski Museum:
King Jan Sobieski III; Regimental Colours.

colours, paintings and miniatures and relics from the Napoleonic era.

The whole comprehensive display of Poland's military achievements is augmented by the **archives** and **libraries** relating to its history which include important documents, registers, journals of action, reports, diaries etc. which all had a bearing on the period before World War II, the 1939 campaign and the period of fighting outside Poland. The Institute is now virtually the Keeper of central state archives and the main source of information on Polish history during the war.

the essentials

Underground South Kensington (Circle, District, Piccadilly Lines). **Open** Tue-Fri 0930-1600. **Cloakroom. Toilets. Photography. Educational facilities. Visitors services** films, guided tours. **Research** library.

■ POLLOCK'S TOY MUSEUM
1 Scala Street W1P 1LT.   Tel 636 3452
Admission *charge*

The museum is not strictly a children's museum as it is also concerned with keeping alive the traditional English toy theatre. There are also toys from around the world. Particular attention is being given to the acquisition of examples of English dolls and toys thus giving a more specialised focus of interest. The range is wide with exhibits from many countries including ingenious mechanical and constructional toys such as the 1907 Meccano. There are traditional toy soldiers, dolls made of china, wood, rag, celluloid, wax and composition materials, pre-1910 bears and toys made in China, Japan, Russia, India and South America.

The items on display are changed quite frequently. Space in the museum is severely restricted as it is crammed with exhibits and the rooms are small. It is particularly popular during school holidays and your visit will be more enjoyable outside these peak periods. Traditional toys, reprints and working toy theatres are on sale, and attract both children and collectors. The museum is named after Benjamin Pollock (1856-1937) whose shop in East London was well-known for its toy theatres. Its contents were saved for posterity in 1944 by an antiquarian bookseller and are the basis of the museum which was started in 1956.

─────────────── *the essentials* ───────────────
Underground Goodge Street (Northern Line). **Open** Mon-Sat 1000-1700. **Toilets. Shopping. Publications. Photography** for private purposes. **Visitors' services** toy theatre shows in holidays. **Research** library.

■ PRINCE HENRY'S ROOM

17 Fleet Street EC4Y 1AA. Tel 353 7323
Admission *free*

The room is in one of the few buildings to survive the Great Fire of London in 1666, the threat of demolition in the 1890s and the Blitz in 1940-41. Built in 1610 the house became a tavern and eventually a home for a waxworks exhibition from 1795 to 1816. It was believed, incorrectly, that the three feathers motif on the facade identified it as a residence for Prince Henry (1594-1612), eldest son of James I and Prince of Wales at the time. The most outstanding feature of the room is the original, *richly decorated plaster ceiling* incorporating the inscribed letters PH and Prince of Wales feathers. A tenuous association with Samuel Pepys the famous diarist, who was born nearby, is marked by a permanent exhibition of contemporary items, prints and paintings of the diarist and his time.

─────────────── *the essentials* ───────────────
Underground Blackfriars, Temple (Circle, District Lines). **Open** 1345-1700, Sat 1344-1600. **Cloakroom. Shopping** sales desk. **Publications. Photography. Visitors' services** lectures.

■ PUBLIC RECORD OFFICE, KEW

Ruskin Avenue, Kew TW9 4DU. Tel 876 3444
Admission *prior application*

The Public Record Office was established under the Public Record Office Act 1838 and contains the national archives (that is the records of central government and the central courts of England and Wales) from the time of the Norman conquest until the 1950s. The records are divided between two buildings at Kew and at Chancery Lane in central London. The building at Kew is among the most modern archive buildings in the world. The main reading room seats approximately 240 readers and there are small-map and large-document reading rooms. In addition there is a reference room. The building is air-conditioned to provide a controlled environment for document storage and items are requisitioned via computer terminal keyboards which give instant up-to-date information as to availability. Microfilm and microfiche readers are available and there are facilities for researchers to use their own typewriters and tape recorders.

─────────────── *the essentials* ───────────────
Underground Kew Gardens (District Line). **Open** Mon-Fri 0930-1700 (closed first 2 weeks Oct). **Cloakroom. Toilets. Parking. Public telephones. For the disabled** access, toilets. **Refreshments** restaurant, snacks. **Shopping** sales desk. **Educational facilities. Visitors' services** guided tours by prior arrangement. **Research.**

■ PUBLIC RECORD OFFICE MUSEUM

Chancery Lane WC2A 1LR.   Tel 876 3444
Admission *free*

The Public Record Office building in Chancery Lane, drawing by Whitney Lumas.

This Museum of the national archives has been here since 1902, presenting a representative selection chosen to give a public showing to its outstanding treasures, such as *Domesday Book*, compiled on the orders of William the Conqueror in 1086, and to illustrate the evolution of the public records over eight centuries and the range of subjects which they cover, from overseas affairs, war and the economy to law and order and the welfare state. In addition to the small permanent exhibition, a series of temporary exhibitions are planned.

Great and Little Domesday Books on the Domesday Tudor chest. The famous book was rebound into five volumes in 1985, instead of its original two.

the essentials

Underground Chancery Lane (Central Line). **Open** Mon-Fri 1000-1700. **For the disabled** by prior arrangement. **Visitors' services** guided tours for groups by prior arrangement. **Research** reading rooms open to the public Mon-Fri 0930-1700.

■ QUEEN'S GALLERY

Buckingham Palace Road SW1A 1AA.   Tel 799 2331
Admission *charge*

A Buckingham Palace Warden admiring the portrait of Henry V by an unknown artist.

The gallery which is the venue of temporary exhibitions from the British Royal family collections, is not large, but most skilfully designed. In fact, technically, it is as fine as one could wish, and rightly so, because the Queen's Pictures are a collection of astonishing richness. The roll-call of great masters is endless, the examples the choicest, the most perfectly preserved. The Van Dycks, Canalettos, Stubbses and Gainsboroughs are unsurpassed anywhere in the world. The Master Drawings range from Leonardo, Raphael and Michelangelo through Holbein, Canaletto and Hogarth to Augustus John, Stanley Spencer and Topolski.

Exhibitions, changed periodically, are carefully planned to explore various aspects and themes among these priceless treasures, and the catalogues, thoroughly researched and beautifully presented, are models of their kind. No one who cares for great paintings will fail to visit this unique and, whatever the current exhibition, always richly rewarding gallery. You enter by an unobtrusive doorway on the Buckingham Palace Road side of the Palace, and continue along a passageway. Those hoping for a glimpse of life behind the royal scenes will be disappointed. Security is absolute. Gravely courteous attendants in royal livery make sure you do not lose your way.

the essentials

Underground St James's Park (Circle, District Lines), Victoria (Circle, District, Victoria Lines). **Open** Tue-Sat 1030-1700, Sun 1400-1700. Closed Mon except Bank Holidays. **Cloakroom. For the disabled** access. **Shopping** sales desk. **Publications.**

■ RANGER'S HOUSE

Chesterfield Walk, Blackheath SE10 8QX.   Tel 853 0035
Admission *free*

Ranger's House overlooking Blackheath.

In the 1680s one Andrew Snape, the King's Serjeant Farrier, describ-ed by the diarist John Evelyn as 'a man full of projects', built three houses as a speculative venture on 'The Waste' beside Greenwich Park. The centre villa was on the site of Ranger's House which pro-bably owes its present form to Admiral Francis Hosier (1673-1727) who lived here in the early years of the C18. Philip, 4th Earl of Chesterfield (1694-1773), politician and author of letters of wordly advice to his natural son, inherited Ranger's House as an, at first, unwelcome legacy from his younger brother John Stanhope in 1784. He later retired here when, beset by increasing deafness, he left politics for the rural peace of Blackheath.

One of the improvements which Chesterfield made on moving in-to the house was the addition of a **gallery** (1749-50), a happy thought because today it forms the ideal setting for the ***Suffolk Collection.*** This is an astonishing array of full-length portraits, some 53 in all. The heart of the collection is a set of remarkable works by William Larkin (d1619), a shadowy figure. What is certain is that these pic-tures present an invaluable survey of courtly fashion in the first decades of the C17. *Edward Sackville*, 4th Earl of Dorset (No. 4) is dazzling in black satin and white lace with hugely ballooning breeches. He is covered in gold lace and his shoes bear ornate rosettes the size of prize-winning entries at a flower show. Not far behind him in magnificence is Larkin's *Countess of Oxford* (No. 10). She and her twin sister wear identically fantastic slashed dresses. Note the curiously metallic finish of the curtains, an ef-fect much liked by Larkin and characteristic of his work.

There is much else at Ranger's House. Note in the gallery window the splendid Kirckman *harpsichord* of 1772. Recitals are given here in this perfect setting. Upstairs is a selection from the ***Dolmetsch Collection*** of historical musical instruments, and in the corridor the prints include a fine portrait of *John Peter Saloman*, the impresario who brought the great Joseph Haydn to London and to the peak of his achievement as a symphonist, the London Symphonies.

Ranger's House, the Suffolk Collection: A Howard boy by Peake (left) and Richard Sackville, 3rd Earl of Dorset by Larkin (right).

the essentials

Underground New Cross (East London Line) then **Bus** 53. **Open** daily 1000-1700 (1600 Jan-Nov). **Cloakroom. Toilets. Parking. For the disabled** access to ground floor, toilets. **Shopping** sales desk. **Photography** by agreement. **Educational facilities. Visitors' services** guided tours by appointment.

■ REGIMENTAL MUSEUM OF THE ROYAL FUSILIERS

Tower of London, Tower Hill EC3N 4AB.   Tel 709 0765
Admission *charge*

It records the formation and subsequent history of 'Our Royal Regiment of Fuzileers'. This was raised and quartered in the Tower of London on the instructions of King James II in 1685, when the soldiers were armed with a type of flintlock musket known as a 'fuzil'. The original purpose of the new regiment was to guard the guns in the Tower of London. Relics and commemorations of the Regiment's battles are exhibited, together with uniforms, weapons used and captured, silver, china, medals, oil paintings and dioramas of the Battle of Albuhera (1811) and Monte Cassino (1944), and of course, a specimen of the C17 'fuzil'. Note the original *Victoria Cross* struck in 1856 for inspection and approval by Queen Victoria, several VCs won by soldiers of the Regiment in various wars, and the uniform worn by King George V as its Colonel-in-Chief. Separate rooms present the Regiment's history in these periods: 1685-1853, 1854-1918 and 1919-1969. Its association with the City of London was recognised in 1881 when the title 'City of London Regiment' was added to the Royal Fusiliers, from which stemmed the privilege of marching through the City with bayonets fixed and Colours flying.

the essentials

Underground Tower Hill (Circle, District Lines). **Open** daily Apr-Oct 1000-1730, Nov-Mar 1000-1645. **Shopping** sales desk. **Photography.**

■ RIESCO COLLECTION OF CHINESE CERAMICS

Fairfield Halls, Park Lane, Croydon CR9 1DG.   Tel 681 0821
Admission *free*

This collection, amassed by a local businessman and presented to Croydon Council, fills only four showcases but these contain choice specimens from more than 4,000 years of Chinese ceramics, including vigorous Tang dynasty tomb models, subtle Song dynasty stoneware and porcelain, and magnificent Ming, five-colour, and blue-and-white pieces made for the C18 Qing emperors. With the handlist, this is an excellent concise introduction to the world of Chinese ceramics.

─────────── *the essentials* ───────────

BR East Croydon (from Victoria Station). **Open** Mon-Sat 1000-2000. **Cloakroom. Toilets. Public telephones. Refreshments** snacks. **Shopping. Publications** handlist, postcards. **Photography.**

■ ROCK CIRCUS

London Pavilion, Piccadilly Circus W1V 9LB.   Tel 734 7203 (734 8026)
Admission *charge*

A most innovative permanent exhibition of waxworks connected with the world of popular music. About fifty artists are represented, the selection mainly being of those performers who, it is felt, have made the greatest contribution to rock-and-roll, including Elvis Presley, the Beatles and the Rolling Stones. Visitors can listen to their heroes' music and a brief history by means of specially-designed stereo headphones which are worn throughout the exhibition. Not only are there stationary life-size waxworks figures but, as a finale, visitors are seated on a revolving theatre with models of acts past and present performing for the audience, miming to their music, while a brief resumé of rock history is narrated. (FS)

─────────── *the essentials* ───────────

Underground Piccadilly Circus (Bakerloo, Piccadilly Lines). **Open** daily 1000-2200. **Cloakroom. Toilets. Public telephones. For the disabled** access, toilets. **Refreshments** soft drinks. **Shopping. Publications. Photography.**

■ ROYAL ACADEMY OF ARTS

Burlington House, Piccadilly W1V 0DS.   Tel 439 7438
Admission *charge*

The Royal Academy was founded in 1768 to provide a free school of art for promising young students and to give mature and distinguished artists the opportunity of exhibiting and selling their work. By charging for admission to the exhibition the Royal Academy was able to become financially independent and has remained so ever since.

Each of the 50 elected members, called Royal Academicians, have to give an example of their work to the Academy before they receive their Diploma signed by the Sovereign. This forms the nucleus of the ***Royal Academy's permanent collection***. It also includes gifts, bequests and works purchased through certain small trust funds, making a unique collection. The main portion is formed of works that each Academician gave to represent him at the time of his election. This makes an extremely interesting survey

Sir Joshua Reynolds, 1st President of the Royal Academy of Arts, by Alfred Drury RA, at Burlington House.

of British Art of the past 217 years. These works are frequently loaned to important exhibitions and also form travelling exhibitions, taking art to the provinces. Some of them are used to decorate parts of Burlington House. The rest unless on loan can be seen by appointment.

One of the greatest treasures is the *Michelangelo Tondo*. It was carved in Florence about 1505 for Taddeo Taddei and was bought in 1824 by Sir George Beaumont, who was instrumental in the formation of the National Gallery (qv). At his request his heirs gave the tondo to the Royal Academy in 1830.

The Taddei Tondo (c1505), by Michelangelo.

During the summer months the 15 beautiful galleries, built by the Royal Academy on the gardens of Burlington House, contain the famous **Annual Summer Exhibition**, held without a break since 1769. About 1,500 works by living artists are for sale and they make an exhibition with such a variety of styles that there is always something to appeal to everyone.

All year round loan exhibitions of international repute with widely differing subjects are held. The policy is always to have at least one exhibition open, every day of the week, usually from 1000 to 1800. During the past few years the list included such successful exhibitions as: 'Great Japan Exhibition', 'Genius of Venice', the work of the Royal Academy's first President, 'Sir Joshua Reynolds', 'The Age of Chivalry', 'Henry Moore' and 'Italian Art in the 20th Century'.

Series of lectures are arranged to add to the enjoyment and understanding of the exhibitions. Membership of the Friends of the Royal Academy gives free admission, with a guest, to all exhibitions, use of the Friends Room and access to the *Library*, which has about 15,000 volumes. Many of these are C17, C18 and C19 books given or bequeathed by Royal Academicians. The Library is open to all serious scholars and researchers 1400 to 1700, Monday to Friday. (C-AP)

──────────────── *the essentials* ────────────────

Underground Piccadilly Circus (Bakerloo, Piccadilly Lines). **Open** daily 1000-1800. **Cloakroom. Toilets. For the disabled** access, toilets. **Shopping** bookshop. **Publications. Educational facilities. Visitors' services** Acousta Guides. **Research** library.

■ ROYAL AIR FORCE MUSEUM

Grahame Park Way NW9 5LL.   Tel 205 2266
Admission *charge*

The Royal Air Force Museum complex. Two of the original Grahame White Aircraft Factory buildings (1915) house the RAF Museum, attached to which is the Bomber Command Museum. The building on the left is the Battle of Britain Museum.

This important complex comprises three quite separate but complementary displays — the RAF Museum, the Battle of Britain Museum, and the Bomber Command Museum. The **Royal Air Force Museum** is the only British national museum devoted solely to the history of aviation and to the story of the Royal Air Force, past, present and future. The museum, which was established in 1963 and opened by the Queen in 1972, is aptly situated on ten acres of the former historic airfield at Hendon, the cradle of British aviation.

The museum building, of striking modern design, incorporates as its superb aircraft exhibition hall two hangars dating from World War I. The vast hall displays some forty aircraft ranging from the *Bleriot XI* of 1909 through the 'Biggles era' of World War I to the supersonic *Lightning*. The aircraft are positioned as far as possible in chronological order with clear and informative captions, and, from carefully planned vantage points, panoramic views can be obtained from the first floor, while at ground level there is the feeling of walking through a spacious, well-lit hangar.

The RAF Museum, the Main Aircraft Hall.

Linking the two hangars is an area which contains the **Camm Collection** commemorating the late Sir Sidney Camm who designed such famous aircraft as the Hawker Hart, the immortal Hurricane and the P1127 'jump jet', forerunner of the Harrier which proved to be invaluable in the Falkland Islands conflict. Surrounding the hall are eleven galleries on two floors, each dealing with a separate period of aviation from the Royal Engineers' balloon experiments in the 1870s to the Royal Air Force of today. Exhibits include aero-engines, propellers, navigational aids, uniforms, decorations and trophies. Various scenes of early Royal Flying Corps workshops and WRAF huts of both World Wars have been recreated in their contemporary environment, while dramatic audio-visual displays show the work of the Royal Air Force both past and present. The museum also houses a fine collection of paintings, drawings and sculptures.

In 1975 the **Dermot Boyle Wing** was opened. Here temporary exhibitions are displayed. These have included 'The Wings of the Eagle' which portrayed the history of the German Air Force, 'Kings and Queens and Flying Machines' which showed the involvement of royalty in aviation, and sets from the BBC TV series 'The Secret Army'. The Wing has also been used for prestigious events eg 'The Design Council's Annual Awards' where the awards were presented by the Duke of Edinburgh.

Particular mention must be made of the **Department of Aviation Records** which includes the *Archives* and *Library*. The department possesses material of great value to the historian including the important collection of *Brabazon Papers* which range over the entire period of practical powered flight from its inception to 1964. Other treasures include original drawings from the hands of some of the most distinguished aircraft designers, among them Mitchell of Spitfire fame. The library houses an extensive collection of aviation reference books and the reading room is open by prior appointment on weekdays only, 1000 to 1600.

1	Bomber Command Museum:
	1. A Lancaster; 2. A DH9A.
2	Battle of Britain Museum:
3	3. The Spitfire (foreground) and Hurricane, under camouflage.

The museum does not provide conducted tours. However, short introductory talks can be given by prior arrangement with the Education Officer on weekdays, 1000 to 1230, and there are film shows of general aviation interest as well as some of particular value.

Spurred on by the success and world-wide acclaim of the RAF Museum, the **Battle of Britain Museum** was launched in 1978, as a national tribute to the men, women and machines involved in the decisive Air Battle of 1940, and especially to 'The Few'.

The aircraft are displayed along the sides of the hanger-like building with the RAF machines facing their erstwhile adversaries. The *Spitfire MkI*, which is located in an imaginative replica of a wartime dispersal pen, saw action during the Battle of Britain and participated in the 100th 'kill' of No. 609 Squadron. The German aircraft involved in the struggle are well represented and include a *JU88, Heinkel III, Stuka* dive bomber, and *ME109*. Although the main thrust of the exhibition is rightly concerned with the confrontation between fighter and bomber aircraft, there are other exhibits to remind us of the part played by the anti-aircraft defences, searchlights, radar, balloons, Observer Corps, police, fire and ambulance services. The Central area contains a replica of No.11 Group Operations room at RAF Uxbridge as it was at the turning point of the Battle on 15 September 1940, the day which has since been recognised as 'Battle of Britain Day'.

Opened in April 1983, the **Bomber Command Museum** has been designed to display and preserve many unique bomber aircraft and artefacts. It also pays tribute to the courage, determination and perseverance of the men and women who built, maintained and flew these aircraft and in particular to the 126,000 aircrew of Bomber Command and the 8th and 9th USAAF who died in bomber operations during World War II. The museum, which is linked to the RAF Museum, has three inter-connecting halls, carpeted walk-ways and exhibition pavilions. Standing at the entrance to the museum is the magnificent *Lancaster* which bears silent witness to the achievements and sacrifices made by the crews of Bomber Command. The collection includes the only known surviving *Wellington* (apart from the wreck recovered in 1985 from the depths of Loch Ness) and the dramatically-displayed *Halifax* which was raised from a lake in Norway. In April 1942 the aircraft flew its first and last operational sortie when it was shot down while attacking the battleship Tirpitz in a Norwegian fiord.

The World War I era is represented by the immaculately-restored *DH9A* aircraft and tiny *Sopwith Tabloid*. Post war aircraft include two 'V' Bombers, the *Valiant* and the *Vulcan*. The aircraft display is complemented by pavilions which contain exhibits ranging from aircraft models, flying clothing, and photographic reconnaissance equipment, to a full-scale reconstruction of the office of Sir Barnes Wallis, the famous aircraft designer and inventor of the 'Bouncing Bomb', a replica of which is also on view. (WW)

---
the essentials

Underground Colindale (Northern Line). **Open** Mon-Sat 1000-1800, Sun 1400-1800. **Cloakroom** in RAF Museum. **Toilets. Parking. Public telephones** in RAF Museum. **For the disabled** access, toilets. **Refreshments** restaurant, snacks. **Shopping** in RAF Museum. **Publications. Photography. Educational facilities** in RAF Museum. **Visitors' services** films, lectures. **Research** library.

■ ROYAL ARMOURIES

Tower of London, Tower Hill EC3N 4AB. Tel 480 6358
Admission *charge*

The Tower of London has been a royal household, a royal observatory, the royal mint and a royal jail. It still houses the Royal Armouries, the finest historical arsenal in the world, in its oldest part, the C11 White Tower. Newly reorganised and given their royal designation in 1985, the Armouries are also officially entitled the National Museum of Arms and Armour, and constitute Britain's oldest public museum (1660). The collection of arms and armour which now covers four floors of the ancient keep has as its nucleus the personal armours and arsenal of Henry VIII. The collection is still growing so that some aspects are now viewable in other parts of the Tower of London.

Visitors enter the **White Tower** at the **first floor** to find the sporting weapons, from medieval crossbows to the famous Colt·45 revolver of the American West, and including oddities like the C18 musket specially made for a one-armed, one-eyed man. On this floor, too, is tournament armour of the C15 to the early C17. Two galleries on the **second floor** have weapons and armour from the C5 to the end of the Middle Ages in one, and the Renaissance in the other — measure yourself against the suit of armour made for the 6ft 10in German giant in this gallery. Also in the *Renaissance Armoury* is an important recent acquisition, bought at the auction of the contents of Hever Castle in 1984: the magnificent *armour of the Earl of Southampton*, courtier to Queen Elizabeth and patron of Shakespeare. On the **top floor** are the *Tudor and Stuart Armouries*. Here is *Henry VIII's* own *armour*, a suit made for him as a young man and others he wore as he got older and more corpulent. *Charles I's armour* is here too, and that of his small son, later *Charles II*. The **basement**, which is visited last, was originally a store room (used for gunpowder from the mid-C18) but has now been given the appearance of an old-time armoury. Hundreds of muskets, pikes, helmets, swords and other armour and weapons from the C16 to the C19 are arranged here, as well as examples of early cannon and mortars.

The Royal Armoury, like all museums, is still growing, and has had to spread in recent years to other buildings. In the **Waterloo Building** is the *Oriental Armoury* which includes the unique *elephant armour*, believed to have been captured by Robert Clive at the Battle of Plassey in 1757, and two sets of Japanese armour sent to James I.

Next door in the **New Armouries** is the collection of standard issue weapons used by British armed forces from the mid-C17 to the mid-C19, including the equipment used to fire the *Congreve Rocket*, invented in the early years of the C19 and the fore-runner of modern rocketry.

Instruments of torture and punishment are shown in the **Bowyer Tower**, including the axe and block used at the execution of Simon Fraser, Lord Lovat, after the 1745 rebellion led by Prince Charles Edward Stuart.

The honorific 'Royal' justly reflects the world-ranking status of the Armouries not only as a museum, housed in a building which is

Plan of the Royal Armouries
(Tower of London)

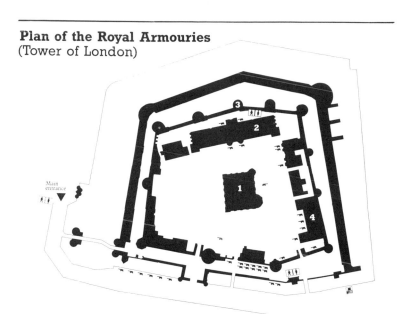

1. **The White Tower:** Cannon Room, Medieval Armoury, Mortar Room, Old Armoury, Renaissance Armoury, Sporting Armoury, Stuart Armoury, Tournament Armoury, Tudor Armoury. **2. Waterloo Barracks:** Oriental Armoury. **3. Bowyer Tower:** Instruments of torture & punishment. **4. New Armouries:** British Military Armoury.

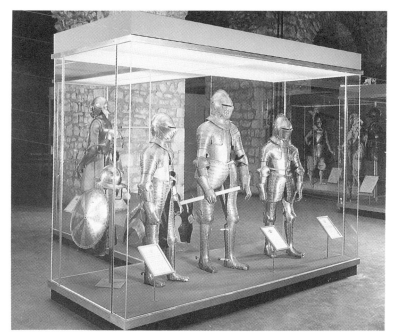

Royal Armouries: Stuart Royal Armour (White Tower). Left to right, armour of Charles I (age 15), made 1610-15. Dutch armour c1612 made for Henry, Prince of Wales. Armour c1609, presented to Prince Henry by Sir Francis Vere.

itself a national monument, but as a scientific institution and repository of weapons scholarship and conservation expertise that has come even to NASA's aid. (ST)

───────────────── the essentials ─────────────────

Underground Tower Hill (Circle, District Lines). **Open** Mar-Oct Mon-Sat 0930-1845, Sun 1400-1730, Nov-Feb Mon-Sat 0930-1630. **Toilets** within the Tower. **Public telephones** within the Tower. **For the disabled** toilets within the Tower. **Refreshments** within the Tower. **Shopping** sales desk. **Publications. Photography. Educational** facilities by prior appointment. **Visitors' services** films, lectures. **Research** library. **Staff opinion.**

■ ROYAL ARTILLERY REGIMENTAL MUSEUM

Academy Road, Woolwich SE18 4DN. Tel 856 5533 ext 2523
Admission *prior application*

This is housed in the Old Royal Military Academy on the first floor of the Tower Block. The numerous exhibits complement the weapons in the not far away Museum of Artillery (qv) with particular emphasis on this famous regiment. The exhibition begins with the early C18 and covers all the wars in which the Royal Regiment of Artillery was involved.

───────────────── the essentials ─────────────────

BR Woolwich Arsenal, Woolwich Dockyard (from Charing Cross Station). **Open** Mon-Fri 1230-1630; Sat and Sun 1400-1600. **Toilets. Parking. For the disabled** access. **Shopping** sales desk. **Photography** by prior written application. **Research** library by arrangement.

■ ROYAL BALLET SCHOOL MUSEUM AND ARCHIVES

White Lodge, Richmond Park, Richmond TW10 5HR
Admission *prior application*

The Museum, in the Royal Ballet School's imposing mansion, in the heart of Richmond Park, possesses many treasures, memorabilia and precious archive material relating to C19 ballet and, in particular, Anna Pavlova (cf Pavlova Memorial Museum) and former distinguished dancers of the Royal Ballet and its predecessors.

───────────────── the essentials ─────────────────

Underground Richmond (District Line). **Open** by prior written appointment. **Research** library and archives by prior arrangement.

■ ROYAL BOTANIC GARDENS: MUSEUMS AND COLLECTIONS

Kew, Richmond, Surrey TW9 3AB. Tel 940 1171
Admission *charge*

Established under royal patronage more than 200 years ago the Royal Botanic Gardens, Kew are world-famous as a tourist attraction providing a thoroughly enjoyable day out for all the family. But although around 1¼ million visitors come here each year, few realise that this is primarily a great scientific institution with an outstanding reputation for the identification and classification of plants, for their conservation and exploitation.

In the *Herbarium and Library*, open only to serious students and qualified researchers, are some 5½ million dried plants and over 120,000 books, 140,000 reprints and other items and some 160,000 prints and drawings. There is also the *Jodrell Laboratory* where ex-

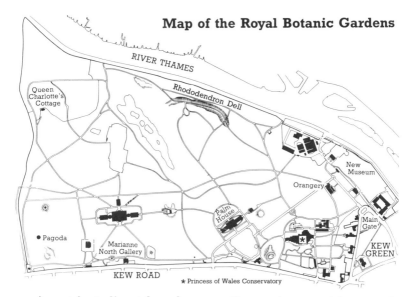

RIVER THAMES

Queen Charlotte's Cottage

Rhododendron Dell

New Museum

Orangery

Palm House

Pagoda

Marianne North Gallery

Main Gate

KEW GREEN

KEW ROAD

★ Princess of Wales Conservatory

perimental studies take place on the anatomy, cytology and biochemistry of plants and at Kew's second garden at Wakehurst Place in Sussex the physiology of seeds takes place and a large Seed Bank is maintained.

But there is much at Kew to interest and delight the ordinary visitor. It is a beautiful and tranquil garden with magnificent trees and impressive vistas. The 50,000 species of plants come from all parts of the world, the more delicate being displayed in the vast *Temperate House* and the world-famous *Palm House.* A major new greenhouse of unique design is the *Princess of Wales Conservatory.* The *Marianne North Gallery* contains an astonishing array of botanical subjects painted by this indefatigable Victorian lady in almost every corner of the globe with enormous dedication and considerable talent. Cambridge Cottage houses the *Kew Gardens Gallery* where art exhibitions are held. For details of current exhibition contact the Public Relations Department. The elegant *Orangery* has displays on

Royal Botanic Gardens: Princess of Wales Conservatory.

the work and history of Kew together with changing exhibitions and a book and gift shop. The details, correct at the time of writing, are liable to be amended as a result of the major restructuring of Kew's Museum and Information services now in progress.

Royal Botanic Gardens, Kew: The Marianne North Gallery.

───────────────── *the essentials* ─────────────────
Underground Kew Gardens (District Line). **Open** ☐ Museums and Marianne North Gallery: 0930-1630; Sun 0930-1730. ☐ Gardens 0930-1600 and 2000 according to season. **Cloakroom. Toilets. Parking. Public telephones. For the disabled** restricted access, toilets. **Refreshments** restaurant, snacks. **Shopping. Publications. Photography** but in greenhouses by application only. **Educational services** by prior arrangement. **Visitors' services** lectures by prior arrangement. **Research** by appointment.

■ ROYAL BRITAIN
Aldersgate Street, Barbican EC2Y 8UH.   Tel 588 0588
Admission *charge*

Located right opposite the Barbican Underground station, this permanent exhibition uses compact disc technology and computer-synchronised visuals to present 1000 years of British royal history from 973 right through to the present day. Twenty-three stage sets recreate major royal events with the aim of giving the visitor a first-hand experience of how British history has evolved. (FS)

───────────────── *the essentials* ─────────────────
Underground Barbican (Circle, Metropolitan Lines). **Open** daily 0900-1730. **Toilets. For the disabled** lift. **Refreshments** restaurant. **Shopping. Publications. Photography. Educational facilities.**

■ ROYAL COLLEGE OF GENERAL PRACTITIONERS MUSEUM
14 Princes Gate, Hyde Park SW7 1PU.   Tel 581 3232 ext 219
Admission *prior application*

The collection, made-up of specialist medical items concerned with General Practice, consists largely of C18 and C19 medical acquisitions. These range from C18 blue and white, cherub and peacock designed drug jars to mahogany-cased amputation and dissection kits. One of the most interesting and unique items is a green-shagreen C18 *Culpeper microscope* with accompanying ivory slides. All items have been kindly donated by Members and interested General Practitioners and their families. (AD)

───────────────── *the essentials* ─────────────────
Underground South Kensington (Circle, District, Piccadilly Lines). **Open** Tue 0930-1730. **Cloakroom. Toilets. Public telephones. Visitors' services** guided tour by arrangement. **Research** library, archive.

■ ROYAL COLLEGE OF MUSIC DEPARTMENT OF PORTRAITS

Prince Consort Road SW7 2BS. Tel 589 3643
Admission *free*

This museum is a treasure-house for those who are interested in the history of music, its performers and their time, but it is not a place to walk in and browse around, since the collections are displayed or stored in different places, at times not accessible to the general public.

The Department of Portraits was started fairly recently, in 1971, although the foundation of the Royal College of Music goes back to 1883. It was due to the patronage given by the Prince of Wales, later King Edward VII. The collection comprises more than 200 original portraits, busts, thousands of engravings and photographs of musicians, plus letters, photographs, programmes, music publishers' catalogues and all kinds of memorabilia connected with the musical world. Its character is more international than might be expected and the department has become a centre for research and reference of worldwide importance. At the start the priority was to repair the damage done by decades of neglect. Most of the canvases have been cleaned and all are now hung either in the department or in the various public rooms of the college.

The collection has been assembled either through commissions or, more frequently, by gift. Among the important donations is that of the late Miss Louise Bonten, in 1984, granddaughter of Sir August Manns, conductor at Crystal Palace for nearly half-a-century. There are two portraits of *Manns*, some 200 *autograph letters* from composers and performers (Brahms, Liszt, Verdi, Dvorak and Grieg), many rare *programmes, photographs* and several splendid presentation items.

--- *the essentials* ---

Underground South Kensington (Circle, District, Piccadilly Lines). **Open** Mon-Fri 1000-1730 (closed 10 days at Easter and Christmas). **Toilets. Public telephones. Refreshments** snacks. **Visitors' services** guided tours by arrangement. Research library.

■ ROYAL COLLEGE OF MUSIC MUSEUM OF INSTRUMENTS

Prince Consort Road SW7 2BS. Tel 589 3643
Admission *charge*

The collection has been built from gifts received since the foundation of the Royal College of Music in 1883. The first donation came in 1884 from the Maharajah Sourindro Mohun Tagore, the Indian musicologist and educator. Ten years later George Donaldson, later Sir George, gave his valuable collection and made a further gift of instruments in 1900. Asian instruments were donated by King Edward VII and in 1911 the collection of A.J. Hipkins, a pioneer in the revival of early keyboard instruments, was presented by his family. Another important addition was in 1968 when Mr E.A.K. Ridley gave his collection of wind instruments. There have been other donations and now the museum has nearly 500 instruments in all. The collection although it might be considered small by international standards includes exhibits of outstanding importance.

The instruments are exhibited on two levels, grouped mainly ac-

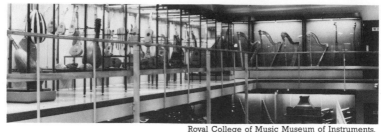
Royal College of Music Museum of Instruments.

cording to type. Among the keyboard instruments is the anonymous *clavicytherium*, probably made in South Germany at the end of the C15. It is believed to be the earliest stringed keyboard instrument. The exquisite decoration, partially missing, can still be appreciated. The *harpsichord* by Alessandro Trasuntino, Venice, 1531, is one of the earliest surviving examples and has inlaid and painted decoration. The anonymous harpsichord, probably Italian, of the C16, has gilded decorations on a green ground with scrolled foliage and birds on the inside of the case. There is also a polygonal *virginal* by Giovanni Celestini, built in 1593. The collection includes English bentside spinets, more harpsichords, early Viennese and English pianos, and a clavichord by Johann Bohak which may have belonged to Haydn. The *regal*, probably made in Germany in 1629, is the only example in a public collection in Britain. There is a varied group of percussion instruments. The wind instruments belong mainly to the **Ridley collection**, assembled with the purpose of demonstrating the development of orchestral woodwind. Flutes and clarinets are particularly well represented. The stringed instruments section is also well equipped with hurdy-gurdies (for this instrument Haydn wrote his concerti and notturni for the King of Naples), violins, pochettes (little fiddles from the C17 and C18 used to accompany dancing lessons), violas, viols, viole d'amore, lutes, octave lutes of Milanese mandolins, citterns, guitars, dulcimers, double psalteries and harps. In the ethnic collection are Asian and African instruments. The museum is primarily a place of study and work for the students of the college and scholars.

--- *the essentials* ---

Underground South Kensington (Circle, District, Piccadilly Lines). **Open** Wed 1100-1630 (term). **Toilets. Public telephones. Refreshments** snacks. **Publications. Photography** no flash. **Visitors' services** guided tours by appointment. **Research** library.

■ ROYAL COLLEGE OF PHYSICIANS PORTRAIT COLLECTION
11 St Andrew's Place, Regent's Park NW1 4LE.   Tel 935 1174 ext 374
Admission *prior application*

The College's much-admired modern building (architect Sir Denys Lasdun) houses a collection of portraits which is not primarily concerned with artistic excellence, though it includes works by Lely, Kneller, Reynolds, Zoffany, Lawrence. Its purpose is to preserve for posterity the features of those closely connected with the College, or who have earned the special esteem of the medical profession. The Founder, Thomas Linacre, is said to be seen in an early C19 copy of a C16 original in the Royal Collection. Sir Theodore de Mayerne (1573-1655) was Court Physician to James I and Charles I and one of the first to use mercury and other chemical remedies. His contemporary William Harvey is seen in a Victorian set-piece explaining the circulation of the blood to James I. Many C18 luminaries had portraits painted specially for presentation, among them Sir Hans Sloane, President 1719-35, and his successor William Pellett. Sir William Browne (1765-66) had himself immortalized full length, gowned and adorned with symbols, by the gifted Thomas Hudson. Later great men include Albert Schweitzer, Lord Moran (Churchill's doctor) by Annigoni, and Isaac Wolfson in a portrait-bust by Sir William Reid Dick. This is a collection of varying artistic merit but full of historical and human interest.

─────────────── *the essentials* ───────────────

Underground Great Portland Street (Circle, District, Metropolitan Lines). **Open** Mon-Fri 1000-1700. **Cloakroom. Toilets. Parking. Public telephones. For the disabled** access, toilets. **Publications. Photography. Visitors' services. Research** library, archive.

■ ROYAL GEOGRAPHICAL SOCIETY MAP ROOM

1 Kensington Gore SW7 2AR.   Tel 589 5466
Admission *prior application*

The Royal Geographical Society was founded in 1830. Its main purpose is to lend support and expertise to initiatives related to geography: geographical education, field research, and explorations such as those of Mulu, the rain forest in Sarawak (Borneo), the Karakoram Mountains in Pakistan, and the Wahibah Sand Sea in Oman. Of famous names of the past, Livingstone, Stanley and Scott were all associated with the Royal Geographical Society. The fellowship and membership system gives any person, private body or enterprise access to the many services of the Society: lectures, the Geographical Journal, library, archive and the Map Room. The last is open to the general public because the Society receives a Parliamentary grant (from 1854) on condition that free access is granted.

The map collection totals 700,000 maps, 4,000 atlases and 36 globes, consulted with help of the staff. It is surpassed only by the British Library, and by the Library of Congress (4 millions). It is enlarged mainly by donations — the Society receives on average 8,000 maps and 50 atlases each year.

─────────────── *the essentials* ───────────────

Underground South Kensington (Circle, District, Piccadilly Lines). **Open** Mon-Fri 1000-1700 (closed 2 weeks in Summer). **Cloakroom. Toilets. Public telephones. Research** on application.

■ ROYAL HOSPITAL CHELSEA MUSEUM

Royal Hospital Road SW3 4SR.   Tel 730 0161 ext 244
Admission *free*

Originally founded by Charles II in 1682 as a retreat for veterans of the regular army, the Royal Hospital still serves that function today, and provides a home for about 400 Chelsea Pensioners. The main part of the buildings is by Sir Christopher Wren (1631-1723), with later additions by Robert Adam (1728-1792) and Sir John Soane (1753-1837). The grounds of the Royal Hospital slope down to the River Thames and provide a beautiful setting for the magnificent architecture. As well as viewing the grounds and the exterior, one can visit the *Chapel* and the *Great Hall*, both containing fine examples of interior design and portraiture of the period. There is also a small museum of objects related to the history of the Hospital, and a particularly interesting collection of *ex-pensioners' medals*, numbering over 1,800.

---
the essentials

Underground Sloane Square (Circle, District Lines). **Open** Apr-Sept   Mon-Sat 1000-1200, 1400-1600, Oct-Mar Sun 1400-1600. **Toilets. Refreshments** cafeteria. **Shopping** sales desk. **Publications. Photography** by prior arrangement. **Visitors' services** guided tours by prior arrangement with the Hospital adjutant.

■ ROYAL MEWS

Buckingham Palace Road SW1W 0QH.   Tel 930 4832 ext 634
Admission *charge*

The stables and coach houses were built in 1825 to a Nash design in the shape of a quadrangle. To the west and north are the stables while the east side contains the state coaches. More buildings behind the stables house a collection of Royal cars. The major attraction is undoubtedly the *Gold State Coach* which was first used by George III at the State Opening of Parliament in 1762 and now reserved for major state occasions involving Her Majesty the Queen herself. This huge ornate vehicle weighs 4 tons and is drawn by eight horses at walking pace. It has exquisite carvings, mouldings and paintings made by leading craftsmen of the day of which the most notable was Cipriani who painted the coach panels. There is now no provision for a coachman to drive the horses which are controlled only by the postillions.

Royal Mews: the Gold State Coach.

The closed *Irish State Coach*, which is a copy of the original destroyed by fire in 1911, is in frequent use for ceremonial occasions and for the State Opening of Parliament. The open body 1902 *State Landau* built for King Edward VII is also in regular use for meeting and conveying foreign heads of government on State visits. Also on show is the *Glass Coach* used by the bride and bridegroom at royal weddings and to take newly appointed ambassadors to the

Palace, the *Scottish State Coach, Queen Alexandra's State Coach, King Edward VII's Town Coach,* various *State Landaus,* open *barouches* and several other town carriages, including two unusual *Phaetons* built for Queen Victoria. Various sets of *harnesses* can be seen of a collection which is probably the finest in the world. Each is separately identified by type and function, some made of red Moroccan leather but all well ornamented in brass or gilt. There are saddles which are of great interest, some specially made for the rider's preference, some conventional but with elaborate decorations and fittings, often given as presents by foreign dignitaries.

The famous *Rolls Royce cars* which are used for state functions can often be seen at close quarters, with their unique features including the transparent cover which enables a clear view to be obtained of the rear passengers. They are not on display but frequently pass through the Main Yard whilst the public are viewing the exhibits.

---
the essentials

Underground Victoria (Circle, District, Victoria Lines). **Open** Wed, Thur 1400-1600 (closed Ascot Week and other times as notified by Press). **Toilets. Public telephones. For the disabled** access, toilets. **Shopping. Publications. Photography.**

■ ROYAL MILITARY SCHOOL OF MUSIC MUSEUM
Kneller Hall, Twickenham TW2 7DY.   Tel 898 5533
Admission *prior application*

The great portrait-painter Sir Godfrey Kneller (1646-1723) built himself a villa here, but it has almost disappeared in the huge Jacobean-style mansion built in 1848. This now houses the Army's musical academy, and its small museum. Amid bandsmen's uniforms and other musical militaria, the instruments are mainly of the wind variety, but there are two notable exceptions, a fine *double-bass* by Amati (1650) and a *basso da camera* or small version used for solo work, by Guarnieri (1615) on which Prince Albert was taught to play by the virtuoso bass-player Dragonetti.

Open-air concerts are presented during the summer months, on occasion with the added extra musical attraction of fireworks.

---
the essentials

BR Whitton (from Waterloo Station). **Open** Mon, Tue, Thur, Fri 1000-1200. 1400-1600. Wed 1000-1200. **Parking. Shopping** sales desk. **Educational facilities. Visitors' services** lectures, guided tours by prior arrangement.

■ ROYAL SOCIETY OF ARTS
8 John Adam Street WC2N 6EZ.   Tel 930 5115
Admission *prior application*

The Society was founded in 1754 as the Society for the Encouragement of Arts, Manufactures and Commerce, a title which, though normally abbreviated, is still valid. After a series of homes it moved in 1774 to its present magnificent premises, built for it as part of the Adam brothers' Adelphi development. Robert Adam's impressive neoclassical exterior is reflected within, with a decorative scheme of extraordinary richness and complexity.

The walls are hung with portraits of the Society's luminaries by Cosway, Herkomer and others, but the pièce de résistance is the

Royal Society of Arts: the Great Room, with Barry's fine paintings and the President's Chair (on the dais). The Room also contains the Grignion Clock. Over the dais, Jacob Bouverie, the first President of the Society, by Gainsborough.

Great Room which, in 1777, James Barry undertook to decorate with a series of paintings, *The Progress of Human Knowledge*, his avowed aim being to rival Greece, Rome and the Renaissance masters, and to 'drag the arts, reluctant, into day'. Johnson, Blake and Benjamin Haydon greatly admired Barry's work, and its effect is indeed striking. Among the Society's treasured possessions are the *Grignion Clock* (1760) and the *President's Chair* (1759) designed by Sir William Chambers.

The **Library** is especially rich in early books and manuscripts relating to practical arts and technology and holds a *treatise on gunnery* dated 1588, an *autograph of Daniel Defoe*, and the earliest proceedings of the Great Exhibition of 1851.

─────────── *the essentials* ───────────

Underground Charing Cross (Bakerloo, Jubilee, Northern Lines). **Visitors' services** films, lectures, guided tours by arrangement for educational bodies only. **Research** library.

■ SAATCHI COLLECTION
98A Boundary Road NW8 0RH.   Tel 624 8299
Admission *free*

This major collection of contemporary art is on view to the public in the spectacular setting of a converted warehouse in St John's Wood. Started in 1970 by Doris and Charles Saatchi, the collection consists of approximately 600 paintings and sculptures by artists such as Robert Ryman, Sol LeWitt, Carl Andre, Andy Warhol, Malcolm Morley, and Frank Stella. A selection from the collection is shown on a rotating basis changing approximately every six months.

The exhibition space, extraordinarily well lit by both artificial and natural sources and covering some 27,000 sq ft, is a magnificent setting for the type of art displayed, much of it on a large scale. For details concerning the current exhibition, telephone the gallery. (MG)

the essentials

Underground St John's Wood (Jubilee Line). **Open** Fri-Sat 1200-1800 also by appointment. **Cloakroom. Toilets. Publications. Research** facilities for scholars.

■ ST BRIDE PRINTING LIBRARY
St Bride Institute, Bride Lane EC4Y 8EE.   Tel 335 4660
Admission *free*

This is essentially a reference library, on one floor. It contains books and periodicals on all aspects of the technique, design and history of printing and related subjects. On a separate floor a collection of C19 hand printing presses is housed. These machines and artefacts can be seen only by arrangement with the Librarian as they are not on regular display. Although the library is easily accessible and freely open to the public without the formality of a reader's ticket, the exhibits are not and those interested in viewing the hardware must either wait for the occasional exhibitions which are held on the premises or visit the Watford Museum [194 High Street, Watford, Herts] which has an extensive permanent display of similar and more complex machines.

the essentials

Underground Blackfriars (Circle, District Lines). **Open** Mon-Fri 0930-1730. **Toilets. Photography** by prior arrangement. **Research.**

■ ST BRIDE'S CHURCH AND CRYPT MUSEUM
Fleet Street EC4Y 8AU.   Tel 353 1301
Admission *free*

The present St Bride's is the eighth church to have stood on this site in the heart of the City of London. It is a reconstruction of the church built by Sir Christopher Wren (1631-1723) following the great fire of London in 1666, and is based on Wren's own plans and drawings. The museum in the crypt presents a history of the various churches that have stood on the site, since the first stone one built in the C6 in honour of St Bride (St Bridget of Kildare). As well as containing an extensive display, the crypt also has remnants of almost every building that has ever been on that site, including a Roman pavement. As well as architectural history and the development of printing and the newspaper industry, the museum contains elements of social history, showing among other things costumes and a body-snatcher-proof coffin! (IO)

──────────────── *the essentials* ────────────────

Underground Blackfriars (Circle, District Lines). **Open** daily 0830-1730. **For the disabled** access to ground floor only. **Shopping** sales desk. **Publications. Photography. Visitors' services** lectures, guided tours by prior arrangement.

■ SALVATION ARMY MUSEUM

117/121 Judd Street WC1H 9NN.   Tel 387 1656 ext 14
Admission *donation*

Salvation Army Museum and the 'music corner'.

The museum, located on the second floor of the Salvation Army Publishing and Supplies building, tells the story of the movement which conquered the world (it is still active in 86 countries) in the name of the Gospel and of social improvement. Among the exhibits are photographs, documents, objects and relics of the everyday life and work of General William Booth (1829-1912), the founder, and his followers. Even the chair which accompanied the General in his extensive world's tours can be found. The collection is undoubtedly of enormous importance for those interested in the Movement, but also enables any visitor to gain an insight into the C19 way of life and gives a fairly tangible idea of the stamina needed to undertake such a mission. A section presents the evolution of uniforms, where special attention is paid to the famous bonnet, which Mrs Booth chose because she wanted a headgear for the girls that would be 'cheap, strong and large enough to protect the heads of the wearers from cold as well as from brickbats and other missiles'.

──────────────── *the essentials* ────────────────

Underground King's Cross (Circle, Metropolitan, Northern, Piccadilly, Victoria Lines). **Open** Mon-Fri 0930-1530, Sat by appointment. **Cloakroom. Toilets. Public telephones. Refreshments** self-service restaurant, snacks. **Shopping. Publications. Photography. Educational facilities. Visitors' services** films, guided tours, lectures **Research** library.

■ SCIENCE MUSEUM

Exhibition Road SW7 2DD.   Tel 938 8000
Admission *charge*

The Science Museum and its near neighbour the Victoria and Albert Museum (qv) originated in the same enterprise, the Great Exhibition of 1851. Its organiser, Sir Henry Cole, founded the South Kensington Museum out of profits, and it opened in 1857 with science and arts sections on the present site of the V&A.

By 1864 the two collections had already grown too big for each other, and the science department was moved across the road, remaining part of the South Kensington Museum even after this was renamed the Victoria and Albert Museum in 1899. When the new V&A building was opened in 1909 the two museums were finally separated administratively as well as physically, and the present Science Museum's building, which was begun in 1913, was opened by George V in 1929. Its full title is the National Museum of Science and Industry, and it includes also the National Railway Museum at York, the National Museum of Photography, Film and Television at Bradford and the Concorde Exhibition at Yeovilton (Devon). Some of the larger objects relating to agriculture, aircraft, transport and space are stored at Wroughton, Wiltshire, and they can be seen either by appointment or at special viewing weekends and open days.

The main South Kensington museum delights millions of visitors each year. It uses the latest push-button information technology to take them on an historical journey of discovery, with the many fascinating byways which technology took along the road to our latest achievements; all the milestones are here.

Science Museum: the Road and Rail Transport Gallery; on the left the Deltic diesel. On the right (centre) the Rocket and beyond, Puffing Billy.

On the **ground floor** the emphasis is on power, starting with the great engines of Newcomen, Watt and Trevithick. Further in, there are the **railway engines** – *Puffing Billy* of 1813, the earliest surviving locomotive; Stephenson's famous *Rocket* of 1829; the Great Western Railway's majestic 1923 *Caerphilly Castle;* and the monstrous *Deltic* diesel locomotive of the mid-fifties dwarfing a 1909 Rolls-Royce. The story of motor cars is told here, too, with examples of automobiles from much earlier than the Silver Ghost, starting with the *Benz three-wheel* çar of 1888. Powered flight is represented, and although the *Wright Brothers' aeroplane* of 1903 is in Washington, an exact replica is here. Also on display is the aircraft which carried Alcock and Brown across the Atlantic for the first time, Amy Johnson's *Gipsy Moth* and the *Supermarine S6B,* forerunner of the Spitfires (on display) of World War II. There is a special high walkway to enable visitors to look at the aircraft close-to.

From late 1986 the most spectacular display on the ground floor is the **Space Gallery**, replacing the Exploration Gallery. The history of rockets is told for the first time, as well as the achievements in manned space flight (with the Apollo 10 lunar command module and reconstructions of the interior of a space shuttle). Satellites are explained here, and there is the opportunity for visitors to see their own homes photographed from a satellite 140 miles high with a system specially developed for the Science Museum. There is also a link with a meteorological satellite so that visitors can judge the weather in any part of Europe, and a direct broadcast satellite monitor showing what is being seen on television in other major European cities. The Space Gallery ends with a remarkable glimpse into the future: a project to fly to what may be the nearest planetary system to our own, 35 billion miles away.

There are five floors above the ground where such phenomena as electricity, photography, printing, chemistry, computing, navigation, aeronautics, nuclear power, telecommunications, meteorology, time measurement, map-making, surveying and astronomy are explained, with many opportunities for practical experiments.

A gallery explains the impact of science and technology on today's food. Called **Food for Thought,** it is lively and interactive. It breaks with traditional Science Museum exhibitions by featuring some of the social and economic factors which influence our choice of food. It takes an objective look at issues such as the use of additives and today's media stories about food hygiene. The aim is to help people to understand the modern food industry and set it in an historical context. The gallery has five main sections: Food and the body; Preparing and preserving food; Food and society; Trading food; Food in the future.

Within the Science Museum is another which, since it opened in 1980, has proved to be one of the most popular elements: the **Wellcome Museum of the History of Medicine**. It is the largest collection of its kind in the world, based on the collection started by Henry Wellcome of the Burroughs Wellcome Company in the C19 which was loaned to the Science Museum by the Wellcome Trustees. It tells the story of healing from the earliest use of medicine to modern discoveries and applications. In the lower gallery full-size dioramas are used; a 1860s bedroom in which a

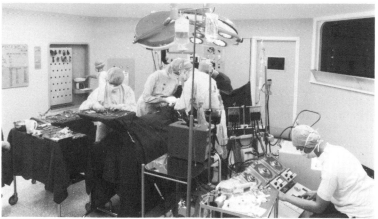

Science Museum:

1. The Babbage Machine; 2. Apollo 10 capsule; 3. The Caerphilly Castle;
4. An open-heart operation in 1980.

Science Museum: the Gibson & Son Pharmacy (Wellcome Museum of the History of Medicine).

child is being born; a pharmacy of 1905; dental surgeries of the 1890s, the 1930s and the 1980s; a modern operating theatre in which open-heart surgery is being performed. The Upper Gallery shows more than 3,500 objects illustrating medical history from all places and periods, fully labelled to describe in detail even the most up-to-date techniques.

The Science Museum was founded as an educational establishment, and it has an extensive education department today (schools and groups are advised to contact the department direct to find out about facilities by telephoning the museum number). Opened in 1986, **Launch Pad** is an interactive gallery in which children are able to discover science for themselves with various experiments varying in complexity – but all of them fun. (ST)

――――――――――――― *the essentials* ―――――――――――――

Underground South Kensington (Circle, District, Piccadilly Lines). **Open** Mon-Sat 1000-1800, Sun 1430-1800. **Cloakroom. Toilets. For the disabled** access, lifts, toilets. **Refreshment** snacks. **Shopping. Publications. Photography. Visitors' services** films, lectures. **Research** library.

■ SCIENCE MUSEUM LIBRARY

Imperial College Road SW7 5NH.   Tel 938 8234
Admission *free*

The Library, an integral part of the Science Museum, but in its own premises, holds important scientific and technological publications, books and periodicals, old and new, with a total stock of about a ½ million volumes, and 19,000 periodicals (6,000 of these current). It also has in its care the Science Museum's **Pictorial Collection** of paintings, prints and drawings, and the **Archives Collection** of historic and manuscript items.

The Library specialises in the history of science and technology. It is open to the public without formality, though those wishing to consult rare books and archive material must produce evidence of identity and address to obtain a reader's ticket.

――――――――――――― *the essentials* ―――――――――――――

Underground South Kensington (Circle, District, Piccadilly Lines). **Open** Mon-Sat 1000-1730. **Cloakroom. Toilets. For the disabled** access. **Publications. Visitors' services** guided tours by arrangement.

■ SCIENCE REFERENCE AND INFORMATION SERVICE

*25 Southampton Buildings, Chancery Lane WC2A 1AW.   Tel 323 7494
**9 Kean Street WC2B 1AT. Tel 323 7288. Fax 323 7930
Admission *free*

Formerly the Science Reference Library, this is now the national reference library for modern science, business and commerce, patents, trade marks and designs and is part of the British Library (qv). Its direct ancestor was the Patent Office Library which opened in 1855, four years after the Great Exhibition had focused public attention on the country's growing technological developments. It was the first public library in the UK to keep all its stock on open access, a tradition maintained today with visitors offered direct access to as high a proportion of stock as space permits.

The reading room at **Holborn** (25 Southampton Buildings) offers literature of the physical sciences, engineering, patents and business; that at **Aldwych** (9 Kean Street) of the life and Earth

The Reading Room at Holborn.

sciences and technologies, biotechnology, medicine, astronomy and pure mathematics.

The collections include more than 31,800 serial titles, 223,000 books and over 30 million world-wide patent specifications. Holdings are uniquely comprehensive. Photography of the world's surface, for instance, extends from Gaspard Felix Tournachon's 1858 invention for aerial balloon photography to recent image data listings from Landat satellite programmes. There is a Computer Search Service available, linguistic aid for non-English material and various specialist services to support British science, technology and industry. Enquiries can be made by telephone, fax, telex and post.

---
the essentials
---

* **Underground** Chancery Lane (Central Line). **Open** Reading Room Mon-Fri 0930-2100; Sat 1000-1300; Foreign Patents Reading Room Mon-Fri 0930-1730. **Cloakroom. Toilets. Public telephones. For the disabled** access by prior arrangement. **Publications. Photography** with prior permission. **Visitors' services** guided tours by arrangements, linguistic aid. **Research** library. **Staff opinion.**
** **Underground** Holborn (Central, Piccadilly Lines). **Open** Mon-Fri 0930-1730. **Cloakroom. Toilets. Public telephones. For the disabled** access, lift. **Photography** by arrangement. **Visitors' services** guided tours by arrangement, linguistic aid. **Research** library. **Staff opinion.**

■ SHAKESPEARE GLOBE MUSEUM
1 Bear Gardens SE1 9ED.   Tel 928 6342
Admission *charge*

The permanent exhibition focuses on the history of the Elizabethan and Jacobean stage based on Bankside in Shakespeare's day. Models and contemporary visual material tell the story of the playhouses, players and audiences from 1576 to 1642. Housed in a converted Georgian warehouse, the museum stands in Bear Gardens, so called after the bear-baiting ring which stood on the site until it was replaced by the Hope Playhouse. This was closed in 1642, when the Puritans suppressed by Parliamentary order all theatres and destroyed their fittings and furniture. The Hope had a temporary stage so that bear-baiting, a very popular sport of C16 and C17 London, could be mounted as well as plays.

The museum presents also, through reproduced documents of the period, the life of Southwark, situated on the south bank of the River Thames next to London Bridge, which was the only permanent crossing of the river in Tudor times. Its position brought a bustling activity to the area: trade, pubs, brothels, entertainments of all kinds from bear-baiting to a lively theatrical life. The Globe, the most famous of the local playhouses because of its close connection with Shakespeare, was only a hundred yards from the present Bear Gardens Museum. A project to reconstruct it as faithfully as possible to the original design is being promoted and plans and a model of the proposed reconstruction are housed within the museum. Shakespeare's own company played at The Globe and the first performance of 'Hamlet', 'King Lear' and 'Macbeth' took place there. The museum also houses a replica 1616 stage and promotes productions of C16 and C17 plays throughout the year.

---
the essentials

Underground Cannon Street, Mansion House (Circle, District Lines), London Bridge (Northern Line). **Open** Tue-Sat 1000-1730, Sun 1400-1800. **Cloakroom. Toilets. For the disabled** limited access. **Refreshments** coffee bar. **Shopping** sales desk. **Photography. Educational facilities. Visitors' service** films, lectures, guided tours by arrangement.

The model for the new Globe (above), and bear greeting visitors to the Shakespeare Globe Museum (below).

■ SILVER STUDIO COLLECTION

Middlesex Polytechnic, Bounds Green Road N11 2NQ.   Tel 368 1299 ext 339
Admission *prior application*

In the form of a print room, archive and research library, this is one of the most comprehensive collections of decorative design material in the country, with about 20,000 designs, 2,000 wallpapers, 50 wallpaper pattern books, about 4,000 design samples, a large library of works on design, and miscellanea (the Silver Studio kept meticulous records of its activity).

The Silver Studio of Design was started in the second part of the C19 by Arthur Silver in London. The enterprise had the aim of 'bringing together a body of men to establish a studio which would be capable of supplying designs for the whole field of fabrics and other materials used in the decoration of the home'. Arthur Silver (1852-1896) combined a considerable talent as a designer with business acumen. He made many useful contacts through the Arts and Crafts Society including William Morris, Walter Crane and Gleeson White. The Silver Studio designed for the more avant-garde firms of the period, including Jeffrey & Co., Charles Knowles, Morton, and Liberty and built up a trade with French, Belgian and American manufacturers. Arthur Silver also had the services of two brilliant Art Nouveau designers, J. Illingworth Kay and Harry Napper. At his death Harry Napper and J.R. Houghton ran the Silver Studio until his son Rex was able to take control in 1900.

Rex Silver (1879-1965) continued and expanded his father's work, helped by his brother Harry. The Silver Studio's output continued to show the great versatility that was its characteristic since its beginning. It contributed to most of the important textile and wallpaper exhibitions in this country and abroad and produced designs for the more design-conscious British firms during the 1920s and 30s. Since many of the firms who bought from Arthur Silver (Liberty, Warner, Morton and Sanderson) were still buying designs from Rex Silver in the early 1960s, the collection also reflects the decorating and furnishing tastes of the English upper and middle classes over almost a century.

─── *the essentials* ───

Underground Bounds Green (Piccadilly Line). **Open** Mon-Fri 0930-1700. **Cloakroom. Toilets. Parking. Public telephones. For the disabled** access, toilets. **Refreshments** restaurant. **Publications. Photography. Visitors' services** lectures. **Research** library.

■ SIR JOHN SOANE'S MUSEUM

13 Lincoln's Inn Fields WC2A 3BP.   Tel 405 2107
Admission *free*

The Museum is crammed with the accumulated treasures acquired by the architect Sir John Soane (1753-1837) in the houses which he designed for his own occupation. As a wealthy professional man, Sir John was able to indulge his taste and fantasies with the best artefacts of Egyptian, Greek, Roman and other civilisations and fill his home with constructions such as the Catacombs, Monk's Parlour, Crypt, and Sepulchral Chamber. As a patron of the arts Soane commissioned works from Academy colleagues and other artists as well as continually adding to his collection from public and private sales of effects by other collectors.

On the **ground floor** is the combined dining room and library which have compartmented ceilings with pictures of various scenes from the Greek classics painted by Henry Howard R.A. This floor, together with the basement and first floor, contains the main display area. In the *Little Study* are many marble fragments from the *Tatham Collection* (1772-1842) which were acquired in Rome during the C18 as relics of the Roman Empire. Glass-fronted cabinets in the Dressing Room show various C15 and C16 objects of art from Italy and

Sir John Soane's Museum, facing Lincoln's Inn Fields.

Sir John Soane's Museum: the Dining Room.

more Roman pieces. Paintings, drawings and engravings on the walls are by several artists, Dutch, English and Italian, including a Canaletto. Passing through the Corridor and then into the Picture Room, gives an unexpected wide view of a good part of the museum. However, it is the **Picture Room** which has a particular appeal as it is dominated by the eight stages of the *Rake's Progress* and the four stages of *The Election*, among the most famous of Hogarth's works. Also in this room are paintings by Turner, Watteau, Piranesi, Henry Howard and a large selection of Soane's own works, including his drawings for the Bank of England.

In the **basement** is the **Sepulchral Chamber** containing the *sarcophagus of Seti I* which is one of the main treasures of the museum. Discovered during the exploration of the Necropolis of Thebes in the early C19, it was first offered to the British Museum, but rejected because of cost, and then promptly acquired by Soane in 1824. Interpretation of the hieroglyphics was not completed until 1908. Another striking feature is the **Dome**, which is the oldest part of the museum and can be seen from the basement. The pillars supporting the Dome are covered with sculptures and fragments, vases and other works.

The contents of the museum include ancient and medieval objects, items from the Renaissance and later periods in W. Europe, Oriental and primitive American artefacts, paintings and drawings, architectural models, drawings and prints, and some furniture. The furniture was, however, only occasionally collected for its artistic and antiquarian interest. In the **library** are nearly 8,000 volumes, manuscripts, early printed works and Soane's collection of 30,000 architectural drawings, by Wren, Robert Adam, George Dance and Soane himself. These can be seen by appointment.

Soane's Museum: the Dome. Antique vases and fragments with the bust of Soane by Sir Francis Chantrey.

---
the essentials

Underground Holborn (Central, Piccadilly Lines). **Open** Tue-Sat 1000-1700. **Toilets. Shopping** sales desk. **Publications. Photography** no flash or tripods. **Visitors' services** guided tours (Sat 1430). **Research** library.

■ SOSEKI MUSEUM IN LONDON
80b The Chase SW4 0NG.   Tel 720 8718
Admission *free*

The Japanese author Natsume Soseki (1867-1916) spent two student years in London at the beginning of the century. This period contributed significantly to his later writing. His final lodgings in the capital faced what is today the Museum. This contains a selection of memorabilia relating to his life over here, including a number of evocative photographs of London at the turn of the century. The **Library** houses the entire body of Soseki's writings and critical works about the author. There is also an impressive collection of books on modern Japanese literature.

---
the essentials

Underground Clapham North (Northern Line). **Open** Wed, Sat 1000-1200, 1400-1700, Sun 1400-1700. **Cloakroom. Toilets. Educational facilities. Visitors' services** guided tours by arrangement. **Research** library.

■ SOUTH LONDON ART GALLERY

Peckham Road SE5 8UH. Tel 703 6120
Admission *free*

South London Art Gallery: Sleeping boots boy, by G. Smith (1829-1901).

Originally a private foundation, initiated by William Rossiter (c1821-1897), this purpose-built gallery was opened in 1891 on its present site (which was in fact Rossiter's garden) with the support of leading artists such as Lord Leighton. The aim of the gallery is two-fold: to house, and, wherever possible, expand the permanent collections (currently in store) and to maintain an annual programme of temporary exhibitions. About 300 works by British artists (c1700 onwards) form the main collection of paintings and drawings. Ford Madox Brown, Val Prinsep, John Ruskin and G.F. Watts are represented here as are John Piper, Stanley Spencer, Graham Sutherland and Christopher Wood. Additionally there is a collection of C20 original prints.

Not on permanent display but readily available on application to the Keeper is the Topographical Collection which is based on 500 paintings and drawings of Southwark. Changing exhibitions cover virtually all artistic subjects and media: ceramics, embroidery, jewellery, photography and sculpture as well as painting and drawing. One-person shows have been held of the works of Martin Bloch, John Bratby, William Coldstream, Mario Dubsky, Anthony Eyton and Carol Robb, and sculpture exhibitions have featured the creations of Karel Vogel and H.A. Gerrard.

---
the essentials

Underground Elephant and Castle (Bakerloo, Northern Lines) then **Bus** 12,171; Oval (Northern Line) then **Bus** 36. **Open** Tue-Sat 1000-1800, Sun 1500-1800 (closed between exhibitions). **Shopping** sales desk. **Publications. Photography** by arrangement. **Educational facilities. Visitors' service** lectures. **Research** enquiries by scholars welcome.

■ TATE GALLERY

Millbank SW1P 4RG.   Tel 821 1313 (821 7128)

Admission *free*

(A wholesale re-hanging is planned for 1990. The numbers here in bold type refer to the Plan on pages 226/227 and reflect the layout of the galleries at the time of going to press.)

The Tate Gallery opened in 1897. Its foundation was primarily the result of increasing demands for the creation of a national gallery of modern British art.

The National Gallery (qv) had, and still has, responsibility for collecting and displaying British art but was deemed not to be discharging this responsibility adequately and in any case it did not, and does not, collect works by living artists.

Henry (later Sir Henry) Tate, a sugar millionaire and collector of contemporary British Art, offered to build such a gallery if the government would provide a site. After much haggling the government offered the present Millbank site, then occupied by London's largest prison, the Millbank Penitentiary, which was duly demolished to make way for the gallery. Henry Tate also donated to the nation his own art collection: 67 English pictures, the most famous of which, *Ophelia* (1851) by the Pre-Raphaelite John Everett Millais, remains one of the great stars of the Tate collections (Gallery 14).

The Tate soon began to grow. Originally its brief was defined as artists born after 1790. Turner, born in 1775, fell outside the Tate's existing responsibilities. However, in 1910 Turner's great bequest of 300 oil paintings and 19,000 water-colours and drawings was transferred from the National Gallery and galleries were specifically built for it by the generosity of Joseph (later Sir Joseph) Duveen.

Then, in 1916, Sir Hugh Lane bequeathed to the nation a remarkable collection of Impressionist paintings and it was decided to house them in the Tate. So in 1917, by means of a Treasury Minute, the Tate's responsibilities were re-defined to include foreign art and British artists born before 1790. Steady growth continued of the collections and of the buildings. The original site, much larger than the building when it first opened, was finally completely filled in 1978 and the Tate is expanding into a new site next door.

The Tate's collections, as they now exist, can be divided broadly into two: the National Collection of Historic British Painting is defined as painting in Britain from the mid C16 to the late C19; the National Collection of Modern Art consists of British and foreign painting and sculpture from about 1880, and a collection of prints from about 1945. The Tate also has an Archive primarily responsible for C20 British Art.

From the left of the lobby area, as you enter the Tate, a sequence of galleries leads off, hung chronologically starting with the oldest, with the Historic British Collection, and on the right is a parallel sequence of galleries in which Modern Art is displayed in a similar chronological way.

The **Historic British Collection** begins in Gallery **3**. Here is the oldest painting in the Tate, *A Man in a Black Cap*, dated 1545, by

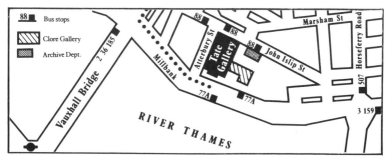

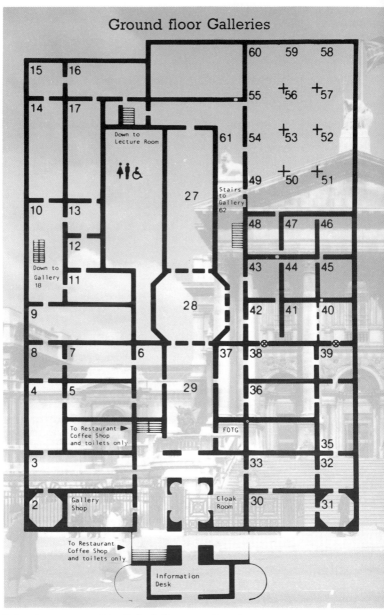

Ground floor Galleries

John Bettes, an English follower of Holbein's sharply focused realism. A few decades later, under Elizabeth I, English painting took on an increasingly stylised and decorative character, exemplified here by the portrait of Elizabeth herself from the studio of Nicholas Hilliard, her court painter and the first great native-born genius of English painting. Also remarkable examples of the Elizabethan style are *The Cholmondeley Sisters* (artist unknown) with its fascinating inscription, which must be read, and *Captain Thomas Lee* by the Dutch immigrant painter Gheeraerts. Lee was a peace-keeper for Elizabeth I in Ireland – his bare legs were ap-

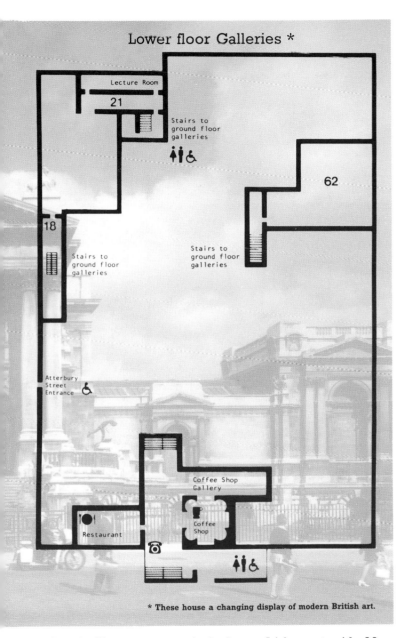

Lecture Room

21

Stairs to
ground floor
galleries

18

Stairs to
ground floor
galleries

Stairs to
ground floor
galleries

62

Atterbury
Street
Entrance

Coffee Shop
Gallery

Restaurant

Coffee
Shop

* These house a changing display of modern British art.

parently to facilitate movement in the boggy Irish countryside. Moving into the reign of Charles I, there are two other fascinating paintings, the portrait of *Sir Richard Saltonstall and his family* by David Des Granges, which, painted to commemorate the birth of a child by his second wife, also includes a ghostly portrait of his dead first wife, and *Endymion Porter*, a portrait by William Dobson, the short-lived successor to Van Dyck as court painter to Charles I. Porter is shown as a 'complete' man, his intellectual interests, symbolised by the bust of Apollo, complementing the image of soldier and huntsman.

| 1 | Tate Gallery: |
| 2 | 1. The Cholmondeley Sisters, British School C17.
2. Hogarth, The painter and his pug. |

229

In Gallery **2** we come to William Hogarth and the first important group of works by a single artist in the Tate. Hogarth is sometimes said to be 'the father of English painting' and in the first half of the C18 he created a wide-ranging art based primarily on English life and a personal theory of art, as well as founding an art academy and acting as a vociferous art politician. His most notable works here are the famous *Self-Portrait* with his pet pug dog, his theatre scene *The Beggar's Opera*, and the anti-French satire *The Roast Beef of Old England*.

After Hogarth, in the second half of the C18, English art bloomed: in Gallery **4** are important groups of work, hung on facing walls, by Stubbs and Gainsborough, whose sheer brilliance as painters, allied to great originality of vision, makes them the dominating geniuses of English art from about 1760-80; Stubbs as a painter of animals and occasionally people; Gainsborough as a painter of people and occasionally landscape. Most notable among the Stubbses are *Mares and Foals in a Landscape*, the great pair of paintings of *Reapers* and *Haymakers* and not least, three of the scenes of a wild horse attacked by a lion which is Stubbs's most famous subject (17 variations are known altogether). Each picture shows a different phase of the encounter and struggle between the two animals. Gainsborough's *Ben Truman* is considered his greatest male portrait, characteristically beautiful in colour and paint handling, while *Giovanna Baccelli* shows his brushwork at its most flowing and dynamic, depicting life and movement in this portrait of a ballerina as no other artist of the time could have done.

Gainsborough's great rival was Reynolds, first President of the Royal Academy of Arts. In his official position, Reynolds did much for the status of artists in England but his painting lacks the sensuous brilliance of Gainsborough and often has not lasted well physically. However, in the substantial group of paintings by Reynolds in Gallery **5** there are three famous and revealing *self-portraits*, and one of Reynolds's most successful and celebrated grand portraits *Three Ladies Adorning a Term of Hymen* (The Montgomery Sisters). Also not to be missed is the portrait, demonstrating a new attitude to nature, of *Sir Brooke Boothby* by Joseph Wright of Derby, like Stubbs and Gainsborough an original and unconventional artist in his time.

The oddest genius of English art was William Blake, the only English artist to develop the figure art of Michelangelo and Raphael in a significant way. The Blake collection at the Tate, the largest anywhere, fills the whole of Gallery **7** (walk through **6** and **5**). It is installed in special conditions of low light, since most of Blake's works are on paper. At the end of the Blake room is a group of works by his friend and follower, Samuel Palmer, and by the group of artists around Palmer who called themselves 'The Ancients'.

Of the two great English painters of natural phenomena, J M W Turner and John Constable, the latter is the less well represented at the Tate but the famous *Flatford Mill,* one of his most typical Suffolk scenes, is in Gallery **11** together with, of particular note, two of his 'six foot' canvases, the breezy *Chain Pier, Brighton* and the dark and stormy *Hadleigh Castle,* painted just after his wife's death.

The Tate's great Turners are now shown in the handsome **Clore Gallery** built specially for them on the north side of the building.

In his will J M W Turner left the finished paintings remaining in his studio to the nation, wishing them to be kept and displayed in a home of their own. At long last the dream is fulfilled in the Clore Gallery. This L-shaped building, to the north of the Tate Gallery main entrance, was designed by the firm of James Stirling, architect of the acclaimed Staatsgalerie at Stuttgart, and is probably the most technically advanced gallery in the world. It was opened by H M The Queen in April 1987. It houses most of Turner's rich and diverse output of 300 major oil paintings and over 20,000 drawings and watercolours, many of them in nearly 300 sketchbooks. Superb facilities for study and research, including a Study Room where many thousands of drawings and watercolours acquired by the nation at the artist's death can be examined at leisure, assure the Clore Gallery's future as a focus for Turner studies. Above all, its elegant and sumptuously carpeted rooms display in its entirety the Tate's huge collection of canvases by this giant among C19 landscape artists.

A gallery full of lesser contemporaries of Turner and Constable is dominated by the enormous and amazing biblical fantasies of John Martin and Francis Danby, and James Ward's huge canvas of *Gordale Scar*, another of the Tate's well known favourites. The climax of the Tate's Historic British Collection comes with the Pre-Raphaelites, the group of young artists founded in 1848 by John Everett Millais, William Holman Hunt and Dante Gabriel Rossetti to create a new, realistic art dealing with serious subjects. The Pre-Raphaelite Collection fills Gallery **14** and much of **15**. Most notable works are the already mentioned Millais's *Ophelia*, Hunt's *Awakening Conscience*, Rossetti's *Beata Beatrix* and Burne-Jones's *King Cophetua and the Beggar Maid*. Finally, in Gallery **17** are works by the American-born James McNeill Whistler whose increasingly abstract views of the Thames of the 1870s mark the beginning of Modernism in Britain. The Tate has one of the most famous of these, *Nocturne in Blue and Gold: Old Battersea Bridge*.

In order to view the Tate's Modern Collection in correct sequence the visitor must return from Gallery 17 to the front of the building and start again.

The **Modern Collection** begins with Impressionism and the early modern movements in Galleries **30-32**. Highlights include one of Cézanne's last paintings, *The Gardener*, and a great Gaugin from his Tahitian period *Faa Iheihe (Decoration)*. There is a famous pair of Fauve paintings by the founders of that movement, *André Derain* by Matisse, and *Matisse* by Derain done in 1905, and a fine group of paintings by Bonnard including one of the pictures of his wife in the bath. The Tate's representation of Picasso begins in his 'Blue' period with the haunting *Young Girl in a Chemise* and continues with the early Cubist *Seated Nude, 1909-10*. The high point of Cubism about 1911 is illustrated by a superb Braque, *Clarinet and Bottle of Rum on a Mantelpiece*. Italian Futurism is represented by the famous Futurist sculpture of a running man, Boccioni's *Unique Forms of Continuity in Space* of 1913, and there is an important group of works by the British Vorticists led by Wyndham Lewis.

The handsome and spacious Gallery **35**, painted white, is devoted to the early development of pure abstract art and contains one of the first abstract paintings, *Dynamic Suprematism* of 1915, a rare canvas by the Russian pioneer of abstraction Kasimir Malevich. There is a good group of paintings by Mondrian and very fine examples of the work of Ben Nicholson, the first consistent English practitioner of pure abstraction. Modern Sculpture is represented here by an early masterpiece by Brancusi, the bronze *Maiastra* (a mythical bird) and by works by Naum Gabo, Barbara Hepworth and Henry Moore. The Tate has large collections of these three major C20 artists. Much of the Hepworth collection remains in the artist's house, now the **Hepworth Museum** in St Ives, Cornwall, where it is beautifully displayed. The Hepworth Museum and the Tate Gallery Liverpool, opened in 1988, are outstations of the Tate Gallery.

The development of Expressionism is marked by another of the Tate's great modern masterpieces *The Sick Child* by the Norwegian Edvard Munch in Gallery **39**, and there are works by artists of the German 'Brücke' group (founded 1905), notably Kirchner's *Bathers at Moritzburg* and Nolde's *The Sea*, as well as by the great individualist George Grosz (*Suicide*) and Max Beckmann (*Carnival*).

The Tate has one of the best collections of Surrealist art of any museum in the world. The source of Surrealist painting is represented by the celebrated painting by De Chirico of a nude and a bunch of bananas, *The Uncertainty of the Poet*, and early Surrealism by no less than three of that extraordinary group of Surrealist masterpieces painted by Max Ernst in the period of the formation of the movement in Paris in the early 1920s. There is also a group of Dali's most important works of the 1930s, including *The Metamorphosis of Narcissus* and paintings and sculpture by all the other major Surrealists. Picasso between the wars is represented by three outstanding paintings. *The Three Dancers* of 1925 is a grand canvas with themes of love, death and the femme fatale and marks Picasso's break with Cubism. *Nude woman in a Red Armchair* is a lyrical tribute to Marie-Thérèse Walther, one of his greatest loves. His paintings inspired by her are considered to be among his greatest works. A more recent addition *Weeping Woman* (1937) on loan for years from the Penrose Collection, was acquired for the nation in 1987.

Tate Gallery: Picasso, Nude Woman in a Red Armchair.

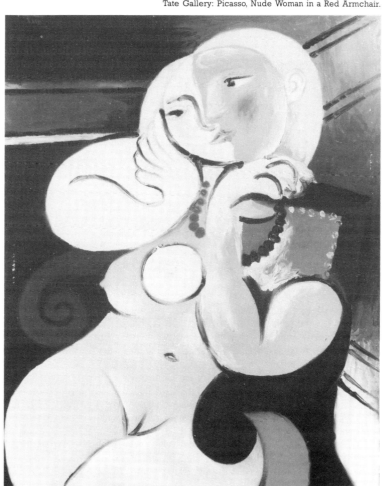

The Tate's post-war collections are displayed in Galleries **38-60** with the most recent art in the central hall (Galleries **27**, **28**) but the detailed arrangement tends to vary. Some highlights of the post-war collection up to the early 1960s are: Matisse's huge, brilliantly coloured late collage *The Snail,* one of the greatest C20 works in the Tate; important groups of works by Giacometti (partly given by the artist), Dubuffet and Bacon; substantial holdings of American Abstract Expressionism including Barnet Newman's *Adam and Eve* and the *Rothko Room,* a remarkable group of enormous mural paintings originally intended for the Four Seasons Restaurant in New York but given to the Tate by Rothko in the year of his death; three major paintings by Jackson Pollock *Birth* (c.1941), *Number 14 (1951)* and *Summertime: Number 9A* (1948); substantial holdings of British and American Pop Art including major works by the British Richard

Tate Gallery: Dali, Metamorphosis of Narcissus.

Hamilton *(Swinging London)*, Peter Blake *(Self-Portrait with Badges)*, and David Hockney *(Mr & Mrs Clark and Percy)* and by the Americans Claes Oldenburgh, Roy Lichtenstein and Andy Warhol, these last two represented respectively by the equally celebrated paintings *Whaam!* and *Marilyn Diptych*.

The Tate also has substantial holdings of the colourful large-scale abstract sculpture of Caro and his school that flourished in the 1960s and of the similarly large scale abstract painting of the same decade whose leading figures were Noland and Louis in the US and Hoyland, Smith, Denny and Cohen in Britain. The dominant movements of the 70s Minimal and Conceptual Art, are also well represented in the Tate although only a selection of work is on view at any given time. The School of London is well represented with works by Bacon, Auerbach, Freud and Kossoff. Also represented is

| 1 | Tate Gallery: |
| 2 | 1. Hepworth, Pelagos, 1946;
2. Caro, Early One Morning, 1962. |

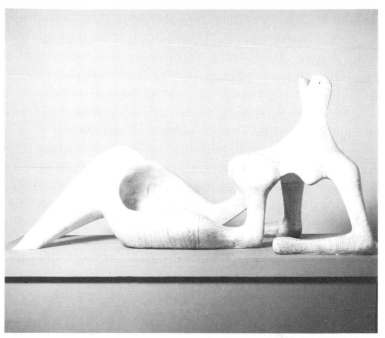

Tate Gallery:
1. Moore, Reclining Figure, 1951;
2. Brancusi, Maiastra;
3. Giacometti, Man Pointing.

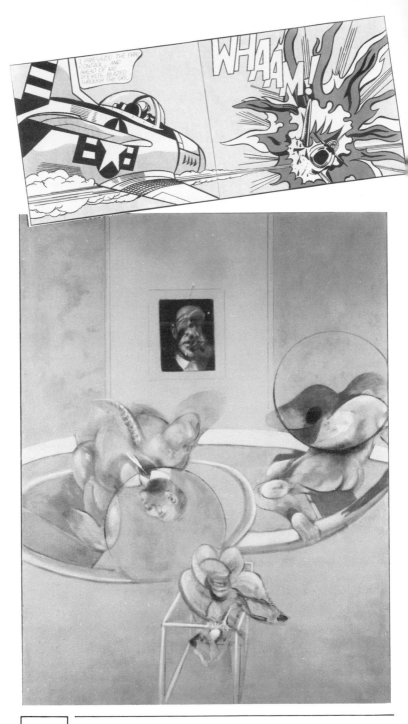

Tate Gallery: Broodthaers,
Casserole and Closed Mussels.

international painting and sculpture of the last decade with works by Americans such as Robert Longo, David Salle, Julian Schnabel and Jenny Holzer. Europeans include Georg Baselitz, Anselm Kiefer, Francesco Clemente, Sandro Chia. Of particular interest is the strong collection of recent British sculpture, including works by Stephen Cox, Richard Long, Barry Flanagan, Richard Wentworth, Bill Woodrow, Anish Kapoor, Alison Wilding, Shirazeh Houshiary, Richard Deacon and Tony Cragg.

There is an important programme of temporary exhibitions consisting of 2-3 major one-artist or one-movement retrospectives, both Historic British and Modern, each year and up to 10 small exhibitions. Recent major shows have included late Picasso, David Hockney and Hogarth ('Manners and Morals'). The Educational Department provides extensive free tours, lectures and documentary audio-visual programmes for the adult public as well as services for schools and teachers. Details of all Tate programmes are published in the monthly calendar obtainable free from the Information Desk just inside the front door. The Tate has a coffee bar and restaurant famous for its murals by Rex Whistler and its outstanding, and outstandingly good-value, wine list. (SW)

─────────────── *the essentials* ───────────────

Underground Pimlico (Victoria Line). **Open** Mon-Sat 1000-1750; Sun 1400-1750. **Cloakroom. Toilets. Public telephones. For the disabled** access, toilets, special tours by appointment. **Refreshments** restaurant (Sun closed), coffee shop. **Shopping** bookshop, sales desk for special exhibitions. **Publications. Photography** for private use only, no flash, no tripod, no cine camera. **Educational facilities. Visitors' services** guided tours Mon-Fri, lectures, films. **Research** library (limited access).

■ TELECOM TECHNOLOGY SHOWCASE
135 Queen Victoria Street EC4V 4AT.   Tel 248 7444
Admission *free*

Opened in 1982 it records over 200 years of progress in communications from the early slow mechanical devices situated on prominent hilltops to the latest instantaneous microtechnology used in voice transmission. Many examples are shown of the technical progress from the semaphore to the electric telegraph which was so vital to railway signalling, and the telephone which has been demystified since the early days when it was rarely available to the average person. The importance of microwave radio is also highlighted in the exhibition as is the way global links are made using space satellites. This started with the Early Bird in 1965 with only 240 voice circuits or one TV channel.

-------------------------- *the essentials* --------------------------
Underground Blackfriars (Circle, District Lines). **Open** Mon-Fri 1000-1700. **Toilets. Public telephones. For the disabled** access. **Shopping. Visitors' services** lectures. by prior arrangement. **Research** archives and study facilities by prior arrangement.

■ THAMES POLICE MUSEUM
98 Wapping High Street E1 9NE.   Tel 488 5196
Admission *prior written application*

This former carpenter's shop dates from 1872, but the story of the River (properly, Marine) Police goes back to 1798. The display includes portraits, documents, uniforms, equipment and a variety of models of police craft, plus a Thames Sailing Barge. A flag from the 'Princess Alice' is a reminder of the day in 1879 when this passenger vessel was in collision, and 500 lives were lost. The tragic delay in the arrival of the police craft, a rowing boat, hastened the introduction of powered boats. Paintings, prints and photographs illustrate the story of this most colourful section of the Metropolitan Police.

-------------------------- *the essentials* --------------------------
Underground Wapping (East London Line). **Open** by arrangement. **Toilets. Photography** by arrangement. **Educational facilities** lectures, tours, films by arrangement.

■ THEATRE MUSEUM
Russell Street WC2.   Tel 836 7891 (836 7624)
Admission *charge*

This museum is a branch of the Victoria and Albert Museum (qv). It is devoted to all the performing arts – theatre, opera, ballet, pantomime, music hall, variety, circus and rock and pop and has one of the richest theatrical collections in the world. There is one semi-permanent exhibition telling the history of the theatre through the objects in the collections. There are two other galleries for temporary exhibitions. In addition, there is a paintings gallery and a small theatre seating eighty-five people. There is a full programme of changing exhibitions and other events. Study facilities for scholars are also provided.

-------------------------- *the essentials* --------------------------
Underground Covent Garden (Piccadilly Line). **Open** Tue-Sun 1200-2000. **Cloakroom. Toilets. Public telephones. For the disabled** access, toilets. **Refreshments** snacks. **Shopping. Publications. Photography** by prior arrangement. **Educational facilities. Visitors' services** guided tours for school parties by appointment, lectures. **Research** library. **Staff opinion.**

■ TOWER BRIDGE MUSEUM AND EXHIBITIONS

SE1 2UP. Tel 407 0922
Admission *charge*

Tower Bridge, open for a Thames sailing-barge.

The museum and exhibitions show the interior working of one of London's most famous bridges, the only one to open allowing the passage of tall ships. The steam engines, boilers and water storage tanks (called 'accumulators') that operate the bascules are still in perfect working order. During their active life (1894-1976) they never failed to perform even though called upon up to fifty times per day to pump water to operate the hydraulic system. Their replacement by electric motors, and the raising of the bridge only four to five times a week, has reduced the need for staff from 120 to 15 today.

In the North Tower the exhibition *A Structural Triumph* illustrates the building of the bridge through drawings, photographs and video films. Also displayed are alternative designs to that of Horace Jones who with John Wolfe Barry (a relation of Sir Charles Barry of Houses of Parliament fame) produced the winning project. Their solution gave London its most prominent landmark. A stroll across the high, glass-enclosed walkway, with special windows which open for taking panoramic photographs, to the South Tower leads to the *Wonder Bridge exhibition* with a model, photographs and relics of the construction of the bridge and its later use. At ground level, by the lift exit, can be seen an original control cabin with its operating levers still in place.

The museum known as the *Machinery Exhibition,* a short walk away from the South Tower, houses the historic engines and equipment for the bridge. The massive engines are exactly as they were when the bridge was built and one of them may be seen turning. Here are the giant 'accumulators'; control equipment; boilers; a working technical model; video show and hydraulic drive engine which is push-button operated. Not open to the public is the modern machinery room and the deeply buried chambers containing the twin counterpoises which are concealed within the main towers.

1. Ticket Office
2. Exhibition 'A Structural Triumph'
3. Information and Sales Desk
4. Glass enclosed Walkways
5. Exhibition 'The City's Bridge'
6. Exhibition 'The Wonder Bridge'
7. Public Toilets
8. Museum and Machinery Exhibition

Tower Bridge: the old pumping engines.

the essentials

Underground Tower Hill (Circle, District Lines). **Open** daily Nov-Mar 1000-1645, Apr-Oct 1000-1830. **Toilets. For the disabled** access, toilets. **Shopping** sales desk. **Publications. Photography. Educational facilities.**

■ TREASURY OF THE DIOCESE OF LONDON

St Paul's Cathedral's Crypt, EC4 8AE. Tel 248 2705
Admission *charge*

The treasury was created in the Crypt of St Paul's in 1981 with a new display of ecclesiastical plate, regalia and manuscripts. The earliest items of plate shown date from around 1500 and then extend into the 1980s with two gold goblets marking the wedding of Prince Charles and Lady Diana.

The exhibits cover the whole period of the Church of England. Much of it is on loan from parishes and institutions in London. The contribution from the C19 is particularly interesting as it shows a gradual change in the ceremonial conventions of the Church of England after a long period of relative austerity following the Reformation. This is especially noticeable in the colourfully embroidered vestments which were reintroduced to Anglican worship in the late C19. A central case contains the Jubilee Cope of the Bishop of London which shows London church spires.

───────────────── *the essentials* ─────────────────

Underground St Paul's (Central Line). **Open** Summer Mon-Fri 1000-1615, Sat 1100-1615, Winter Mon-Fri 1000-1515, Sat 1100-1515 (closed for special services). **For the disabled** on application in advance. **Shopping** sales desk. **Photography. Educational facilities** on application. **Visitors' services** guided tours of the Cathedral, films.

■ VALENCE HOUSE MUSEUM

Becontree Avenue, Dagenham RM8 3HT. Tel 592 2211
Admission *free*

The present building, partly moated, dates mainly from the C17 and is the only manor house remaining in Dagenham. The manor was held in the C14 by Aymer de Valence, Earl of Pembroke. The house

Valence House: Fanshawe Room.

(timber framed and plastered) contains various artefacts from the area: Stone Age and Bronze Age implements, Roman pottery, Anglo-Saxon ornaments and weapons, topographical paintings and maps, and above all some fine portraits of the Fanshawe family executed by renowned court artists like Marcus Gheeraedts, William Dobson, Sir Peter Lely, Sir Godfrey Kneller and others.

--- *the essentials* ---

BR Becontree, Chadwell Heath, (from Liverpool Street Station), **Open** Mon-Fri 1000-1600. **Toilets. Parking Shopping** sales desk. **Publications. Visitors' services** lectures, guided tours by arrangement.

■ VESTRY HOUSE MUSEUM

Vestry Road, E17 9NH.   Tel 527 5544 ext 4391
Admission *free*

Vestry House Museum, seen from the garden.

In a quiet 'villagey' setting not far from Walthamstow's busy shopping centre, a handsome brick workhouse of 1730 houses one of London's most rewarding local history museums. Here you will find Britain's very first motor-vehicle, the locally-built *Bremer Car,* which made its debut in 1894/1895. Alongside is the charming little Wadley Dairy milk-cart and the rather grander crimson bread van of Simmons the bakers.

Upstairs is a remarkable *High-Victorian Parlour* in all its crowded glory, and a comprehensive collection of kitchenalia. Do not miss the Cell which survives from 1840 when the building contained the local police station. One of the pleasures of Vestry House is that everything is intelligently captioned and explained.

This is also the home of Waltham Forest Borough Archives; the museum also holds an extensive collection of old photographs, many of which can be bought as postcards. The educational resources are energetically managed, and the atmosphere of this delightful museum is helpful and welcoming. When you leave, walk along and inspect the Squire's Almshouses provided in 1795 for 'Six Decayed Tradesmen's Widows', and further on, the Ancient House, a most impressive timber-framed mansion, an extraordinary survivor in workaday Walthamstow.

--- *the essentials* ---

Underground Walthamstow Central (Victoria Line). **Open** Mon-Fri 1000-1300, 1400-1730, Sat 1000-1300, 1400-1700. **Toilets. For the disabled** by prior arrangement. **Shopping** sales desk. **Publications. Photography** by application only. **Educational facilities** by appointment only. **Visitors' services** lectures, guided tours by appointment only. **Research** library by appointment only.

| 1 | Vestry House Museum: |
| 2 | 1. The 'Hearth and Home' display; 2. The Laundry display (1985). |

■ VICTORIA AND ALBERT MUSEUM
Cromwell Road SW7 2RL.
Tel: 938 8500 (938 8441)
Admission *donation*

Victoria and Albert Museum, main entrance, surmounted by Lanteri's 'Fame'.

The Victoria and Albert Museum (or simply the V&A) is the National Museum of Art and Design; others know it more affectionately and less grandly as 'Britain's Attic'. It is both, with the most magnificent examples of the fine and applied decorative arts.

The V&A sprang from the Great Exhibition of 1851, a brainchild of a civil servant called Henry Cole, who persuaded the government and his friend Prince Albert, who was to be an encouragement and an inspiration to Cole and his enterprise for the rest of his life, that the £186,000 profits from the exhibition should be used to found a museum whose purpose would be not just to entertain but, in the spirit of the exhibition, to show the best in art and design and so encourage manufacturers and industrialists as well as artists and designers to strive to produce a matching best. It began in Marlborough House in London's Pall Mall and became established at its present site in 1857 in rather ugly iron buildings. Cole even had the name of the area changed from Brompton to something which he thought would attract more visitors, South Kensington, and his new venture was called the South Kensington Museum.

In the 1870s the old iron buildings were moved to London's East End and still serve as the Bethnal Green Museum of Childhood (qv). A new building was designed by Aston (later Sir Aston) Webb and in her last major public duty Queen Victoria laid the foundation stone in 1899 and gave the museum its new title. The Victoria and Albert Museum as we see it now was opened by King Edward VII ten years later. In 1987 Pirelli UK sponsored the redesigning of the central quadrangle in the Italian Renaissance manner to form what is now the Pirelli Garden.

There are several million objects in the seven miles of gallery space in this enormous museum. They are looked after by nine curatorial departments:

Victoria and Albert Museum: Rossellino, Virgin and Child, terracotta, C15.

Ceramics; Designs, Prints and Drawings (which includes paintings and photographs); **Far Eastern; Furniture and Interior Design; Indian; Metalwork; Sculpture; Textiles, Furnishing and Dress,** and the **National Art Library** (qv). There is also an Education Department which provides daily lectures and gallery talks as well as written information.

The Bethnal Green Museum of Childhood (qv), the Wellington Museum (qv), and Ham House (qv) and Osterley Park House (both administered on behalf of the National Trust) are branches of the V&A. The Theatre Museum opened as a branch of the V&A at Covent Garden in the Spring of 1987.

The V&A is a place of superlatives. It is the largest of the South Kensington museums by far, covering 13 acres, and in 1983 it took over

Victoria and Albert Museum Cast Courts: Trajan's column. The plaster cast was made in 1864.

the adjoining former Huxley Building — now the Henry Cole Wing,
once part of the Imperial College of Science and Technology —
to house the huge collections of prints, drawings, paintings and
photographs in a unique and specially designed storage system.
The entire central core of the eight-storey wing is a massive store
for over a million works of art, and members of staff boast they can
bring any piece out for inspection within ten minutes of its being
requested by a visitor to the **Print Room**. Five of the **Cole Wing's**
eight floors are open to the public, and include the first permanent exhibition space dedicated to photography in an art museum.

There is also a display of printing techniques, and the only panorama — a 360-degree landscape painting which the viewer stands in the centre of to see — on show in Britain. Another gallery in the wing (Level Four) houses the **National Collection of Portrait Miniatures**, including the famous *Young Man Among the Roses* by Nicholas Hilliard, while on the top floor is the biggest single display of paintings and sketches by one of England's finest landscape painters, John Constable — his sketch books alone are worth a special visit to Level Six. On the ground floor of the Henry Cole Wing is the New Restaurant. The Cole Wing is linked to the main museum by the new Exhibition Road Entrance, which is itself a small gallery containing *sculptures by Rodin*, most of them given by the sculptor himself.

In the main building, objects are displayed in two distinct manners. Primary galleries are designed to take pieces from all relevant departments to express the style of an age from Medieval to Modern times, but there are also study collections of types of objects for those wishing to go into greater detail. The V&A's galleries have a delightful way of catching the visitor by surprise. The **Cast Courts** are two huge galleries containing Victorian plaster casts of Europe's great pieces of monumental sculpture and masonry, made as teaching aids. They represent, in some cases, a more accurate expression of the original than the actual piece: the real *Trajan's Column* in Rome, for instance, is now so badly corroded by C20 pollution as to be hardly recognisable, while the 1870s plaster cast shows none of this degradation; other originals have, of course, disappeared in the two European wars. Also to be seen is a cast of the *Porta de la Gloria*, the doorway of the Church of Santiago de Compostela, goal for millions of pilgrims over the centuries, and of Michelangelo's *David* (search for the fig-leaf which a Victorian custodian had made, now separately displayed). In the corridor between the two courts is a display of fakes and copies of Medieval and Renaissance works of art made in the C19 including sculptures by the amazing counterfeiter of portrait busts, Bastianini. Near the casts and up a short flight of stairs is the collection of *wax sculptures*, amazingly life-like representations and tableaux for which there was a delightful vogue in the C18 and early C19.

But still on the **ground floor**, in another large court is the **Dress Collection**, where costume and its creation is seen as a decorative art with everything from the beautiful *shirt worn by Prince Rupert of the Rhine* in the C17 to a *modern suit* by Tommy Nutter. In between are the clothes worn by the best-dressed men and women of four centuries. The C20 is especially closely examined, with two thirds of the pieces on show coming from the modern period. Immediately above the Costume Court, up a short staircase, is the **Historic Musical Instruments Collection.**

Opposite the Dress Collection is the **Raphael Cartoon Court**, in which the paintings which the Renaissance artist made as patterns for tapestry are shown, on loan from the Queen. Other important galleries on this level include the **Indian Gallery**, where you will find *Tippoo's Tiger* — a toy made for an Indian sultan in the C18 showing a tiger mauling a British soldier to death and emitting a horribly realistic noise (now, sadly, not workable); the gigantic *Ardabil Carpet* (34ft 6ins by 17ft 6ins) is also here. The **Chinese Gallery**

1	Victoria and Albert Museum:
	1. The Great Bed of Ware, c1590;
2	2. Tippoo's Tiger.

Victoria and Albert Museum: Constable, Dedham Vale.

has, among its treasures, a jar dating from 2000 BC and there is also a gallery of **Islamic Art**. The **Continental Galleries**, displaying the styles of Europe from the C16 to the C18, are near the main entrance, opposite a new set of rooms dedicated to Continental art of the C19.

Two other important galleries are on the ground floor. First the **Medieval Treasury** with perhaps the most valuable pieces in the entire collections, both because of their intrinsic value and because of their rarity. The centrepiece is the C12 *Eltenburg Reliquary*.Secondly, the **Toshiba Gallery**, the biggest Japanese Gallery in Europe, showing objects which have never been on display before. Indeed, the Japanese Collections are so extensive that even here the displays have to be changed to show all that should be seen, and the unique collection of lacquer work is at last paid its due respect, as are the delightful netsuke, the carved ivory buttons from which tobacco pouches were hung.

On the **second level** — of what is a very complicated building — is, literally, a treasure house which has to be under constant guard and can only be entered through manually controlled turnstiles. It is the **Jewellery Gallery**, and the value of its holdings cannot be estimated. It is the largest single display of Medieval and

The Toshiba Gallery of Japanese Art and Design

The Toshiba Gallery of Japanese Art and Design, sponsored through the generosity of the Toshiba Corporation, opened in December 1986.

The exhibits are arranged primarily by theme, and date mainly from the period 1550-1900 (late Muromachi to Meiji periods). Two small sections concerned with Buddhist art and early ceramics contain older objects such as a fine C13 Amida Nyorai and a splendid early C15 Shigaraki jar. The section on tea utensils contains several Momoyama period ceramic masterpieces, notably a Black Raku teabowl by Honami Koetsu (1558-1637), a Yellow Seto drum-shaped vase and a powerfully sculpted Bizen freshwater jar. Works by Nonomura Ninsei (1640-1690) include an incense burner in the shape of a conch-shell. The central area of the gallery is devoted to the Museum's extensive collections of inro, netsuke, arms and armour, and woodblock prints. The collection of Edo period lacquer is also well represented, ranging from a traditional and exquisitely made writing table of about 1620 to an inventively decorated paper box and box for writing utensils by Ikeda Taishin (1825-1903). The stars of the export lacquer collection are the Mazarin chest and the Van Diemen box, made to order for Maria Van Diemen, the wife of Anton Van Diemen, Governor-General of the Dutch East Indies from 1636 to 1645. The export theme is carried over into the section devoted to Blue and White, Imari and Kakiemon style porcelains from Arita, and also into the display of Meiji period crafts. This includes many objects of sorts not often seen in Japan. Technically brilliant, they are often decorated with the excess of ornament that appealed so strongly to Victorian and Edwardian taste.

There is also a fine collection of Edo period costume and an important group of folkcraft items. Efforts to collect works by C20 Japanese artists can be seen in a folding screen by Serizawa Keisuke (1895-1984), a Red Shino dish by Kitaoji Rosanjin (1883-1959) and a sculpture entitled 'Cloud Image' by Susuki Osamu (born 1934). (RF)

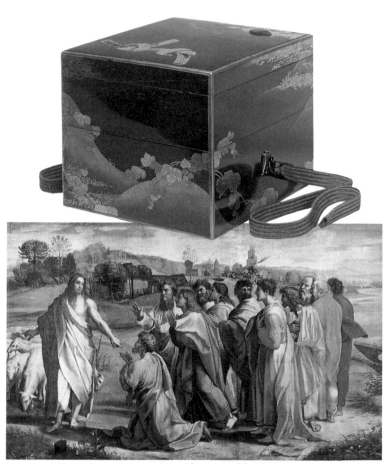

Victoria and Albert Museum: Lacquered wood Japanese cabinet for the incense ceremony, C18. Raphael cartoon: Christ's Charge to St Peter.

Renaissance jewellery in the world, matched with changing displays of the very latest designs. There is also celebrated jewellery, and among the prizes here are *pieces from the Russian Crown Jewels*, part of the suite of jewels which Napoleon gave to his adopted daughter as a wedding present and the bracelet clasps of Marie Antoinette.

On the same level is the **Renaissance Gallery** which includes, as well as Torrigiani's famous *bust of Henry VII* and *Henry VIII's gloves*, perhaps the most popular single object in the V&A, the *Great Bed of Ware*. This oak four-poster, 12 feet wide, appears in Shakespeare and in Dickens, and bears the carved signatures of hundreds of temporary occupants during its days of hotel service. One of the newest galleries to be seen on this floor is dedicated to **C20 British Art and Design**, rewarding both for scholars and for casual visitors.

———————————— *the essentials* ————————————

Underground South Kensington (Circle, District, Piccadilly Lines). **Open** Mon-Sat 1000-1750; Sun 1430-1750. **Cloakroom. Toilets. Public telephones. For the disabled** access, toilets. **Refreshments** restaurant, snacks. **Shopping. Publications. Photography. Educational services. Visitor's services** guided tours Mon-Fri, films, lectures. **Research** library. **Staff opinion.**

■ VINTAGE WIRELESS MUSEUM

23 Rosendale Road SE21 8DU. Tel 670 3667
Admission *prior application*

Vintage Wireless Museum: wireless over the years.

Opened in 1974, this is very much a private collection assembled by Mr Gerald Wells over a long period of time. The wireless sets on display are mostly representative of the period from 1917 to 1940 but some examples can be seen which lead up to the 'transistor age' of the 1960s. There are over 1,000 items to be seen, mainly of British origin but with a good contribution especially from the USA and Netherlands. Several pre-war TV sets are also shown in the collection, which is on display in a large Victorian house.

For the technically minded there is ample scope to follow developments from a trench set dating from 1917 and the simplest kits, often for self-assembly, bought through department stores in the 1920s, to the more complex, powerful and refined models which appeared at the end of the period. A particularly interesting exhibit is the 1924 HMV prototype crystal set and gramophone which was not put into production. Many people's interest will be in the cabinets which housed the radios, some incredibly elaborate as in many homes the wireless set provided a focal point in the living room until it was eventually eclipsed by the TV set. A booklet which describes the exhibits and the background to the collection is available and there is a small reference library.

the essentials

BR Herne Hill (from Blackfriars Station). **Open** daily 1100-1900, other times by arrangement. **Cloakroom. Toilets. Parking. Refreshment** snacks. **Publications. Photography. Visitors' services** guided tours, lectures: **Research** library.

■ WALLACE COLLECTION

Hertford House, Manchester Square W1M 6BN. Tel 935 0687
Admission *free*

The Wallace Collection is one of the outstanding private collections in the world, including among its treasures an array of C18 French paintings to rival the Louvre, a remarkable assembly of furniture and applied art and a number of unexpected masterpieces such as The Laughing Cavalier and Fragonard's The Swing.

Wallace Collection: Hals, The Laughing Cavalier.

Built up in the C19 by the third and fourth Marquesses of Hertford and the latter's illegitimate son, Sir Richard Wallace, the collection was bequeathed to the nation in 1897 by Lady Wallace. The family was a colourful and cosmopolitan one entertaining close, sometimes scandalous, connections with the English Royal and French Imperial families; perhaps its most interesting figure was the third Marquess himself, a wildly extravagant man who is memorably portrayed as the dissolute Lord Stayne in Thackeray's Vanity Fair.

Entering the house one is immediately confronted with a magnificent scene centred around the *Grand Staircase*, parts of which were made originally for Louis XV. Turn right into the first of three galleries originally used as State rooms. Here are fine *C18 and C19 English paintings* including Sir Thomas Lawrence's lively portrait of the Countess of Blessington, a lady best known for her reminiscences of Lord Byron. **Gallery 2** contains splendid examples of *Boulle furniture*, exquisitely veneered in brass and tortoiseshell, and a monumental gilt-bronze *chandelier* by Jacques Caffieri, one of the great Rococo craftsmen.

Works of ***Medieval and Renaissance art*** are displayed in **Gallery 3** along with a number of curiosities. To the left of the entrance stands a bust by German Pilon of Charles IX of France, a melancholy portrait of a King chiefly remembered for having ordered the massacre of Protestants on St Bartholomew's Day in 1572. Among the most interesting items in this room are a collection of C16 Limoges enamels, including a colourful interpretation of Raphael's Apollo and the Muses (wall-case B), a Venetian glass dish mould-blown with the figure of a lion (wall-case B) and, on the East wall,

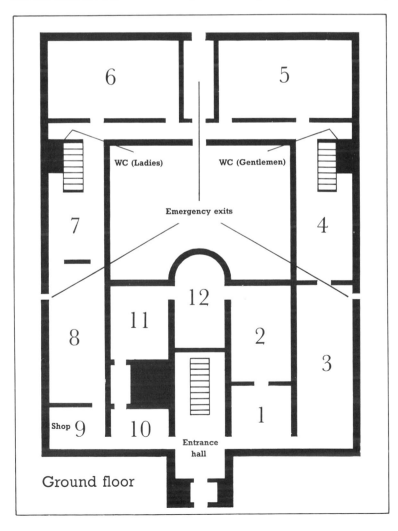

a charming fresco by Vincenzo Foppa of the young Cicero reading.

The adjoining **Gallery 4** was once Wallace's Smoking Room; although its original Victorian tiles were removed in 1937, earlier ceramic wares remain on display. These include radiant examples of Italian Majolica, Turkish Isnik earthenware and French Palissy ware with its unappetising assortment of shells and lizards. A curious memento is the Bell of S. Mura of C10 Irish origin and once credited with healing properties.

We now come to four galleries which house the **Arms and Armour** collections, one of the most important assemblies of its kind in the world. Here is a complete set of armour for man and horse, a slightly comical sight; also a fine Italian bronze cannon cast with scenes from classical mythology. In **Gallery 5** are to be seen a number of presentation sporting guns exquisitely decorated on lock, stock and barrel. *Oriental arms* in **Gallery 8** are complemented by a number of French C19 Orientalist paintings some of which show the weapons being put to use. Peace returns with **Galleries 9-12**

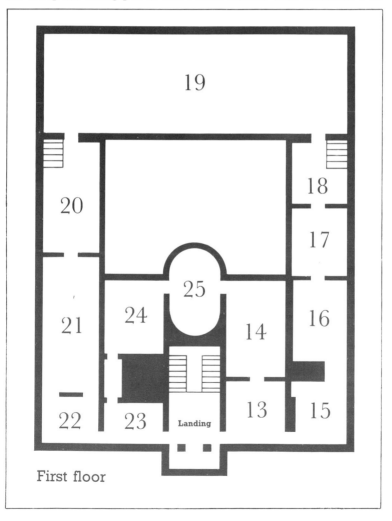

First floor

Wallace Collection: Astronomical Régulateur Clock, c1745, with movement by Alexandre Fortier and Michel Stollewerck.

which display contemporary paintings purchased by the fourth marquess in London and Paris, among them characterful animal subjects by Landseer, literary and historical works by Delacroix and Delaroche (including the poignant *Princes in the Tower*) and delightful landscape water-colours by Richard Bonington, a remarkably gifted artist who died at the age of twenty-six.

To reach the first floor ascend the Grand Staircase hung with allegorical paintings by Boucher once belonging to Madame de Pompadour. In contrast, **Gallery 13**, on the left, enjoys the cool, clear restraint of C17 Venetian paintings by Canaletto as well as a number of works by his pupil, Francesco Guardi. The *Régulateur Clock* in **Gallery 14** is perhaps the most remarkable of all the wonderful clocks in the collection: it shows Greenwich Mean Time, true Solar time, the phases, age and longitude of the Moon, the rising and setting of the Sun and the date. Now begins a tour of some of the great masterpieces of European paintings, beginning with Rembrandt's *The Good Samaritan* (1630), an extraordinarily lucid treatment of the popular parable. The same artist's *Landscape with a Coach* (1637) appears in **Gallery 17** with other splendid views of the Dutch landscape by Ruisdael, Hobbema and Wijnants. **Gallery 19**, over a hundred feet long and containing a host of magnificent paintings, compares favourably with some of the greatest galleries in the world. Opposite the entrance is Titian's *Perseus and Andromeda*, one of seven great canvases by the artist illustrating the works of Ovid. This one was once owned by Van Dyck. To its left is Poussin's *Dance to the Music of Time* in which the personifications of poverty, work, riches and pleasure are shown treading the circle of life. Rubens's superb *Rainbow Landscape* describes gloriously and minutely a scene near to the artist's home outside Brussels. On the opposite wall hangs the world-famous *Laughing Cavalier* by Frans Hals, a portrait full of life, though hardly laughing.

By no means an anti-climax, **Gallery 21** contains perhaps the finest assembly of French C18 paintings to be seen in a single room. In among the colourful fêtes galantes of Watteau is a melancholy portrait of Gilles and his family. Fragonard's *Gardens of the Villa d'Este* is a wonderful evocation of an Italian summer's evening: whilst *The Swing*, a well-known amorous picture, conveys a fine sense of movement. The final galleries include Lady Wallace's bedroom, **Gallery 22**, hung with a portrait of Mme Pompadour and the room where the second Marchioness used to entertain the Prince Regent. Return down the Grand Staircase and notice how, in the Entrance Hall, a few choice items from different areas of the collection are displayed for your final delectation. (MG)

———————————————— *the essentials* ————————————————

Underground Bond Street (Central, Jubilee Lines). **Open** Mon-Sat 1000-1700, Sun 1400-1700. **Cloakroom. Toilets. Public telephones. For the disabled** access, lift. **Shopping** sales desk. **Publications. Visitors' services** guided tours (once a week). **Research** library by appointment.

■ **WANDSWORTH MUSEUM**
Disraeli Road SW15 2DR.   Tel 871 7074
Admission *free*

The Museum tells the story of everyday life in Battersea, Balham, Putney, Tooting, Wandsworth, Roehampton, Earlsfield and Southfields. People have been living in these areas for thousands of years. The museum illustrates local life with objects dating from prehistoric times to the C20. Paintings, photos and maps show the changing landscape of the Wandsworth area – the homes of rich and poor, the farms, factories, watermills and windmills, the busy rivers, the peaceful countryside and the bustling suburban streets.

--- *the essentials* ---

Underground East Putney (District Line). **Open** Mon, Wed, Fri, Sat 1300-1700. **Toilets. Public telephones. For the disabled** access to ground floor only. **Shopping. Photography. Educational facilities. Visitors' services** by prior arrangement. **Research** by prior arrangement. **Staff opinion.**

■ WELLCOME INSTITUTE FOR THE HISTORY OF MEDICINE

183 Euston Road NW1 2BP. Tel 387 4477
Admission *prior application*

The institute had its origin in the very extensive collection of Henry S. Wellcome (1853-1936), entrepreneur and philanthropist. His first museum and library was established as early as 1913, and was intended to illustrate the history of man in a medical context, and to encourage research. In 1932 it was installed in the newly-built Wellcome Research Institution (now the Wellcome Building) in Euston Road. After various reorganisations, in 1977-80 the museum objects were transferred to the Science Museum (qv) and the institute at Euston Road now concentrates on teaching and research in the history of medicine and the allied sciences.

At the heart of the institute is the *Library* based on the books and manuscripts acquired by Sir Henry Wellcome and since his death constantly added to so that today it is the largest and most comprehensive of its kind in Europe. Over five centuries of medical and related literature are represented in approximately 400,000 books. The range is extraordinary, reflecting Henry Wellcome's wide interests and subsequent purchases. His aim to acquire a copy of every significant printed text on Western medical science from antiquity to the present has nearly been accomplished. The famous names include Aristotle, Galen and Hippocrates whose works were first printed in the C15. *First editions* of Bacon, Galileo, Kepler, Descartes, Hooke, Newton, Boyle and William Harvey are also held. Classic works from a later period are represented by Hunter, Jenner, Lister, Pasteur and Roentgen. The earliest European *manuscript* is in Anglo-Saxon and there are others in a variety of European languages, original C15 anatomical and medical illustrations, and many more treasures. In addition there are letters by Florence Nightingale, Pasteur, Lister, Jenner, Paget, Huxley, von Humboldt and other important medical and scientific personalities.

A *Contemporary Medical Archives Centre* is the most recent addition and its purpose is to preserve C20 records, documents, and archive collections relating to medical care and research in Britain. It holds the most complete register of British hospital records in the country. The institute has a continuing programme of seminars, lectures and exhibitions.

--- *the essentials* ---

Underground Euston Square (Circle, Metropolitan Lines). **Open** Mon-Fri 0930-1715. **Cloakroom. Toilets. Shopping** sales desk. **Photography. Visitors' services** lectures, guided tours by prior arrangement. **Research** library.

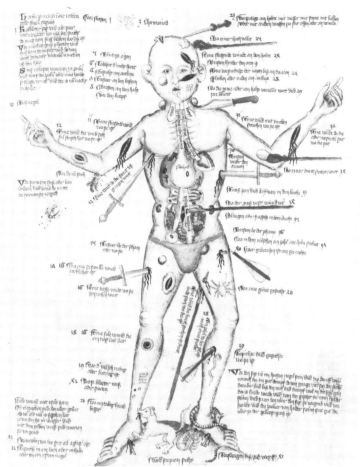
Wellcome Institute: 'Wound man', from the Apocalypsis, Wellcome MS 49.

■ WELLCOME MUSEUM OF HUMAN ANATOMY

Royal College of Surgeons of England, 35-43 Lincoln's Inn Fields WC2A 3PN.   Tel 405 3474 ext 3101
Admission *prior application*

The museum has a comprehensive collection of dissections demonstrating human anatomy, arranged according to the regions of the body, and skeletal material of different ages including foetal skeletons. Illustrated keys to specimens are available. Special features of the museum include resin corrosion casts of blood vessels, tracheobronchial trees, biliary and renal tracts. Serial sections through the adult head, neck and trunk and several dissected temporal bones are displayed together with atlases of the same. There are radiological, histological and cytological demonstrations with explanatory texts. The museum is open to medical and dental practitioners, and undergraduates introduced by their tutors. (REMB)

––––––––––––––––––– *the essentials* –––––––––––––––––––
Underground Holborn (Central, Piccadilly Lines). **Open** Mon-Fri 0900-1800; closed all August. **Cloakroom. Toilets. Public telephones. Visitors' services** by prior arrangement. **Staff opinion.**

■ WELLCOME TROPICAL INSTITUTE MUSEUM

183 Euston Road NW1 2BP.   Tel 387 4477 ext 3240
Admission *prior application*

Established by Sir Henry Wellcome, founder of the huge Wellcome Foundation pharmaceutical empire, the museum occupies the upper ground floor of the Wellcome Building. It is a teaching museum, for doctors, nurses, pharmacists, and members of other paramedical professions, including teachers and students of the natural sciences, only. Admission is by ticket obtainable at the main entrance to the building.

From its inception the collection dealt with tropical medicine, epidemic bacteriology, applied entomology and similar subjects, but today it deals also with broader issues such as nutrition, virology, immunology, cardiology and cancer. It contains two galleries which are divided into cubicles for study according to the disease or topic being dealt with. Many of the information displays are periodically revised and up-dated by consultant specialists.

––––––––––––––––––––––––––––––– *the essentials* –––––––––––––––––––––––––––––––

Underground Euston Square (Circle, Metropolitan Lines). **Open** Mon-Fri 0900-1700. **Cloakroom. Toilets. Public telephones. Publications. Visitors' services** films, lectures, guided tours by arrangement. **Research library,** interpreters by arrangement.

■ WELLINGTON MUSEUM

Apsley House, 149 Piccadilly W1V 9FA.   Tel 499 5676
Admission *charge*

Apsley House. On the left, the Decimus Burton screen, forming an entrance to Hyde Park, and Wellington, on his horse 'Copenhagen'.

The first house to be encountered after the Knightsbridge toll gate by coaches entering London, Apsley House became known as 'Number One', London, and it still is. Robert Adam built it for Baron Apsley in the 1770s. Thirty years later it was sold to Marquess Wellesley, who in turn sold it to his brother, the first Duke of Wellington, in 1817; it remained the Iron Duke's London home for the rest of his life. In 1947 the seventh Duke gave the house to the nation and it has been administered by the V&A ever since, one of London's most splendid palaces and now the Wellington Museum.

Wellington, the hero of the Peninsular War and Waterloo who became a leading statesman and prime minister, had the architect Benjamin Dean Wyatt make alterations to the house, and added the magnificent **Waterloo Gallery**, where he held his annual dinner with his old comrades-in-arms to commemorate the battle which vanquished Napoleon. The V&A has restored this room, and much of the rest of the house, to the way the Duke would remember it, and it is a supreme example of the revived Louis XIV style popular in the early C19.

Wellington was a fine judge and an avid collector of pictures, and he festooned his walls with what is still probably the finest private collection of master paintings. Velazquez — his *Water Seller* must not be missed — Rubens, Van Dyck, Murillo and Breughel are all here. The Duke disliked the Goya mounted portrait, and kept it in store, but it is on display in the Waterloo Gallery now. But his favourite painting, which he would inspect every morning, is a small Correggio entitled *The Agony in the Garden*.

Wellington Museum: The Waterloo Gallery.

264

Wellington Museum: The Wellington Boot, by Paul Pry (left) and the Sèvres vase, with quagga and Cape of Good Hope scenery (right).

England's hero, Wellington was also perceived as the saviour of Europe, with many honorary titles — batons in the ground floor plate and china room bear witness. Many of the magnificent gifts with which he was showered are here, and perhaps the most splendid is the *Sèvres Egyptian Service* which was originally made as a divorce present for the Empress Josephine from Napoleon; she rejected it, and the restored Louis XVIII gave it to Wellington in 1818.

At the foot of the staircase which leads to the first floor and the rooms which include the Waterloo Gallery is the huge Canova *statue of Napoleon*. This stands 11 feet 4 inches high and was commissioned by the Emperor in 1802, but he did not see it until 1811 when he rejected it as being too undignified. The British Government bought it in 1816 and gave it to Wellington.

In the dining room on the first floor is the great dining table with chairs, which the Duke used for his annual dinners, and on the table is the 26 feet long silver centrepiece, presented by Portugal in 1816 and described by the curators as 'the single great monument of neoclassical silver'.

Before leaving, it would be a mistake not to visit the basement where there is a delightful display of caricatures of Wellington, who must have been a most popular subject for cartoonists for much of his long life (he was 83 when he died). (ST)

─────────── *the essentials* ───────────

Underground Hyde Park Corner (Piccadilly Line). **Open** Tue-Thur, Sat 1000-1800, Sun 1430-1800. **Cloakroom. Toilets. For the disabled** access, toilets. **Shopping** sales desk. **Publications. Photography. Visitors' services** guided tours on application.

Wellington Museum: Napoleon, by Canova.

■ WESLEY'S HOUSE

49 City Road EC1Y 1AU. Tel 253 2262
Admission *charge*

The home from 1779 to 1791 of John Wesley (1703-1791), the founder of the Methodist Church, the **house** is located next to the chapel where Wesley preached and was based for the final years of his life. It contains an excellent collection of objects relating to Wesley and his work including letters and clothes. The *library* on the first floor houses many of his books containing notes and corrections in the margins. The most unusual item in the collection is an electric shock machine that Wesley used for treating cases of depression, an extremely advanced idea for the period. The **chapel** is the Mother Church of World Methodism and still retains the columns made out of ships' masts presented by George III. The small Foundery Chapel contains benches from Wesley's first base in London and an organ from the house of Charles Wesley, younger brother of John. In the crypt of the chapel is the **Museum of Methodism** which illustrates the history of Methodism from the C18 to the present day. (IO)

Wesley's House: John Wesley's bedroom.

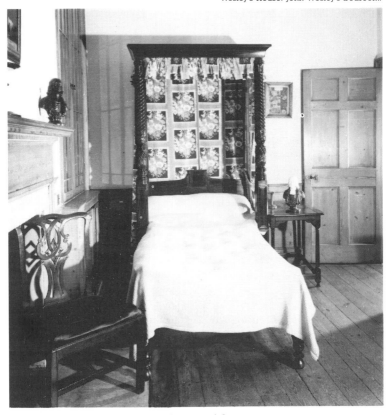

the essentials

Underground Moorgate (Circle, Metropolitan, Northern Lines), Old Street (Northern Line). **Open** Mon-Sat 1000-1600, other times by appointment. **Toilets. Public telephones. For the disabled** access to the Chapel and ground floor of the House. **Refreshments** snacks. **Shopping. Photography. Educational facilities. Visitors' services** guided tours on request, audio-visual.

■ WESTMINSTER ABBEY MUSEUM

Westminster Abbey SW1P 3PA.   Tel 222 5152
Admission *charge*

This collection is situated in the oldest part of Westminster Abbey, the Norman Undercroft of the Monks Dormitory, built between 1066 and 1100 following the Norman invasion of Britain. Recently the display has been completely re-designed so as to enhance the beautiful architectural setting and to enable the unique collection of royal and other *effigies* to be seen to advantage.

Westminster Abbey Museum: Effigy of Queen Anne.

Westminster Abbey Museum: Effigy of Lord Nelson.

The earlier effigies are of wood, and of all but two only the heads survive. Modelled from death-masks, they give an amazingly realistic impression of medieval and Tudor monarchs. The later wax effigies, dating from the C17 and C18, are equally vivid representations, and their clothes and paste jewellery represent in themselves a unique collection of contemporary costume.

The Duchess of Richmond (d1702) has her pet parrot beside her, which is believed to be the oldest stuffed bird to have survived in the country, if not in Europe. Besides the effigies, the Museum also contains examples of Romanesque carving, a fine *relief portrait of Sir Thomas Lovell* by Torrigiano, objects connected with the life of the Benedictine Abbey, an *architectural model and drawings by Sir Christopher Wren,* and a selection of copes and of silvergift plate, mainly of the C17.

--- *the essentials* ---

Underground St James's Park, Westminster (Circle, District Lines). **Open** daily 1000-1630. **For the disabled** access. **Shopping** main Abbey bookshop nearby, sales desk. **Research** library

■ WILLIAM MORRIS GALLERY

Lloyd Park, Forest Road E17 4PP.   Tel 527 5544 ext 4390
Admission *free*

William Morris Gallery: William Morris, from an original photograph.

The boyhood home from 1848 to 1856 of William Morris (1834-96), architect, painter, poet, designer and social reformer, this house, set in an attractive park, contains the *Morris Collection* and the *Sir Frank Brangwyn Collection* of C19 and early C20 painting. It is a monument to all aspects of C19 art and design, with paintings, ceramics, furniture and textiles by the leading contemporary artists. The main emphasis is on Morris himself, with clear explanations of his techniques, his political views, and the stages of his career. Particularly interesting items are the Kelmscott Chaucer, the Woodpecker Tapestry, William de Morgan tile panels, and the Martin Brothers' ceramics. The gallery also houses a reference library of material related to Morris and his circle, which can be consulted by appointment. (IO)

--- *the essentials* ---

Underground Walthamstow Central (Victoria Line). **Open** Tue-Sat 1000-1300. 1400-1700. 1st Sunday in each month 1000-1200, 1400-1700. **For the disabled** access to ground floor only. **Shopping** sales desk. **Publications. Photography** by prior permission and for study purposes only. **Educational facilities. Visitors' services** films, lectures, guided tours by previous appointment. **Research** library.

William Morris Gallery: tapestry, The Woodpecker, woven by Morris & Co at Merton Abbey, 1885.

■ WIMBLEDON LAWN TENNIS MUSEUM

The All England Club, Church Road SW19 5AE.   Tel 946 6131
Admission *charge*

Situated adjacent to the world-famous Centre Court, it is worth a
visit, even for those who are not particularly tennis fans, providing
as it does a fascinating glimpse into the social life of the past
century. The museum was first opened in 1977 to celebrate the
Centenary of the Championships but between the 1984 and 1985
tournaments completely new exhibitions galleries were designed
and constructed. Displays cover the history of Lawn Tennis from
its origins to the present day.

Wimbledon Lawn Tennis Museum: the Victorian Parlour, one of the series of displays.

Some of the most popular features are the racket maker's workshop
c1900 and the gentlemen's dressing room from the original All
England Club site in Worple Road. The centre-piece of the main
gallery is an eye-catching display where figures in tennis dresses
of the appropriate period attend a Victorian tennis tea party on a
vicarage lawn, indulge in an Edwardian picnic, and sip something
rather stronger in the 1920s tennis club pavilion. These settings
afford scope for displaying the museum's collection of sometimes
elaborate and often (by our standards) uncomfortable tennis clothes
as they were worn in times past. The equipment used to play the
game from Victorian times to the present day is on show as are,
for most of the year, the Championship Trophies, presented on
court to the winners each year. Every visitor has a chance to view
the Centre Court as well as watching a film in the museum's audio-
visual theatre. Serious researchers can make an appointment to visit
the Kenneth Ritchie Library wherein all sorts of interesting facts
can be gleaned on various aspects of the game. (VW)

---
the essentials

Underground Southfields (District Line). **Open** Tue-Sat 1100-1700, Sun 1400-1700 (special
arrangements during Championships). **Toilets. Parking. Public telephones. For the
disabled** access, toilets. **Shopping. Visitors' services** films. **Research** library.

1	2
	3

Wimbledon Lawn Tennis Museum:

1. Early Lawn Tennis racket with unusual stringing, c1885;.
2. Ceramic tennis figure, c1890;
3. Victorian and Edwardian tennis costumes from the 1890s to the early 1900s.

■ WIMBLEDON SOCIETY MUSEUM

26 Lingfield Road SW19 4QD.
Admission *free*

Wimbledon Society Museum, facing The Ridgeway.

A small but delightful local history museum, founded in 1908 and staffed by knowledgeable voluntary staff. It is entered from The Ridgeway where it occupies a single large upstairs room on the premises of the Wimbledon Village Club, and is subdivided into sections: archives and manuscripts, books, ephemera, photographs, watercolours and prints, maps, archaeology, and natural history specimens illustrative of Wimbledon past. A good number of items are on display and clearly labelled. The strongest collections, well catalogued, are those of *old photographs, prints* and *watercolours* of the area. The Wimbledon Society (formerly the John Evelyn Society) is also involved in publishing works related to one of the most desirable boroughs within Greater London.

--- *the essentials* ---

Underground Wimbledon (District Line). **Open** Sat 1430-1700. **Toilets. Shopping** sales desk. **Educational** facilities by arrangement. **Visitors'** services guided tours by arrangement.

■ WIMBLEDON WINDMILL MUSEUM

Windmill Road, Wimbledon Common SW19 5NR.   Tel 788 7655
Admission *charge*

The Wimbledon windmill, built in 1817, has an interesting history, having been designed and constructed by a local carpenter in a style unusual in Britain. Functionally it was based on Dutch practice known as 'hollow post', but the structure is believed to have been copied from a unique design of a mill in Southwark near the site of the old Globe Theatre. Disused since 1864, the mill was substantially restored in 1893 to prevent its collapse. Although many of the original timbers remain, the restoration to some extent changed its appearance.

The Wimbledon Windmill.

Wimbledon Windmill Museum: machinery and milling equipment, with explanatory display.

Nevertheless it has remained a significant landmark since it was built. It was the scene for a famous duel nearby between the Earl of Cardigan and Captain Tuckett in 1840, and it was here that Lord Baden-Powell wrote his 'Scouting for Boys' in 1907. In 1976 the building was turned into a museum to record the history and development of windmills in Britain.

The display comprises pictures and drawings, detailed models and examples of machinery and tools used. Most of the exhibits can be handled and there are working models which will particularly interest children. However the models are not simply for amusement, but are intended to instruct, and so contain a considerable amount of technical detail and show not only the more familiar types of windmill but also the less well-known uses of wind power. Wall displays include detailed drawings and photographs of the construction and working of mills.

─────────── *the essentials* ───────────

Underground Wimbledon (District Line). **Open** Apr-Oct Sat, Sun, 1400-1700, also at other times by prior arrangement. **Toilets** nearby. **Refreshments** snacks **Shopping** sales desk. **Publications. Photography. Educational facilities. Visitors' services** guided tours, lectures by arrangement.

■ WOODLANDS ART GALLERY AND LOCAL HISTORY CENTRE

90 Mycenae Road, Blackheath SE3 7SE. Tel 858 4631
Admission *free*

Woodlands Local History Centre.

Woodlands was built in 1774 for John Julius Angerstein, whose collection of old-master paintings formed the nucleus of the National Gallery (qv). The local history library holds a large collection of books, pamphlets, photographs, postcards, maps, prints and drawings relating to the boroughs of Greenwich and Woolwich which were amalgamated in 1965. A Plumstead deed of 1387 is the oldest document in the collection.

The art gallery, opened in 1972, has a large and growing collection of local topographical watercolours and drawings from the mid-C18 to the present. The material, which is well catalogued, is put on display in theme exhibitions from time to time. Contemporary art exhibitions are held every month at the gallery. The gallery is also responsible for the **Tudor Barn Art Gallery** [Well Hall Road SE9 6SZ, Tel 850 2340], an exhibition space for local artists to show their work.

--- *the essentials* ---

BR Westcombe Park (from Charing Cross Station). **Open** Mon, Tue, Thur-Sat 1000-1800, Sun 1400-1800. **Toilets** upon request. **Parking. Shopping** sales desk. **Publications. Photography** general views only. **Research** library.

● Americana

All Hallows by the Tower Undercroft Museum; British Library Map Room; HM Customs and Excise Museum and Exhibition; Dickens House Museum and Library; National Maritime Museum; Public Record Office Museum; Sir John Soane's Museum; Vintage Wireless Museum; Wesley's House.

● Anthropology and Ethnography

Bromley Museum; Commonwealth Institute; Cuming Museum; Darwin Museum; Hackney Museum; Horniman Museum; Museum of Mankind; Natural History Museum; Royal College of Music Museum of Instruments; Sir John Soane's Museum.

● Archaeology and Antiquities

All Hallows by the Tower Undercroft Museum; Harrow School Old Speech Room Gallery; Ashmole Archive; Bexley Museum; British Museum; Bromley Museum; Erith Museum; Greenwich Borough Museum; Horniman Museum; Museum of London; National Maritime Museum; National Monuments Record; Passmore Edwards Museum; Petrie Museum of Egyptian Archaeology; St Bride's Church and Crypt Museum; Sir John Soane's Museum; Valence House; Wimbledon Society Museum.

● Astronomy and Space Exploration

Madame Tussaud's (London Planetarium); National Maritime Museum (Old Royal Observatory); Science Museum; Science Reference and Information Service; Telecom Technology Showcase.

● Biographical and Personal Collections

Ashmole Archive (Archaeology); Cabinet War Rooms (W. Churchill and World War II); Carlyle's House; Charles King Collection of Historical Anaesthetic Apparatus; Darwin Museum; Dickens House Museum; Fawcett Library (The Women's Movement); Flaxman Gallery (Neoclassical casts); Florence Nightingale Museum; Freud Museum; Hogarth's House; Hunterian Museum (Medicine); Keats House; Leighton House (Victorian studio-house, furniture and paintings); Linley Sambourne House (Victorian house, furniture and memorabilia); Lloyd's Nelson Collection; Mander and Mitchenson Theatre Collection; Martinware Pottery Collection; Marx Memorial Library; Museum of Zoology and Comparative Anatomy (founded by Prof R.E. Grant); Percival David Foundation of Chinese Art; Petrie Museum of Egyptian Archaeology; Riesco Collection of Chinese Ceramics; Rock Circus; Royal Ballet School Museum and Archives; Royal Botanic Gardens, Kew (Marianne North Gallery); Saatchi Collection (C20 art); Shakespeare Globe Museum (Elizabethan theatre and Southwark); Sir John Soane's Museum (Neoclassical house, Archaeology and paintings); Soseki Museum (Japanese writer); Tate Gallery (Clore Gallery for the Turner Collection); Wallace Collection (especially French C18 paintings); Wellington Museum; Wesley's House and Museum of Methodism.

● Books and Manuscripts (inc. Newspapers)

British Library; Dickens House Museum and Library; Fawcett Library; Harrow School Old Speech Room Gallery; India Office Library and Records; Lambeth Palace and Library; Marx Memorial Library; National Art Library; National Book League; National Portrait Gallery Archives and Library; Newspaper Library; Oriental Collections; Public Record Office, Kew; Public Record Office Museum; St Bride Printing Library; Science Museum Library; Science Reference and Information Service.

● Ceramics

British Museum; Fenton House; Kingston upon Thames Museum; Leighton House; Mander and Mitchenson Theatre Collection; Martinware Pottery Collection; Museum of the Pharmaceutical Society; Museum of the United Grand Lodge of England; Passmore Edwards Museum (Bow porcelain); Percival David Foundation of Chinese Art; Pitshanger Manor Museum; Riesco Collection of Chinese Ceramics; Royal College of General Practitioners Museum; Victoria and Albert Museum; Wallace Collection; Wellington Museum; William Morris Gallery.

● Ceremonial and Regalia

City Livery Companies Collections; Crown Jewels; Guards Museum; Heralds' Museum; Inns of Court and City Yeomanry Museum; Lloyd's Nelson Collection; Museum of London; Museum of the Order of St John; Museum of the United Grand Lodge of England; National Army Museum; Polish Institute and Sikorski Museum; Regimental Museum of the Royal Fusiliers, Tower of London; Royal Britain; Treasury of the Diocese of London, St Paul's Cathedral; Victoria and Albert Museum.

● Clocks and Watches

British Museum; Clockmakers' Company Collection; Museum of the United Grand Lodge of England; National Maritime Museum (Old Royal Observatory); Wallace Collection.

● Costume, Fashion and Jewels

Barnet Museum; Bethnal Green Museum of Childhood; British Museum (jewels); Court Dress Collection; Crown Jewels; Grange Museum of Local History; Iveagh Bequest (shoe buckles and jewels); Museum of London; Museum of Mankind; Museum of the United Grand Lodge of

England; National Portrait Gallery Archive and Library; Passmore Edwards Museum; Petrie Museum of Egyptian Archaeology (oldest known linen garment); Treasury of the Diocese of London, St Paul's Cathedral; Theatre Museum; Victoria and Albert Museum; Westminster Abbey Museum; Wimbledon Lawn Tennis Museum.

● Crafts and Craftsmanship

British Museum; City Livery Companies Collections; Courtauld Institute of Art; Crafts Council Collection; Jewish Museum; Kingston upon Thames Museum; Martinware Pottery Collection; Museum of London; Museum of Mankind; Osterley Park House; Pitshanger Manor Museum; Silver Studio Collection; Victoria and Albert Museum; William Morris Gallery.

Design

Crafts Council Collection; Design Museum; Science Reference and Information Service; Silver Studio Collection; Victoria and Albert Museum; William Morris Gallery.

● Drawings (inc. Architectural)

Arts Council of Great Britain Collection; British Architectural Library Drawings Collection; British Council Collection; British Museum; Chiswick House; Corporation of London Permanent Collection; Courtauld Institute of Art; Linley Sambourne House; Queen's Gallery, Buckingham Palace; Sir John's Soane's Museum; South London Art Gallery; Tower Bridge Museum and Exhibitions; Victoria and Albert Museum; Westminster Abbey Museum; Wimbledon Society Museum; Wimbledon Windmill Museum; Woodlands Art Gallery.

Ecclesiastical Art and Religious Objects

All Hallows by the Tower Undercroft Museum; British Library; British Museum; Harrow School Old Speech Room Gallery; Jewish Museum; Lambeth Palace and Library; Petrie Museum of Egyptian Archaeology; Treasury of the Diocese of London, St Paul's Cathedral; Victoria and Albert Museum; Wesley's Museum and Museum of Methodism; Westminster Abbey Museum.

Effigies and Waxworks

British Museum; Florence Nightingale Museum; Guards Museum; Guinness World of Records; London Dungeon; Madame Tussaud's; Rock Circus; Royal Britain; Victoria and Albert Museum; Westminster Abbey Museum.

Films and Sound Archives

Imperial War Museum; Mander and Mitchenson Theatre Collection; Museum of London; Museum of the Moving Image (MOMI); National Film Archive; National Sound Archive.

Furniture and Interiors

Bank of England Museum; Barnet Museum; Bethnal Green Museum of Childhood; Carlyle's House; Chiswick House; City Livery Companies Collections; Court Dress Collection; Darwin Museum; Dickens House Museum and Library; Fenton House; Forty Hall; Freud Museum; Geffrye Museum; Grange Museum of Local History; Ham House; Harrow Museum and Heritage Centre; Hogarth's House; India Office Library and Records; Iveagh Bequest; Jewish Museum; Keats House; Leighton House; Linley Sambourne House; Marble Hill House; Museum of London; Museum of Richmond; Osterley Park House; Pitshanger Manor Museum; Prince Henry's Room; Royal Society of Arts; Sir John Soane's Museum; Vestry House Museum; Victoria and Albert Museum; Wallace Collection; Wellington Museum; William Morris Gallery.

Geology and Gemmology

Bexley Museum; Erith Museum; Museum of Mankind; Natural History Museum; Passmore Edwards Museum; Science Reference and Information Service.

● Glass

British Museum; City Livery Companies Collections (Grocers'); Herald's Museum; Museum of London; Museum of the United Grand Lodge of England; Petrie Museum of Egyptian Archaeology; Wallace Collection; Wellington Museum.

Industrial Archaeology

Brunel's Engine House; Gunnersbury Park Museum; Heritage Motor Museum; Kew Bridge Steam Museum; London Gas Museum; London Transport Museum; National Monuments Record; North Woolwich Station Museum; Tower Bridge Museum and Exhibition; Wimbledon Windmill Museum.

Local History Collections

Barnet Museum; Bexley Museum; Bromley Museum; Bruce Castle Museum; Burgh House; Church House Museum; Cuming Museum; Epping Forest Museum; Erith Museum; Grange Museum of Local History; Greenwich Borough Museum; Hackney Museum; Hammersmith and Fulham Local History Collections; Harrow Museum and Heritage Centre; Museum of London; Museum of Richmond; Orleans House Gallery; Shakespeare Globe Museum; South London Art Gallery; Valence House Museum; Vestry House Museum; Wandsworth Museum; Wimbledon Lawn Tennis Museum; Wimbledon Society Museum; Woodland Art Gallery.

Maps and Globes

British Library; Kingston upon Thames Museum; Museum of London; National Army Museum; National Maritime Museum; National Monuments Record; Public Record Office; Royal Geographical Society Map Room; Science Museum; Valence House Museum; Wimbledon Society Museum; Woodlands Art Gallery.

● Medicine and Medical Sciences

British Dental Association Museum; British Optical Association Foundation Museum; Charles King Collection of Historical Anaesthetic Apparatus; City Livery Companies Collections (Apothecaries'); Florence Nightingale Museum; Freud Museum; Gordon Museum; Hunterian Museum; Museum of the Institute of Ophthalmology; Museum of the Order of St John (St John Ambulance Museum); Museum of the Pharmaceutical Society; Odontological Museum; Old St Thomas' Operating Theatre; Royal College of General Practitioners Museum; Royal College of Physicians Portrait Collection; Science Museum (Wellcome Museum of the History of Medicine); Science Reference and Information Service; Wellcome Institute of the History of Medicine; Wellcome Museum of Human Anatomy; Wellcome Tropical Institute Museum.

● Metalwork

All Hallows by the Tower Undercroft Museum; Bank of England Museum; British Museum; City Livery Companies Collections; Courtauld Institute of Art; Heralds' Museum; Jewish Museum; Lloyd's Nelson Collection; Museum of the United Grand Lodge of England; Royal Armouries, Tower of London; Treasury of the Diocese of London, St Paul's Cathedral; Wallace Collection; Wellington Museum; Westminster Abbey Museum.

● Militaria, Arms and Armour, Uniforms

All Hallows by the Tower Undercroft Museum; Barnet Museum; HMS Belfast; Bruce Castle Museum; Cabinet War Rooms; City Livery Companies Collections (Armourers' and Brasiers'); HM Customs and Excise Museum and Exhibition; Florence Nightingale Museum; Guards Museum; Heralds' Museum, Imperial War Museum; Inns of Court and City Yeomanry Museum; Lloyd's Nelson Collection; Museum of Artillery; Museum of the Order of St John; NAAFI Historical Collection; National Maritime Museum; Polish Institute and Sikorski Museum; Regimental Museum of the Royal Fusiliers; Royal Air Force Museum (inc Battle of Britain Museum and Bomber Command Museum); Royal Artillery Regimental Museum; Royal Hospital Chelsea Museum; Royal Military School of Music Museum; Thames Police Museum; Wallace Collection; Wellington Museum.

● Models

Bethnal Green Museum of Childhood; London Toy and Model Museum; Museum of London; Museum of Richmond; National Army Museum; National Maritime Museum; National Postal Museum; Natural History Museum; North Woolwich Station Museum; Pollock's Toy Museum; Science Museum; Thames Police Museum; Tower Bridge Museum and Exhibitions; Wimbledon Windmill Museum.

● Music (printed and MSS) and Musical Instruments

British Library; Coram Foundation for Children; Fenton House; Horniman Museum; Musical Museum; Ranger's House; Royal College of Music Department of Portraits; Royal College of Music Museum of Instruments; Royal Military School of Music Museum; Victoria and Albert Museum.

● Natural Sciences

Bexley Museum; Chelsea Physic Garden; Darwin Museum; Epping Forest Museum; Greenwich Borough Museum; Harrow School Old Speech Room Gallery; Horniman Museum; London Zoological Gardens Collections; Museum Interpretative Centre and Nature Reserve; Museum of Garden History; Museum of Zoology and Comparative Anatomy; National Maritime Museum; Natural History Museum; Passmore Edwards Museum; Royal Botanic Gardens, Kew.

● Numismatics

Bank of England Museum; British Museum; Bromley Museum; Inns of Court and City Yeomanry Museum; Museum of London; Museum of the Order of St John; Museum of the United Grand Lodge of England; National Army Museum; Museum of the United Grand Lodge of England; National Maritime Museum; Regimental Museum of the Royal Fusiliers; Royal Hospital Chelsea Museum.

● Oriental

British Library; British Museum; City Livery Companies Collections (Saddlers'); India Office Library and Records; Museum of the United Grand Lodge of England; Oriental Collections; Percival David Foundation of Chinese Art; Riesco Collection of Chinese Ceramics; Sir John Soane's Museum; Soseki Museum; Victoria and Albert Museum; Wallace Collection.

● Paintings and Watercolours

Arts Council of Great Britain Collections (C20); Bankside Gallery; Banqueting House (Rubens ceiling); British Council Collection (C20); Bromley Museum; Coram Foundation for Children; Corporation of London Permanent Collection ; Courtauld Institute Galleries; Courtauld Institute of Art (photographic archive); Dulwich Picture Gallery; Ham House; Hammersmith and Fulham Local History Collections; Harrow School Old Speech Room Gallery; Imperial War Museum; Iveagh Bequest; Lambeth House; Leighton House; Marble Hill House; National Army Museum; National Gallery; National Maritime Museum; National Portrait Gallery; Orleans House Gallery; Ranger's House; Royal Academy of Arts; Royal Botanic Gardens, Kew; Royal College of Music Department of Portraits; Saatchi Collection (C20); South London Art Gallery; Tate Gallery; Valence House; Victoria and Albert Museum; Wallace Collection; Wellington Museum; William Morris Gallery; Wimbledon Society Museum.

● Performing Arts

Mander and Mitchenson Theatre Collection; Musical Museum; National Sound Archive; Pavlova Memorial Museum; Pollock's Toy Museum; Rock Circus; Royal Ballet School Museum and Archives; Royal College of Music Department of Portraits; Shakespeare Globe Museum; Theatre Museum.

● Philately and Postal History

British Library; Bruce Castle Museum; National Postal Museum.

● Photographs

Arts Council of Great Britain Collection; Ashmole Archive; Bromley Museum; Bruce Castle Museum; Courtauld Institute of Art; Erith Museum; Fawcett Library; Greenwich Borough Museum; Hammersmith and Fulham Local History Collections; India Office Library and Records; Inns of Court and City Yeomanry Museum; Kingston upon Thames Museum; Linley Sambourne House; National Army Museum; National Maritime Museum; National Monuments Record; National Portrait Gallery; National Portrait Gallery Archive and Library; Photographers' Gallery Library; Royal College of Music Department of Portraits; Science Museum; Soseki Museum; Wimbledon Society Museum; Wimbledon Windmill Gallery; Woodlands Art Gallery.

● Portraits (inc. Miniatures)

City Livery Companies Collections; Coram Foundation of Children; Corporation of London Permanent Collection; Dulwich Picture Gallery; Ham House; Harrow School Old Speech Room Gallery; Iveagh Bequest; Mander and Mitchenson Theatre Collection; National Army Museum; National Gallery; National Maritime Museum; National Portrait Gallery; National Portrait Gallery Archive and Library; Ranger's House; Royal College of Music Department of Portraits; Royal College of Physicians Portrait Collection; Royal Society of Arts; Tate Gallery; Valence House Museum; Victoria and Albert Museum; Wallace Collection; Wellington Museum.

● Prints and Etchings

Arts Council of Great Britain Collection; Bankside Gallery; British Museum; Bromley Museum; Corporation of London Permanent Collection; Cutty Sark; Hogarth's House; Dr Johnson's House; Museum of London; National Army Museum; National Book League; National Portrait Gallery; National Portrait Gallery Archive and Library; South London Art Gallery; Victoria and Albert Museum; Wimbledon Society Museum.

● Science and Technology

Bank of England Museum; Barnet Museum; British Dental Association Museum; British Optical Association Foundation Museum; Charles King Collection of Historical Anaesthetic Apparatus; Design Museum; Faraday Museum; Gordon Museum; Grange Museum of Local History; Imperial War Museum; Kew Bridge Steam Museum; Kingston upon Thames Museum; London Gas Museum; Museum of the Institute of Ophthalmology; National Maritime Museum; Natural History Museum; Royal Air Force Museum (inc Battle of Britain Museum and Bomber Command Museum); Royal Armouries; Royal College of General Practitioners Museum; Royal Society of Arts; St Bride Printing Library; Science Museum; Science Reference and Information Service; Telecom Technology Showcase; Vintage Wireless Museum; Wellcome Institute for the History of Medicine; Wellcome Museum of Human Anatomy; Wellcome Tropical Institute Museum.

● Sculpture and Carvings

All Hallows by the Tower Undercroft Museum; Arts Council of Great Britain Collection; Ashmole Archive (photographic archive); British Council Collection; British Museum; Corporation of London Permanent Collection; Courtauld Institute of Art (photographic archive); Cutty Sark; Flaxman Gallery; Geffrye Museum; Heralds' Museum; India Office Library and Records; Jewish Museum; Leighton House; National Portrait Gallery; Petrie Museum of Egyptian Archaeology; Royal Botanic Gardens, Kew (woodwork); Saatchi Collection; Sir John Soane's Museum; Tate Gallery; Victoria and Albert Museum; Wellington Museum.

● Ships and the Sea

HMS Belfast; Clockmakers' Company Collection (chronometers); HM Customs and Excise Museum and Exhibition; Cutty Sark; Erith Museum; Gipsy Moth IV; India Office Library and Records (East India Company); Kathleen and May; Kew Bridge Steam Museum; Lloyd's Nelson Collection; National Maritime Museum; Science Museum; Thames Police Museum.

● Social History

Bank of England Museum; Barnet Museum; Bethnal Green Museum of Childhood; Bexley Museum; Bromley Museum; Bruce Castle Museum; Burgh House; Chartered Insurance Institute Museum; Church Farm House Museum; Coram Foundation for Children; Court Dress Collections; Cuming Museum; HM Customs and Excise Museum and Exhibition; Epping Forest Museum; Erith Museum; Fawcett Library; Florence Nightingale Museum; Geffrye Museum; Grange Museum of Local History; Greenwich Borough Museum; Gunnersbury Park Museum; Hammersmith and Fulham Local History Collections; Harrow Museum and Heritage Centre; Jewish Museum; Kingston upon Thames Museum; Linley Sambourne House; London Cab Company Museum; Museum of London; NAAFI Historical Collection; National Portrait Gallery Archive and Library; Newspaper Library; North Woolwich Station Museum; Passmore Edwards Museum; Rock Circus; St Bride's Church and Crypt Museum; Salvation Army Museum; Shakespeare Globe Theatre; Thames Police Museum; Vestry House Museum; Wandsworth Museum; Wesley's House; Wimbledon Society Museum; Woodlands Art Gallery.

● Sport

Cricket Memorial Gallery; Wimbledon Lawn Tennis Museum.

● Textiles (inc. tapestries, carpets and rugs)

City Livery Companies Collections; Museum of Mankind; Osterley Park House; Silver Studio Collection; Sir John Soane's Museum; Victoria and Albert Museum; Wallace Collection.

● Toys, Games and Children's Books

Bethnal Green Museum of Childhood; British Library (books); Hackney Museum (Matchbox toys); London Toy and Model Museum; National Art Library (books); National Book League (books); Pollock's Toy Museum.

● Transport (excluding ships)

Chartered Insurance Institute Museum (fire-engines); Gunnersbury Park Museum; Heritage Motor Museum; Imperial War Museum; London Cab Company Museum; Royal Air Force Museum; Science Museum; Vestry House Museum (Bremer Car).

MUSEUMS AND COLLECTIONS BY BOROUGHS AND CITIES

The boroughs and cities are the local authorities (municipalities) into which Greater London is administratively divided.

BARKING AND DAGENHAM
Valence House Museum

BARNET
Barnet Museum; Battle of Britain Museum; Bomber Command Museum; Church Farm House Museum; Newspaper Library; Royal Air Force Museum.

BEXLEY
Bexley Museum; Erith Museum.

BRENT
Grange Museum of Local History.

BROMLEY
Bromley Museum; Darwin Museum.

CAMDEN
British Library; British Museum; Burgh House; Charles King Collection of Historical Anaesthetic Apparatus; Coram Foundation for Children; Dickens House Museum and Library; Fenton House; Flaxman Gallery; Freud Museum; Inns of Court and City Yeomanry Museum; Iveagh Bequest; Jewish Museum; Keats House; Museum of the Institute of Ophthalmology; Museum of Zoology and Comparative Anatomy; Oriental Collections; Pavlova Memorial Museum; Percival David Foundation of Chinese Art; Petrie Museum of Egyptian Archaeology; Pollock's Toy Museum; Royal College of Physicians Portrait Collection; Saatchi Collection; Salvation Army Museum; Sir John Soane's Museum; Wellcome Institute for the History of Medicine; Wellcome Tropical Institute Museum.

CITY OF LONDON
All Hallows by the Tower Undercroft Museum; Apothecaries' Company; Armourers' and Brasiers' Company; Bank of England Museum; Chartered Insurance Institute Museum; Clockmakers' Company Collection; Clothworkers' Company; Corporation of London Permanent Collection; HM Customs and Excise Museum; Drapers' Company; Fishmongers' Company; Goldsmiths' Company; Grocers' Company; Haberdashers' Company; Ironmongers' Company; Dr Johnson's House; Lloyd's Nelson Collection; Mercers' Company; Merchant Taylors' Company; Museum of London; National Postal Museum; Pewterers' Company; Royal Britain; Saddlers' Company; St Bride Printing Library; St Bride's Church and Crypt Museum; Salters' Company; Telecom Technology Showcase; Tower Bridge Museum and Exhibitions; Treasury of the Diocese of London, St Paul's Cathedral.

CROYDON
Riesco Collection of Chinese Ceramics.

EALING
Martinware Pottery Collection; Pitshanger Manor Museum.

ENFIELD
Forty Hall.

GREENWICH
Cutty Sark; Gipsy Moth IV; Greenwich Borough Museum; Museum of Artillery; National Maritime Museum; Ranger's House; Royal Artillery Regimental Museum; Woodlands Art Gallery.

HACKNEY
Geffrye Museum; Hackney Museum.

HAMMERSMITH AND FULHAM
Hammersmith and Fulham Local History Collections.

HARINGEY
Bruce Castle Museum; Silver Studio Collection.

HARROW
Harrow Museum and Heritage Centre; Harrow School Old Speech Room Gallery.

HOUNSLOW
Chiswick House; Gunnersbury Park Museum; Heritage Motor Museum; Hogarth's House; Kew Bridge Steam Museum; Musical Museum; Osterley Park House.

ISLINGTON
Marx Memorial Library; Museum of the Order of St John; Wesley's House.

KENSINGTON AND CHELSEA
Carlyle's House; Chelsea Physic Garden; Commonwealth Institute; Court Dress Collection; Leighton House; Linley Sambourne Collection; National Army Museum; National Sound Archive; Natural History Museum; Polish Institute and Sikorski Museum; Royal College of General Practitioners Museum; Royal College of Music Department of Portraits; Royal College of Music Museum of Instruments; Royal Geographical Society; Royal Hospital Chelsea Museum; Science Museum; Science Museum Library; V. & A.

KINGSTON UPON THAMES
Kingston-upon Thames Museum and Heritage Centre.

LAMBETH
Imperial War Museum; Lambeth Palace and Library; London Cab Company Museum; Florence Nightingale Museum; Museum of Garden History; Museum of the Moving Image (MOMI); Museum of the Pharmaceutical Society; NAAFI Historical Collection; Soseki Museum.

LEWISHAM
Horniman Museum; Mander and Mitchenson Theatre Collection; National Portrait Gallery Archive and Library.

MERTON
Wimbledon Lawn Tennis Museum; Wimbledon Society Museum; Wimbledon Windmill Museum.

NEWHAM
Museum Interpretative Centre and Nature Reserve; North Woolwich Station Museum; Passmore Edwards Museum.

RICHMOND UPON THAMES
Ham House; Marble Hill House; Museum of Richmond; Orleans House Gallery; Public Record Office, Kew; Royal Ballet School Museum and Archives; Royal Botanic Gardens; Royal Military School of Music Museum.

SOUTHWARK
Bankside Gallery; HMS Belfast; Brunel's Engine House; Cuming Museum; Design Museum; Dulwich Picture Gallery; Gordon Museum; India Office Library and Records; Kathleen and May; London Dungeon; Old St Thomas' Hospital; Shakespeare Globe Museum; South London Art Gallery.

TOWER HAMLETS
Bethnal Green Museum of Childhood; Crown Jewels (Tower of London); Fawcett Library; Heralds' Museum (Tower of London); London Gas Museum; Regimental Museum of the Royal Fusiliers (Tower of London); Royal Armouries (Tower of London); Thames Police Museum.

WALTHAM FOREST
Epping Forest Museum; Vestry House Museum; William Morris Gallery.

WANDSWORTH
National Book League Collections; Wandsworth Museum.

WESTMINSTER, CITY OF
Arts Council of Great Britain, Ashmole Archive; Banqueting House; British Architectural Library Drawings Collection; British Dental Association Museum; Cabinet War Rooms; Courtauld Institute Galleries; Courtauld Institute of Art; Crafts Council Collection; Cricket Memorial Gallery; Faraday Museum; Guards Museum; Guinness World of Records; Hunterian Museum; London Toy and Model Museum; London Transport Museum; London Zoological Gardens Collections; Madame Tussaud's Waxworks and London Planetarium; Museum of Mankind; Museum of the United Grand Lodge of England; National Film Archive; National Gallery; National Monuments Record; National Portrait Gallery; Odontological Museum; Photographers' Gallery Library; Public Record Office Museum; Queen's Gallery; Rock Circus; Royal Academy of Arts; Royal Mews; Royal Society of Arts; Science Reference and Information Service; Tate Gallery; Theatre Museum; Wallace Collection; Wellcome Museum of Human Anatomy; Wellington Museum; Westminster Abbey Museum.

MUSEUMS AND COLLECTIONS IN THE CENTRAL AREA

(Map References pp 290-304)

A

All Hallows by the Tower Undercroft Museum	3 Rg
Apothecaries' Hall	3 Nf
Armourers' and Brasiers' Hall	3 Pe
Arts Council of Great Britain Collection	5 Hg
Ashmole Archive (King's College)	2 Lf

B

Bank of England Museum	3 Pf
Bankside Gallery	3 Ng
Banqueting House	4 Kg
HMS Belfast	3 Rg
British Architectural Library Drawings Collection	5 Gf
British Council Collection	5 He
British Dental Association Museum	5 He
British Library	2 Ke
British Museum	2 Ke

C

Cabinet War Rooms	4 Kh
Carlyle's House	7 El
Charles King Collection of Historical Anaesthetic Apparatus	2 Ke
Chartered Insurance Institute Museum	3 Pe
Chelsea Physic Garden	7 Fl
Clockmakers' Company Collection (Guildhall Library)	3 Pe
Clothworkers' Hall	3 Rf
Commonwealth Institute	10 Bj
Coram Foundation	2 Kd
Corporation of London Permanent Collection (Guildhall)	3 Pe
Courtauld Institute Galleries	2 Lf
Courtauld Institute of Art	2 Lf
Court Dress Collection (Kensington Palace)	9 Ch
Crafts Council Collection (Crafts Council)	4 Jg
Cricket Memorial Gallery (Lord's Cricket Ground)	1 Ec
Crown Jewels (Tower of London)	3 Sg
HM Customs and Excise Museum and Exhibition	3 Rg

D

Design Museum	3 Sh
Dickens House Museum	2 Ld
Drapers' Hall	3 Pe

F

Faraday Museum (The Royal Institution)	5 Hg
Fawcett Library (City of London Polytechnic)	3 Se
Fishmongers' Hall	3 Pg
Flaxman Gallery (University College)	2 Jd
Florence Nightingale Museum (St Thomas' Hospital)	4 Lh

G

Goldsmiths' Hall	3 Ne
Gordon Museum	3 Pg
Grocers' Hall	3 Pf
Guards Museum	5 Jh
Guinness World of Records (Trocadero)	4 Jf

H

Haberdashers' Hall	3 Ne
Hayward Gallery	4 Lg
Heralds' Museum (Tower of London)	3 Sg
Hunterian Museum (Royal College of Surgeons)	2 Lf

I

Imperial War Museum	4 Mj
India Office Library	4 Mh
Inns of Court and City Yeomanry Museum	2 Le
Ironmongers' Hall	3 Ne

J

Jewish Museum	2 Kd
Dr Johnson's House	2 Mf

K

Kathleen and May (schooner)	3 Pg

L

Lambeth Palace and Library	4 Lj
Leighton House	10 Bj
Linley Sambourne House	10 Bj
Lloyd's Nelson Collection (Lloyd's of London)	3 Rf
London Dungeon	3 Pg
London Toy and Model Museum	8 Df
London Transport Museum	2 Lf
London Zoological Gardens Collections (London Zoo)	1 Gb

M

Madame Tussaud's	1 Gd
Marx Memorial Library	2 Md
Mercers' Hall	3 Pf
Merchant Taylors' Hall	3 Rf
Museum of Garden History	4 Lj
Museum of London	3 Ne
Museum of Mankind	5 Hg
Museum of the Institute of Ophthalmology	2 Kd
Museum of the Moving Image (MOMI)	4 Lg
Museum of the Order of St John (St John's Gate)	3 Nd
Museum of the Pharmaceutical Society	4 Lj
Museum of the United Grand Lodge (Freemasons' Hall)	2 Lf
Museum of Zoology and Comparative Anatomy	2 Jd

N

National Army Museum 7 Fl
National Art Library (V&A) 8 Ej
National Film Archive 5 Jf
National Gallery 4 Kg
National Monuments Record 5 Hf
National Portrait Gallery 4 Kg
National Postal Museum 3 Ne
National Sound Archive 8 Eh
Natural History Museum 8 Dj

O

Odontological Museum (Royal
  College of Surgeons) 2 Lf
Old St Thomas' Operating Theatre 3 Pg
Oriental Collections 2 Je

P

Percival David Foundation 2 Kd
Petrie Museum of Egyptian Archae-
  ology (University College) 2 Jd
Pewterers' Hall 3 Ne
Photographers' Gallery Library 2 Kf
Polish Institute and Sikorski
  Museum 8 Eh
Pollock's Toy Museum 2 Je
Prince Henry's Room 2 Mf
Public Record Office Museum 2 Mf

Q

Queen's Gallery 6 Hh

R

Regimental Museum of the Royal
  Fusiliers (Tower of London) 3 Sg
Rock Circus 5 Jg
Royal Academy of Arts 5 Jg
Royal Armouries (Tower of
  London) 3 Sg
Royal Britain 3 Ne
Royal College of General
  Practitioners Museum 8 Eh
Royal College of Music:
  Department of Portraits and
  Museum of Instruments 8 Dj
Royal College of Physicians
  Portrait Collection 1 Hd
Royal Geographical Society 8 Eh
Royal Hospital Chelsea Museum
  (Chelsea Royal Hospital) 7 Gl
Royal Mews 6 Hj
Royal Society of Arts 4 Kg

S

Saddlers' Hall 3 Nf
St Bride Printing Library 2 Mf
St Bride's Church 2 Mf
St John Ambulance Museum
  (St John's Gate) 3 Nd
Salters' Hall 3 Pe
Salvation Army Museum 2 Kc
Science Museum 8 Ej
Science Museum Library 8 Dj
Science Reference and
  Information Service (Aldwych) 2 Lf
Science Reference and
  Information Service (Holborn) 2 Me
Shakespeare Globe Museum 3 Ng
Sir John Soane's Museum 2 Le
Skinners' Hall 3 Pf

T

Tate Gallery 4 Kk
Telecom Technology Showcase 3 Nf
Theatre Museum 2 Lf
Tower Bridge Museum 3 Sg
Treasury of the Diocese of
  London (St Paul's Cathedral) 3 Nf

V

Victoria and Albert Museum 8 Ej
Vintners' Hall 3 Pf

W

Wallace Collection 5 Ge
Wellcome Institute for the
  History of Medicine
  (Wellcome Building) 2 Jd
Wellcome Museum of Anatomy 2 Lf
Wellcome Tropical Institute
  Museum (Wellcome Building) 2 Jd
Wellington Museum 5 Gh
Wesley's House 3 Pd
Westminster Abbey Museum
  (Westminster Abbey) 4 Kj

MUSEUMS AND COLLECTIONS IN THE OUTER AREA
(Diagram References)

Barnet Museum (Barnet); Bethnal Green Museum of Childhood (Tower Hamlets); Bexley Museum (Bexley); British Optical Association Foundation Museum (Hammersmith and Fulham); Bromley Museum (Bromley); Bruce Castle Museum (Haringey); Brunel's Engine House (Southwark); Burgh House (Camden).

Chiswick House (Hounslow); Church Farm House Museum (Barnet); Cuming Museum (Southwark); Cutty Sark (Greenwich).

Darwin Museum (Bromley); Dulwich Picture Gallery (Southwark).

Epping Forest Museum (Waltham Forest); Erith Museum (Bexley).

Fenton House (Camden); Forty Hall (Enfield); Freud Museum (Camden).

Geffrye Museum (Hackney); Gipsy Moth IV (Greenwich); Grange Museum of Local History (Brent); Greenwich Borough Museum (Greenwich); Gunnersbury Park Museum (Hounslow).

Ham House (Richmond upon Thames); Hammersmith and Fulham Local History Collection (Hammersmith and Fulham); Hackney Museum (Hackney); Harrow Museum and Heritage Centre (Harrow); Harrow School Old Speech Room Gallery (Harrow); Heritage Motor Museum (Hounslow); Hogarth's House (Hounslow); Horniman Museum (Lewisham)

Iveagh Bequest (Camden).

Keats House (Camden); Kew Bridge Steam Museum (Hounslow); Kingston upon Thames Museum and Heritage Centre (Kingston upon Thames).

London Cab Co Museum (Lambeth); London Gas Museum (Tower Hamlets).

Mander and Mitchenson Theatre Collection (Lewisham); Marble Hill House (Richmond upon Thames); Martinware Pottery Collection (Ealing); Museum Interpretative Centre and Nature Reserve (Newham); Museum of Artillery (Greenwich); Museum of Richmond (Richmond upon Thames); Musical Museum (Hounslow).

NAAFI Historical Collection (Lambeth); National Book League Collections (Wandsworth); National Maritime Museum (Greenwich); National Portrait Gallery Archive and Library (Lewisham); Newspaper Library (Barnet); North Woolwich Station Museum (Newham).

Orleans House Gallery (Richmond upon Thames); Osterley Park House (Hounslow).

Passmore Edwards Museum (Newham); Pavlova Memorial Museum (Barnet); Pitshanger Manor Museum (Ealing); Public Record Office, Kew (Richmond upon Thames).

Ranger's House (Greenwich); Riesco Collection (Croydon); Royal Air Force (RAF) Museum (Barnet); Royal Artillery Regimental Museum (Greenwich); Royal Ballet School Museum and Archives (Richmond upon Thames); Royal Botanic Gardens, Kew (Richmond upon Thames); Royal Military School of Music Museum (Richmond upon Thames).

Saatchi Collection (Camden); Silver Studio Collection, Middlesex Polytechnic (Haringey); South London Art Gallery (Southwark)

Thames Police Museum (Tower Hamlets).

Valence House Museum (Barking and Dagenham); Vestry House Museum (Waltham Forest); Vintage Wireless Museum (Lambeth).

Wandsworth Museum (Wandsworth).

William Morris Gallery (Waltham Forest); Wimbledon Lawn Tennis Museum (Merton); Wimbledon Society Museum (Merton); Wimbledon Windmill Museum (Merton); Woodlands Art Gallery (Greenwich).

The shaded area is mostly covered by the set of maps on pages 290-304.

UNDERGROUND STATIONS

Saturdays and Sundays
Certain stations are Closed

288

UNDERGROUND NETWORK

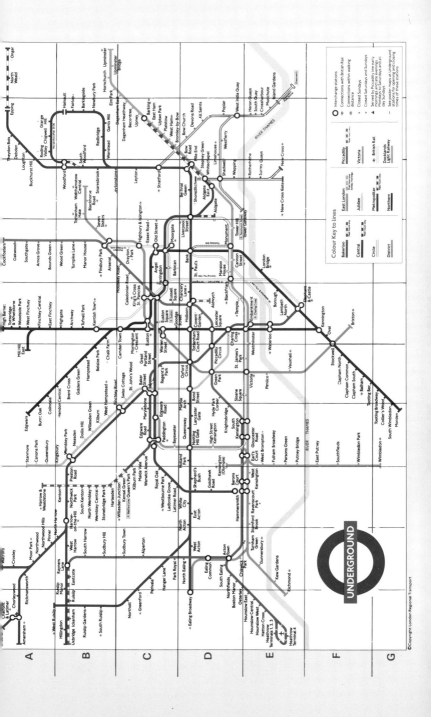

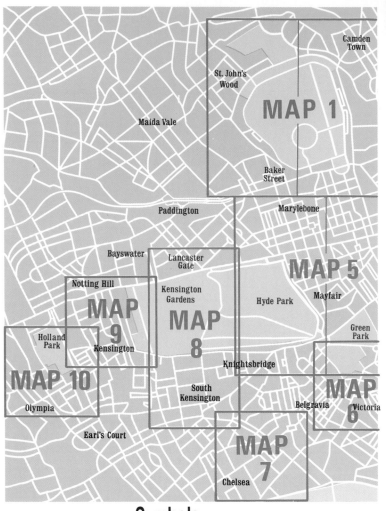

Symbols

Principal Thoroughfare	STRAND
Place of Interest	■
Cinema or Theatre..	☻
Street Market	═
Underground Station	● ⊖
British Rail Station..	■ ⇌
Information Centre	𝒊
Embassy	★
Church	✝

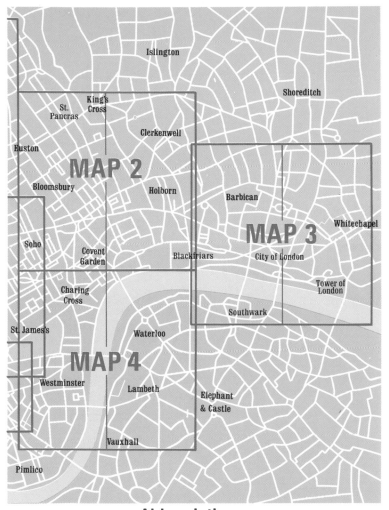

Abbreviations

AVE	AVENUE	PL	PLACE
BGS.	BUILDINGS	RD	ROAD
CRES.	CRESCENT	SQ	SQUARE
GDNS	GARDENS	ST	STREET
GT.	GREAT	TER	TERRACE
LA.	LANE	UPR.	UPPER
	YD	YARD	

Scale (for sectional maps)

Miles   0   ¼   ½

Kilometres 0   ¼   ½   ¾   1

Map 1

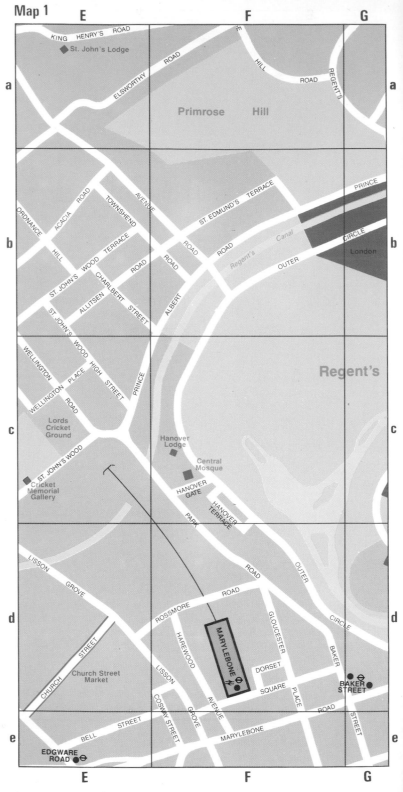

E · F · G

KING HENRY'S ROAD

St. John's Lodge

ELSWORTHY ROAD

Primrose Hill

HILL ROAD

REGENT'S

a

PRINCE

ORDNANCE HILL

ACACIA ROAD

TOWNSHEND

AVENUE

ST. EDMUND'S TERRACE

Regent's Canal

CIRCLE

London

b

ST. JOHN'S WOOD TERRACE

CHARLBERT STREET

ALLITSEN

ROAD

ROAD

ROAD

ALBERT

ROAD

OUTER

ST. JOHN'S

WELLINGTON PLACE

ST. JOHN'S WOOD HIGH STREET

WELLINGTON ROAD

PRINCE

Regent's

Lords Cricket Ground

Hanover Lodge

Central Mosque

c

Cricket Memorial Gallery

ST. JOHN'S WOOD

HANOVER GATE

HANOVER TERRACE

PARK

LISSON GROVE

ROAD

ROAD

OUTER

CIRCLE

ROSSMORE ROAD

GLOUCESTER

BAKER

d

CHURCH STREET

Church Street Market

HAREWOOD

MARYLEBONE

DORSET

SQUARE

PLACE

BAKER STREET

LISSON

COSWAY STREET

GROVE

AVENUE

ROAD

STREET

e

BELL STREET

MARYLEBONE

EDGWARE ROAD

E · F · G

292

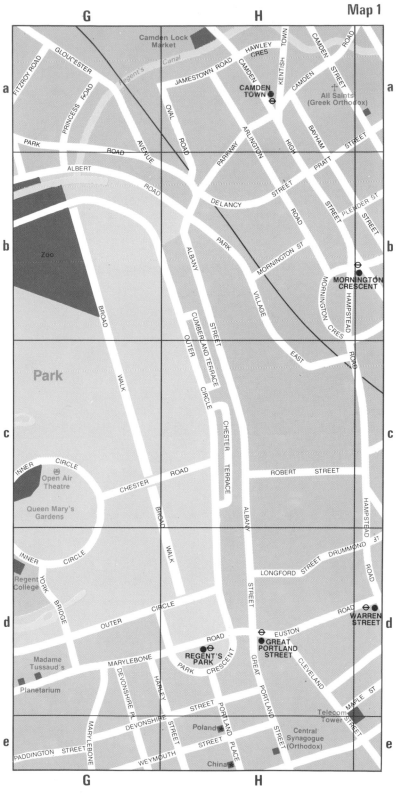

Map 1

G H

Camden Lock Market

Regent's Canal

HAWLEY CRES

CAMDEN TOWN

FITZROY ROAD

GLOUCESTER

PRINCESS ROAD

JAMESTOWN ROAD

CAMDEN STREET

KENTISH TOWN

CAMDEN ROAD

a

All Saints (Greek Orthodox)

PARK ROAD

AVENUE

OVAL ROAD

ARLINGTON

PARKWAY

HIGH STREET

BAYHAM STREET

CAMDEN

ALBERT ROAD

DELANCY

PARK STREET

PRATT STREET

PLENDER ST

Zoo

b

ALBANY

PARK

MORNINGTON ST

ROAD

MORNINGTON CRESCENT

MORNINGTON CRES

HAMPSTEAD

BROAD

VILLAGE

STREET

EAST

ROAD

WALK

Park

CUMBERLAND TERRACE

OUTER

CIRCLE

CHESTER TERRACE

c

INNER CIRCLE

Open Air Theatre

CHESTER ROAD

ROBERT STREET

HAMPSTEAD

Queen Mary's Gardens

BROAD

ALBANY STREET

INNER CIRCLE

DRUMMOND ST

d

Regent College

YORK BRIDGE

WALK

OUTER CIRCLE

LONGFORD STREET

DRUMMOND ROAD

WARREN STREET

Madame Tussaud's

MARYLEBONE

ROAD

EUSTON

GREAT PORTLAND STREET

CLEVELAND

GREAT PORTLAND STREET

REGENT'S PARK

CRESCENT

Planetarium

DEVONSHIRE PL

HARLEY STREET

PORTLAND PLACE

PORTLAND STREET

MAPLE ST

Telecom Tower

MARYLEBONE

DEVONSHIRE STREET

Poland

Central Synagogue (Orthodox)

e

PADDINGTON STREET

WEYMOUTH STREET

China

G H

Map 2

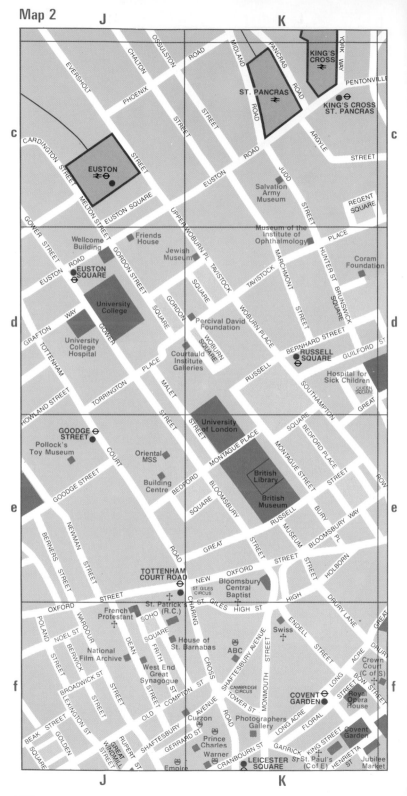

Map 2

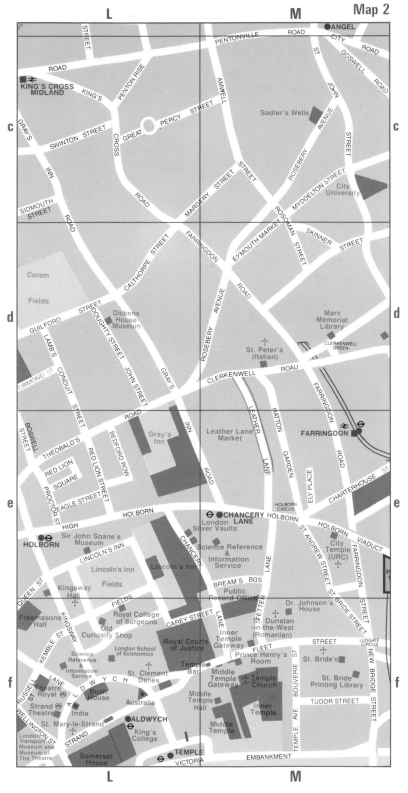

L M

ANGEL
PENTONVILLE ROAD
CITY ROAD
GOSWELL ROAD
STREET
KING'S CROSS MIDLAND
ROAD
PENTON RISE
KING'S
JOHN
AMWELL
Sadler's Wells
AVENUE

c

GRAY'S
SWINTON STREET
GREAT
PERCY STREET
STREET
City University
MYDDELTON STREET
ROSOMAN STREET
ROSEBERY
MARGERY STREET

INN
CROSS
ROAD
SIDMOUTH STREET
ROAD

SKINNER STREET
E/MOUTH MARKET
FARRINGDON

Coram
Fields
CALTHORPE STREET

ROAD
Dickens House Museum
DOUGHTY STREET
GUILFORD STREET
LAMB'S
CONDUIT STREET
ORMOND ST
JOHN STREET
GRAY'S

ROSEBERY AVENUE
ROAD
St. Peter's (Italian)
CLERKENWELL ROAD
LEATHER LANE
HATTON GARDEN

Marx Memorial Library
CLERKENWELL GREEN
FARRINGDON

d

BOSWELL STREET
THEOBALD'S
RED LION SQUARE
BEDFORD ROW
RED LION STREET
Gray's Inn
INN ROAD
Leather Lane Market

FARRINGDON
ROAD
CHARTERHOUSE ST.

e

PROCTOR ST
EAGLE STREET
HIGH
HOLBORN
HOLBORN
London Silver Vaults
CHANCERY LANE
HOLBORN
HOLBORN CIRCUS
ELY PLACE
HOLBORN VIADUCT
ST ANDREW STREET
FARRINGDON
City Temple (URC)

HOLBORN
Sir John Soane's Museum
LINCOLN'S INN
Lincoln's Inn
Lincoln's Inn Fields
Science Reference & Information Service
CHANCERY
LANE

QUEEN ST
Kingsway Hall
FIELDS
BREAM'S BGS
Public Record Office

Dr. Johnson's House
ST BRIDE STREET

Freemasons Hall
KINGSWAY
KEMBLE ST
Royal College of Surgeons
Old Curiosity Shop
CAREY STREET
LANE
Inner Temple Gateway
FETTER LANE
St. Dunstan -in-the-West (Romanian)

STREET
St. Bride's
LUDGATE CIRCUS
NEW BRIDGE STREET

f

RUSSELL ST
LANE
Science Reference & Information Service
London School of Economics
Royal Courts of Justice
FLEET
Prince Henry's Room
BOUVERIE ST
St. Bride Printing Library

Theatre Royal
A L D W Y C H
Bush House
St. Clement Danes
Temple Bar
Middle Temple Gateway
Temple Church

Strand Theatre
India
Australia
Middle Temple Hall
Inner Temple
TUDOR STREET
TEMPLE AVE

ST. Mary-le-Strand
WELLINGTON ST
ALDWYCH
King's College
Middle Temple

London Transport Museum and Museum of The Theatre
STRAND
Somerset House
TEMPLE
VICTORIA
EMBANKMENT

L M

295

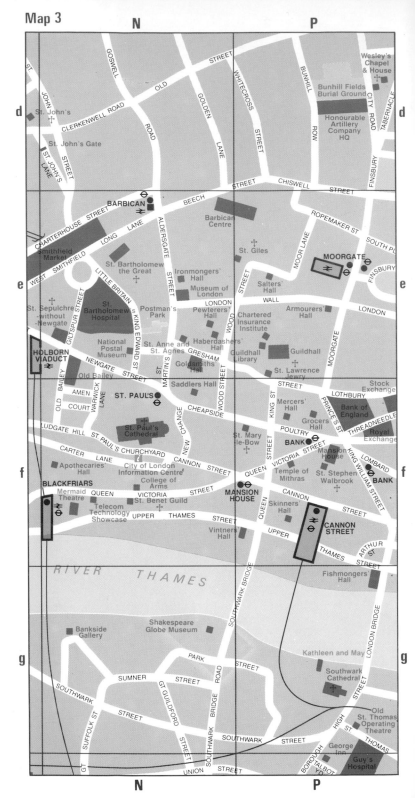

Map 3

N

P

d

BARBICAN

St. John's

St. John's Gate

CLERKENWELL ROAD

GOSWELL STREET

OLD STREET

GOLDEN LANE

WHITECROSS STREET

BUNHILL ROW

CITY ROAD

Wesley's Chapel & House

Bunhill Fields Burial Ground

Honourable Artillery Company HQ

FINSBURY

TABERNACLE

ST. JOHN'S LANE

ST. JOHN'S STREET

CHISWELL STREET

e

CHARTERHOUSE STREET

Smithfield Market

WEST SMITHFIELD

St. Sepulchre -without -Newgate

LONG LANE

ALDERSGATE STREET

BEECH

Barbican Centre

ROPEMAKER ST

SOUTH PL

MOORGATE

FINSBURY

LITTLE BRITAIN

St. Bartholomew the Great

St. Bartholomew's Hospital

GILTSPUR STREET

KING EDWARD STREET

Ironmongers' Hall

Museum of London

Postman's Park

St. Giles

MOOR LANE

LONDON WALL

Salters' Hall

Armourers' Hall

LONDON

HOLBORN VIADUCT

National Postal Museum

St. Anne and St. Agnes

Pewterers' Hall

Haberdashers' Hall

Chartered Insurance Institute

WOOD STREET

Guildhall Library

Guildhall

MOORGATE

NEWGATE STREET

OLD BAILEY

Old Bailey

GRESHAM STREET

Goldsmiths Hall

ST. MARTIN'S

St. Lawrence Jewry

Saddlers Hall

f

AMEN COURT

WARWICK

ST. PAUL'S

CHEAPSIDE

KING ST

Mercers' Hall

LOTHBURY

Stock Exchange

Bank of England

LUDGATE HILL

ST. PAUL'S

St. Paul's Cathedral

NEW CHANGE

Grocers' Hall

PRINCE'S ST

THREADNEEDLE

Royal Exchange

CARTER LANE

ST. PAUL'S CHURCHYARD

CANNON STREET

St. Mary le-Bow

POULTRY

BANK

QUEEN STREET

VICTORIA STREET

Mansion House

KING WILLIAM STREET

LOMBARD

Apothecaries' Hall

City of London Information Centre

College of Arms

Temple of Mithras

St. Stephen Walbrook

BANK

BLACKFRIARS

Mermaid Theatre

QUEEN VICTORIA

St. Benet Guild

Telecom Technology Showcase

UPPER THAMES STREET

Skinners' Hall

CANNON

CANNON STREET

ARTHUR ST

MANSION HOUSE

QUEEN

UPPER THAMES STREET

Vintners' Hall

Fishmongers' Hall

LONDON BRIDGE

g

RIVER THAMES

Bankside Gallery

Shakespeare Globe Museum

PARK STREET

SOUTHWARK BRIDGE

Kathleen and May

Southwark Cathedral

HIGH STREET

THOMAS STREET

SUMNER STREET

SOUTHWARK STREET

GT GUILDFORD STREET

SUFFOLK ST

SOUTHWARK BRIDGE ROAD

SOUTHWARK STREET

Old St. Thomas Operating Theatre

George Inn

Guy's Hospital

GT SUFFOLK ST

UNION STREET

BOROUGH HIGH ST

TALBOT YD

N

P

296

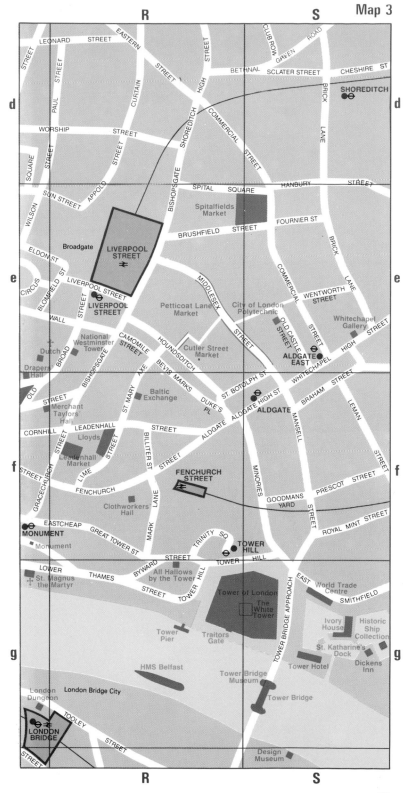

Map 3

R S

LEONARD STREET
EASTERN STREET
CLUB ROW
GREEN ROAD
CHESHIRE ST

STREET
PAUL STREET
CURTAIN STREET
HIGH STREET
BETHNAL
SCLATER STREET
BRICK LANE
SHOREDITCH

d d

WORSHIP STREET
SHOREDITCH
COMMERCIAL STREET

SQUARE
STREET
APPOLD
BISHOPSGATE
SPITAL SQUARE
HANBURY STREET

WILSON
SUN STREET
Spitalfields Market
FOURNIER ST

ELDON ST
Broadgate
LIVERPOOL STREET
BRUSHFIELD STREET
COMMERCIAL
BRICK LANE

e e
CIRCUS
BLOMFIELD ST
LIVERPOOL STREET
LIVERPOOL STREET
Petticoat Lane Market
MIDDLESEX STREET
City of London Polytechnic
WENTWORTH STREET
OLD CASTLE STREET
Whitechapel Gallery

WALL
BROAD
National Westminster Tower
CAMOMILE STREET
HOUNDSDITCH
Cutler Street Market
ALDGATE EAST
STREET
HIGH

Dutch
Drapers' Hall
BISHOPSGATE
BEVIS MARKS
ST. BOTOLPH ST
WHITECHAPEL

OLD STREET
Merchant Taylors' Hall
ST MARY AXE
Baltic Exchange
DUKE'S PL
ALDGATE HIGH ST
ALDGATE
BRAHAM STREET
LEMAN STREET

CORNHILL
LEADENHALL STREET
ALDGATE
MANSELL STREET

Lloyds
BILLITER ST

f f
GRACECHURCH STREET
Leadenhall Market
LIME STREET
FENCHURCH STREET
MINORIES
PRESCOT STREET

FENCHURCH
MARK LANE
FENCHURCH STREET
GOODMANS YARD
STREET

Clothworkers' Hall
TRINITY SQ
ROYAL MINT STREET

EASTCHEAP
MONUMENT
GREAT TOWER ST
TOWER HILL
TOWER HILL

Monument
BYWARD STREET
TOWER

LOWER THAMES STREET
All Hallows by the Tower
EAST
World Trade Centre
SMITHFIELD

St. Magnus the Martyr
TOWER HILL STREET
Tower of London
TOWER BRIDGE APPROACH
Ivory House
Historic Ship Collection

Tower Pier
Traitors Gate
The White Tower
St. Katharine's Dock
Dickens Inn

g g
HMS Belfast
Tower Hotel

London Dungeon
London Bridge City
Tower Bridge Museum

TOOLEY STREET
Tower Bridge

LONDON BRIDGE
STREET
Design Museum

R S

297

Map 4

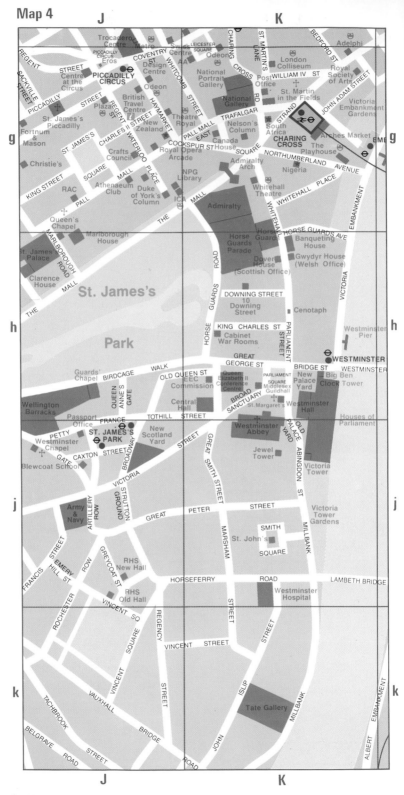

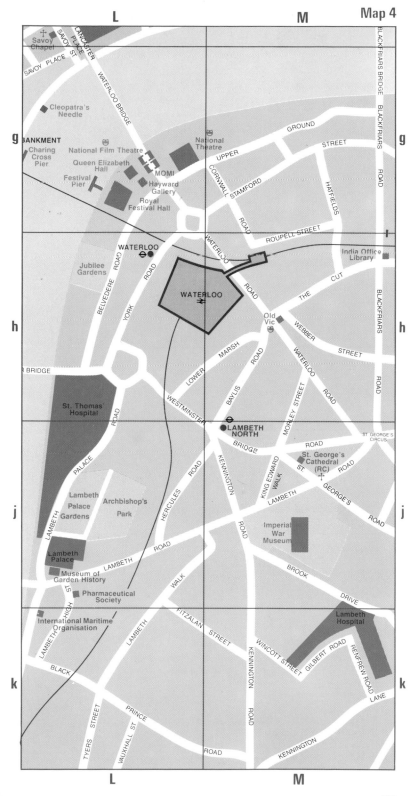

Map 4

L

M

Savoy
Chapel

SAVOY ST

LANCASTER PLACE

SAVOY PLACE

WATERLOO BRIDGE

BLACKFRIARS BRIDGE

BLACKFRIARS

Cleopatra's
Needle

GROUND

STREET

ROAD

g

EMBANKMENT

Charing
Cross Pier

National Film Theatre

Queen Elizabeth Hall

Festival
Pier

Royal
Festival
Hall

MOMI

Hayward
Gallery

National
Theatre

UPPER

CORNWALL

STAMFORD

ROAD

HATFIELDS

ROUPELL STREET

g

WATERLOO

India Office
Library

Jubilee
Gardens

BELVEDERE ROAD

YORK ROAD

WATERLOO

WATERLOO

THE CUT

BLACKFRIARS

h

WATERLOO

Old
Vic

WEBBER

STREET

ROAD

h

BRIDGE

St. Thomas'
Hospital

WESTMINSTER

ROAD

LOWER MARSH

MARSH ROAD

BAYLIS ROAD

WATERLOO ROAD

MORLEY STREET

LAMBETH

PALACE ROAD

LAMBETH NORTH

BRIDGE

KENNINGTON ROAD

ST GEORGE'S CIRCUS

St. George's
Cathedral
(RC)

KING EDWARD WALK

ST.

ROAD

ST. GEORGE'S

ROAD

j

Lambeth
Palace
Gardens

Archbishop's
Park

HERCULES ROAD

Imperial
War
Museum

j

Lambeth
Palace

Museum of
Garden History

Pharmaceutical
Society

LAMBETH

LAMBETH

WALK

ROAD

BROOK

DRIVE

International Maritime
Organisation

Lambeth
Hospital

k

LAMBETH HIGH ST

BLACK

FITZALAN STREET

WINCOTT STREET

KENNINGTON ROAD

GILBERT ROAD

RENFREW ROAD

LANE

k

T'YERS STREET

VAUXHALL ST

PRINCE

ROAD

KENNINGTON

L

M

Map 5

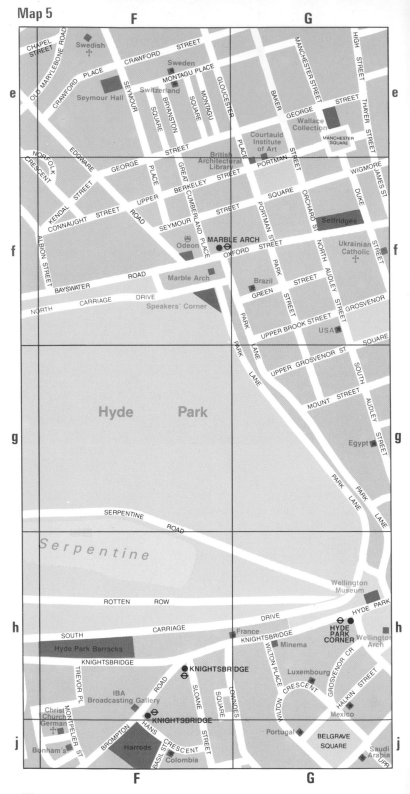

F   G

CHAPEL STREET

Swedish ✝

CRAWFORD STREET

Sweden

MANCHESTER STREET

HIGH STREET

OLD MARYLEBONE ROAD

CRAWFORD PLACE

MONTAGU PLACE

Switzerland

BAKER STREET

GEORGE STREET

THAYER STREET

e   Seymour Hall

SEYMOUR

SQUARE

BRYANSTON

MONTAGU SQUARE

GLOUCESTER PLACE

Wallace Collection

MANCHESTER SQUARE e

NORFOLK CRESCENT

EDGWARE

STREET

GEORGE

PLACE

BERKELEY

GREAT CUMBERLAND

Courtauld Institute of Art

PORTMAN

WIGMORE

JAMES ST

British Architectural Library

KENDAL STREET

CONNAUGHT STREET

ROAD

UPPER

SEYMOUR STREET

STREET

PLACE

PORTMAN SQUARE

ORCHARD ST

DUKE STREET

Selfridges

ALBION STREET

BAYSWATER ROAD

Odeon

MARBLE ARCH

OXFORD STREET

PORTMAN ST

NORTH AUDLEY STREET

Ukrainian Catholic ✝

f   f

NORTH CARRIAGE DRIVE

Marble Arch

Brazil

PARK GREEN STREET

GROSVENOR

Speakers' Corner

PARK STREET

UPPER BROOK STREET

USA

SQUARE

PARK LANE

UPPER GROSVENOR ST

SOUTH AUDLEY STREET

Hyde   Park

LANE

MOUNT STREET

g   Egypt STREET g

SERPENTINE ROAD

PARK LANE

PARK LANE

Serpentine

ROTTEN ROW

Wellington Museum

HYDE PARK

h   SOUTH   CARRIAGE   DRIVE   France   **HYDE PARK CORNER** Wellington Arch h

Hyde Park Barracks

KNIGHTSBRIDGE

Minema

WILTON PLACE

KNIGHTSBRIDGE

TREVOR PL

ROAD

SLOANE STREET

LOWNDES STREET

Luxembourg

WILTON CRESCENT

GROSVENOR CR

HALKIN STREET

IBA Broadcasting Gallery

KNIGHTSBRIDGE

SQUARE

Mexico

Christ Church ✝

MONTPELIER ST

KNIGHTSBRIDGE

German

j   Bonham's   Harrods   Portugal   **BELGRAVE SQUARE**   Saudi Arabia j

BROMPTON

BASIL ST

HANS CRESCENT

Colombia

F   G

Map 5

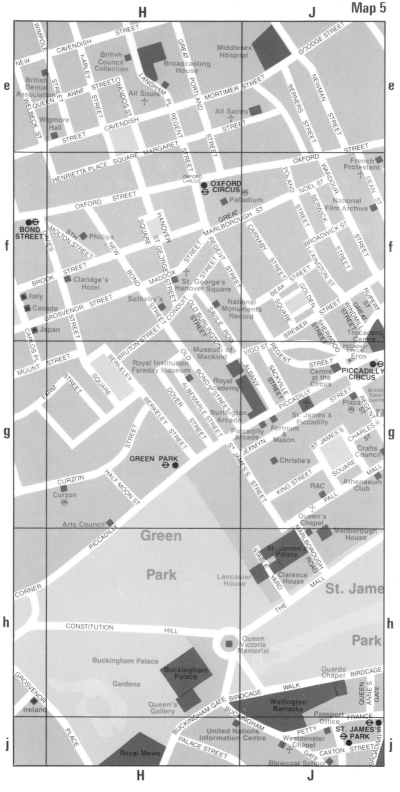

Map 6

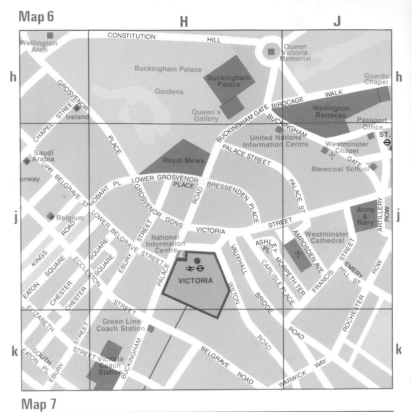

Map 7

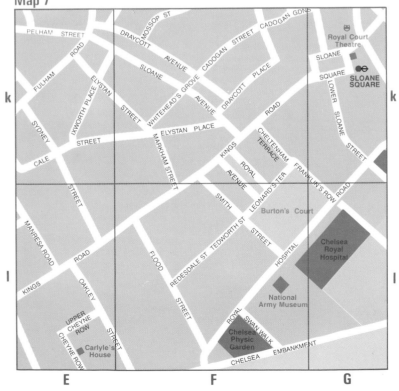

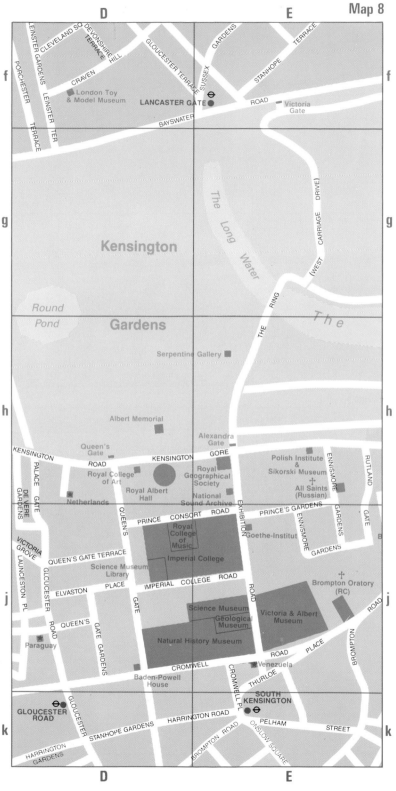

Map 8

D

E

f

PORCHESTER TERRACE

LEINSTER GARDENS

CLEVELAND SQ

DEVONSHIRE TERRACE

CRAVEN HILL

LEINSTER TER

GLOUCESTER TERRACE

London Toy & Model Museum

LANCASTER GATE

BAYSWATER

GARDENS

SUSSEX

STANHOPE

TERRACE

ROAD

Victoria Gate

f

g

Kensington

Round Pond

The Long Water

THE RING (WEST CARRIAGE DRIVE)

The

g

Gardens

Serpentine Gallery

h

KENSINGTON PALACE GARDENS

DE VERE GARDENS

VICTORIA GROVE

LAUNCESTON PL

GLOUCESTER ROAD

QUEEN'S

Albert Memorial

Queen's Gate

ROAD

KENSINGTON

Royal College of Art

Royal Albert Hall

Netherlands

GATE

QUEEN'S GATE TERRACE

Science Museum Library

ELVASTON PLACE

GATE GARDENS

Paraguay

GATE

PRINCE CONSORT ROAD

Royal College of Music

Imperial College

IMPERIAL COLLEGE ROAD

Science Museum

Geological Museum

Natural History Museum

GORE

Alexandra Gate

Royal Geographical Society

National Sound Archive

EXHIBITION

ROAD

Baden-Powell House

CROMWELL

Polish Institute & Sikorski Museum

All Saints (Russian)

PRINCE'S GARDENS

ENNISMORE

GARDENS

Goethe-Institut

GARDENS

Victoria & Albert Museum

ROAD

PLACE

Venezuela

CROMWELL PL

THURLOE

ENNISMORE GARDENS

RUTLAND GATE

B

Brompton Oratory (RC)

BROMPTON ROAD

h

j

j

k

GLOUCESTER ROAD

GLOUCESTER ROAD

STANHOPE GARDENS

HARRINGTON GARDENS

HARRINGTON ROAD

BROMPTON ROAD

ONSLOW SQUARE

SOUTH KENSINGTON

PELHAM

STREET

k

D

E

303

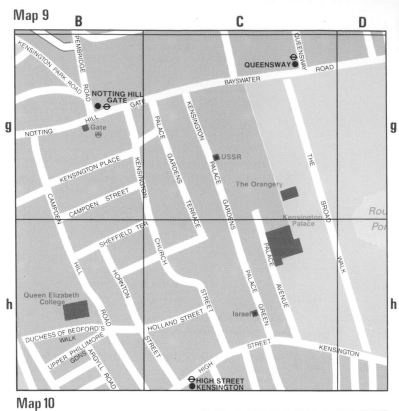

Map 9

B — **C** — **D**

KENSINGTON PARK ROAD
PEMBRIDGE ROAD
KENSINGTON PARK ROAD

QUEENSWAY

QUEENSWAY ⊖●

BAYSWATER ROAD

NOTTING HILL GATE ●⊖

g

NOTTING HILL GATE

Gate

KENSINGTON GARDENS

KENSINGTON PALACE GARDENS

■ USSR

The Orangery ■

g

THE BROAD WALK

KENSINGTON PLACE

KENSINGTON

Kensington Palace ■

CAMPDEN STREET

SHEFFIELD TER

PALACE TERRACE

CHURCH STREET

PALACE AVENUE

Rou
Po

h

Queen Elizabeth College ■

HILL

HORNTON ROAD

HOLLAND STREET

PALACE GREEN

Israel ■

h

DUCHESS OF BEDFORD'S WALK

UPPER PHILLIMORE GDNS

ARGYLL ROAD

STREET

HIGH STREET

KENSINGTON STREET

KENSINGTON

⊖ **HIGH STREET KENSINGTON** ●

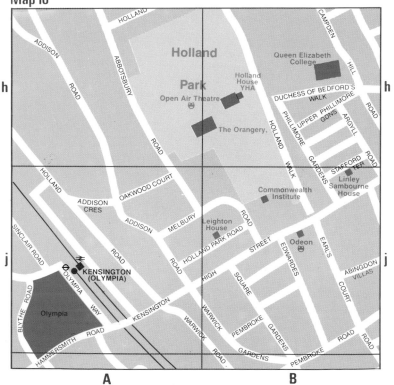

Map 10

HOLLAND

ADDISON ROAD

ABBOTSBURY ROAD

CAMPDEN HILL

Holland

Queen Elizabeth College ■

h

Park

Holland House YHA ■

Open Air Theatre ☺ ■

DUCHESS OF BEDFORD'S WALK

UPPER PHILLIMORE GDNS

ARGYLL ROAD

CAMPDEN HILL ROAD

h

The Orangery, ■

PHILLIMORE GARDENS

HOLLAND WALK

STAFFORD TER

Linley Sambourne House ■

HOLLAND ROAD

OAKWOOD COURT

ADDISON CRES

ADDISON ROAD

MELBURY ROAD

Commonwealth Institute ■

Leighton House ■

HOLLAND PARK ROAD

EARL'S

SINCLAIR ROAD

BLYTHE ROAD

HOLLAND ROAD

OLYMPIA WAY

KENSINGTON (OLYMPIA) ⊖●

KENSINGTON ROAD

HIGH STREET

WARWICK GARDENS

PEMBROKE GARDENS

SQUARE

EDWARDES SQUARE

Odeon ☺

ABINGDON VILLAS

EARL'S COURT ROAD

PEMBROKE ROAD

j

Olympia ■

HAMMERSMITH ROAD

j

A — **B**

304

Postal Districts

307

LONDON: ART MARKET TO THE WORLD
by Antony Thorncroft

With its mighty auction houses, Sotheby's, sprawling over a block of Bond Street, and Christie's, with its palatial mansion in King Street, St James's; with its long established dealers, some like Colnaghi and Agnew, with origins stretching back over centuries; with its major antiques fairs, like the Grosvenor House, a June highlight of the London Season, or more specialist gatherings, like the Ceramics Fair, or the Silver and Jewellery Fair; and with its host of street markets, as in Bermondsey or the Portobello Road, where the sharp-eyed may still pick up an unappreciated Old Master print or a C17 marble bust, London can fearlessly claim to be the centre of the international art market.

New York may have bigger sales of Impressionist and contemporary art; Geneva hold more lavish auctions of silver and jewels; and Hong Kong is now the place to dispose of Chinese porcelain and jades, but no city can compare with London for the range and profusion of its works of art. The nation's history, the wealth that financed the Grand Tours of the C18 Englishman and the empire-building which brought back to Britain the artifacts of Africa and Asia in the C19, has left the country the depository of more than its fair share of the world's treasures. Clever management at Sotheby's and Christie's has ensured that, while other nations may now contain more millionaires and collectors, much of the actual trade in works of art is still handled through London.

Undoubtedly the auction houses lie at the heart of London's prominence. In the 1988-89 season *Sotheby's* sold internationally works of art to the value of over £1.35 billion and *Christie's* disposed of just over £1 billion. Sotheby's may now be American owned, by the real estate developer Mr Alf Taubman, but most of its management and expertise is British and around half its turnover takes place in London. The same is true of Christie's, still British controlled, although the subject of perennial take-over speculation. Auctions in New York may produce greater totals, but there are many more sales in London. Only in August and September, and around Christmas, are the rooms at Sotheby's and Christie's silent, and even then any auction addict can usually attend a sale at one of the smaller auction houses, *Phillips* and *Bonhams*, which concentrate on serving the local antique dealer and the buyer and seller of 'collectibles' – toys, cigarette cards, lead soldiers, fans, automobilia, etc.

A visit to an auction house is one of the great free pleasures of London. In one room, especially in the mornings, a sale will be taking place, perhaps of silver or furniture. If the items are not of earth-shattering appeal perhaps only twenty or thirty people will be spread around the room, the majority of them dealers. You can join in the fun, but these days all potential bidders are issued with a numbered paddle to speed the bidding, and to ensure that the auction house has a record of the identity of a new bidder. Most of the lots in the increasingly lavish and well-illustrated catalogues will show an estimate of the likely price of the object up for auction. The 'low' estimate is usually the reserve price, under which the vendor is unwilling to let the item go. Invariably, in a major sale, prices go for well over the 'high' estimate.

Electronic boards flash up the bidding in all the world's major currencies and the auctioneers are adept at making the sales fun, jollying along the bidding, at least in the early stages of the auction. (Undoubtedly fatigue sets in when around 200 lots have gone under the hammer and then may be the time to find a bargain.) If you make a successful bid there is an added charge of 10 per cent, the buyer's premium, on top of the 'hammer' price.

In other rooms objects in forthcoming sales will be on view, while at the front counter specialists from the various departments will be examining antiques brought in by hopeful members of the public. This free valuation usually gives disappointing news, but it is always worthwhile, if you are using a saleroom to identify and price an antique, to visit more than one: Sotheby's, Christie's and Phillips are conveniently located within fifteen minutes' walk of each other.

Undoubtedly the terrific success of the auction houses in recent years has taken much business away from the dealers. But the dealers cannot live without the salerooms. They are the source of much of their stock, especially in areas like furniture, clocks, silver, arms and armour and books, where specialist knowledge is needed and there are few private buyers. The salerooms also dispose of those antiques that have languished long in the dealer's windows. Also the dealers can get lines of credit from the salerooms. They may object to the lavish marketing campaigns which have convinced so many rich collectors that they can get a better price for their works of art from the auction houses than from a dealer – in fact a good dealer will usually offer a better price than a saleroom – but dealers have now come to terms with the dominance of the salerooms and acknowledge the service they provide in making the public aware of the investment potential in antiques.

Aesthetic and social pleasures combine at Sotheby's...

Rubens's 'Samson and Delilah' sold at Christie's in 1980 to the National Gallery for £2,300,000.

To some extent the London salerooms have been too successful in talking up the price of antiques, especially in Impressionist and C20 art, the main sector for international trading. Few dealers on their own can now afford to bid against the mega-rich private collectors for the best works by Picasso, Van Gogh, Gauguin, and the like. In this area London is the entrepôt rather than the leading player: New York and Paris probably offer better pictures, at least in the dealers. Even so the London premises of *Wildenstein* will always carry some choice Impressionists, as will *Marlborough* and the *Lefevre Gallery,* with its private room of modern masterpieces revealed only to select visitors. Back in Bond Street there is *Thomas Gibson* (famous for once employing the current chairman of Sotheby's UK, Lord Gowrie) who may not have a wide stock but is the kind of dealer who will still pay million-pound prices for 'museum quality' pictures: he set the art world alight, a few years ago by paying about £7m for a work by Braque, lifting Cubist paintings to new heights.

The other major dealer in Impressionists and Moderns is *Richard Green* who has a run of three galleries, two in Dover Street, one around the corner in Bond Street. Green is probably the busiest dealer in pictures operating in London and is unusual in dealing across the field, from C20 art to Old Masters, with forays into sporting pictures and into the recently fast-expanding area of British art from 1880 to 1930. A few years ago Victorian pictures were all the rage and dealers such as *Christopher Wood* (in Motcomb Street), *Peter Nahum* (Ryder Street) and the *Maas Gallery* (Clifford Street) helped to promote and popularise the Pre-Raphaelites and later High Classical Victorian art, all those Greek maidens and Roman slaves. In the last few years the next era of British art – the Newlyn School, Camden Town, the Vorticists, etc, – came to the fore, and dealers such as *David Messum* in Saint George Street and the Fine Art Society, which for a century has occupied grand, arty, premises in Bond Street, have succeeded in marketing artists like Dorothea Sharp and Sir George Clausen to a wider, international, market.

When it comes to contemporary art London can hold its own with any other city, and, conveniently, many of the leading dealers – *Waddington, Kasmin,* the *Redfern, Bernard Jacobson* – are concentrated in Cork Street and its environs. Here you can find examples of those British artists who have broken through to the world stage – Bacon, Moore, Hockney, etc – as well as American and continental modern masters. The galleries continually have shows and even in the summer will be exhibiting new, less familiar, artists. Downstairs there are the permanent stock that the dealers are only too glad to display to interested visitors. Around the corner in Dering Street is another cluster of dealers built around *Anthony d'Offay* who represent Gilbert & George, among other leading lights.

In recent years high rates in the Mayfair region have forced many dealers into peripheral areas. The leading specialist in contemporary sculpture, representing Tony Cragg among many others, is the *Lisson Gallery,* up towards Paddington, and the Portobello Road and Shoreditch areas are alive with artists' studios. The monthly magazine, Galleries, available free in most art galleries, lists the hundreds of dealers now scattered through the metropolis.

Also at Christie's, Van Gogh's 'Sunflowers' fetched £24,750,000 in March 1987, at that time a world-record price for any work of art. This picture went to a Japanese buyer.

One sector where London still dominates the world is Old Masters. Dealers who began by advising C18 English aristocratic collectors on their purchases, notably Agnew and Colnaghi, still face each other in Old Bond Street. *Agnew* has diversified into modern art and *Colnaghi* has made a specialisation of Italian drawings and prints but their vaults will contain some of the finest Old Masters in London, works by Murillo, Turner, Claude, Boucher. And Old Masters are still very cheap when compared with Impressionists, which enables the dealers, with their well-cultivated connections, to compete with the salerooms for the prize pictures. Some dealers specialise, like *Johnny van Haeften* in Duke Street (another haven for Old Master dealers) who dominates in Dutch pictures, especially the now much-sought-after still lifes, and the *Walpole Gallery*, in Dover Street, which has a fine supply of Italian art. Other interesting specialists are *Whitford & Hughes* who stock continental pictures of the late C19 and later, and *Connaught Brown* of Albemarle Street, who were the first to pick up the cult for Scandinavian art.

Pictures may be the most visible works of art but London's eminence is based on the breadth of its treasures. It is particularly strong in exotic foreign wares built on an expertise acquired from Imperial times. Chinese works of art abound, with *Eskenazi* in Piccadilly perhaps the most erudite dealer, with a penchant towards the earlier periods, Chinese archaic bronzes and the like, rather than the more fanciful Ching wares now so popular. Other well established dealers in oriental items are *Bluett* and *Vanderkar. Spink,* just along from Christie's in King Street, and one of the oldest established dealers in London, offers oriental along with virtually every other traditional top quality antique – silver, pictures, objets d'art, coins and medals. It is perhaps the closest London has to an antiques Harrods.

For antiquities there is *Robin Symes* in Jermyn Street and the *Mansour* in Davies Street; for silver London is lavishly endowed, dealers like *Koopman, S.J. Phillips* (also strong in jewels), *ADC Heritage* and

Bibliophily at Maggs, Berkeley Square.

Spink and Son in King Street (corner with Duke Street), St James's.

How of Edinburgh (actually based in Albemarle Street), the equal of any suppliers in the world. For C18 ceramics try the *Haughtons* in Burlington Gardens; for icons, the *Mark Gallery*.

London also leads in furniture, the dealers spread along Mount Street and the Fulham Road, with satellite stars like *Norman Adams* near Harrods and *Mallett* in Bond Street. London's antiquarian book dealers, too, tend to have traditions stretching back centuries, and the finest books and illuminated manuscripts in the world can be found at *Maggs* in Berkeley Square and *Quaritch*, off Golden Square. There is really no end to the roll call. For oriental carpets the best spot is the Highgate warehouse where the dealers, often still Armenian, serve the trade, and also important private collectors. For coins and paper money there are many small shops around the British Museum which is also home, in Museum Street, to *Abbott & Holder*, which, in a rickety building ascending up many floors, houses the biggest collection of inexpensive paintings, watercolours and drawings in London.

Then there are the antiques arcades, notably *Grays* off Davies Street, and *Antiquarius* on the King's Road, in Chelsea, where scores of traders offer the small change of the antiques world – jewels, coins, costumes, prints, all the paraphernalia of the past enlivened with the odd masterpiece.

No city can match London in its range and in its profusion, from the salerooms with its auctions that attract all the major dealers and collectors in the world, especially in late November, in March, and in June, when really exceptional sales of Impressionists, Old Masters and furniture are held, to its knowledgable dealers clustered near the salerooms in St James's or off Bond Street, to its myriad small specialists, experts in folk art, or C17 clocks, in scientific instruments or in militaria. Most can be discovered by browsing, but the British Antique Dealers Association will give more information and the press offices of the salerooms, while anxious to push their upcoming auctions, will also direct interested buyers towards those experts trading in their fancy.

USEFUL ADDRESSES

Abbot & Holder	30 Museum Street WC1	☎ 637 3981
Adams, Norman	8 Hans Road SW3	☎ 589 5266
Agnew	43 Old Bond Street W1	☎ 629 6167
Anthony d'Offay	9 Dering Street W1	☎ 499 4100
Antiquarius Antiques Market	131 King's Road SW3	☎ 351 5353
Bernard Jacobson	14a Clifford Street W1	☎ 439 8355
Bluett	48 Davies Street W1	☎ 629 4018
Bonhams, W. & F.C.	Montpelier Street SW7	☎ 584 9161
British Antique Dealers Association	20 Rutland Gate SW7	☎ 589 4128
Christie's	8 King Street W1	☎ 839 9060
Christopher Wood	15 Motcomb Street SW1	☎ 235 9141
Colnaghi	14 Old Bond Street W1	☎ 491 7408
Connaught Brown	2 Albemarle Street W1	☎ 408 0362
David Messum	34 St George Street W1	☎ 408 0243
Eskenazi	166 Piccadilly W1	☎ 493 5464
Fine Art Society	148 New Bond Street W1	☎ 629 5116
Gray's Antique Market	58 Davies Street W1	☎ 629 7034
Haughton, Brian	3b Burlington Gardens W1	☎ 734 5491
Heritage ADC	2 Old Bond Street W1	☎ 493 5088
How of Edinburgh	28 Albemarle Street W1	☎ 408 1867
International Oriental Carpet C.tre	53 Highgate Road NW5	☎ 267 3346
Johnny Van Haeften Gallery	13 Duke Street SW1	☎ 930 3062
Kasmin Art	34 Warwick Avenue W9	☎ 286 6229
Koopman	25 London Silver Vaults WC2	☎ 242 8365
Lefevre Gallery	30 Bruton Street W1	☎ 493 2107
Lisson Gallery	67 Lisson Street NW1	☎ 724 2739
Maas Gallery	15a Clifford Street W1	☎ 734 2302
Maggs Bros	50 Berkeley Square W1	☎ 493 7160
Mallett & Son	40 New Bond Street W1	☎ 499 7411
Mansour	46 Davies Street W1	☎ 491 7444
Mark Gallery	9 Porchester Place W2	☎ 262 4906
Marlborough Fine Art	6 Albemarle Street W1	☎ 629 5161
Peter Nahum	5 Ryder Street SW1	☎ 930 6059
Phillips	7 Blenheim Street W1	☎ 629 6602
Phillips, S.J.	139 New Bond Street W1	☎ 629 6261
Quaritch, Bernard	5 Lower John Street W1	☎ 734 2983
Redfern Gallery	20 Cork Street W1	☎ 734 1732
Richard Green	39 Dover Street W1	☎ 493 3939
Robin Symes	3 Ormond Yard SW1	☎ 930 9856
Sotheby's	34 New Bond Street W1	☎ 493 8080
Spink & Son	5-7 King Street SW1	☎ 930 7888
Thomas Gibson	44 Old Bond Street W1	☎ 449 8572
Vanderkar	43 Duke Street SW1	☎ 839 1091
Waddington	2 Cork Street W1	☎ 437 8611
Walpole Gallery	38 Dover Street W1	☎ 499 6626
Whitford & Hughes	6 Duke Street SW1	☎ 930 9332
Wildenstein	147 New Bond Street W1	☎ 629 0602

Covers

1. Tate Gallery: 'The Kiss' by Auguste Rodin; 2. Cutty Sark, Greenwich; 3. National Gallery: 'The Virgin and Child with St Anne and St John the Baptist' (detail) by Leonardo da Vinci; 4. British Museum: main entrance.